NS

What to Do When You Don't Want to Call the Cops

| Joan Kennedy Taylor |

What to Do When You Don't Want to Call the Cops

A NON-ADVERSARIAL APPROACH
TO SEXUAL HARASSMENT

A Cato Institute Book

NEW YORK UNIVERSITY PRESS

New York and London

NEW YORK UNIVERSITY PRESS
New York and London

Library of Congress Cataloging-in-Publication Data
Taylor, Joan Kennedy.
What to do when you don't want to call the cops : a
non-adversarial approach to sexual harassment / Joan Kennedy
Taylor.
p.   cm.
"A Cato Institute Book."
Includes bibliographical references (p.   ) and index.
ISBN 0-8147-8232-9 (cloth : perm. paper)
1. Sexual harassment of women—United States. 2. Sex
discrimination against women—United States. 3. Sex role in the
work environment—United States. 4. Sexual harassment—United
States.   I. Title.
HD6060.3 .T39 1999
331.4'133'0973—dc21   99-6652
                                                  CIP

New York University Press books are printed on acid-free paper,
and their binding materials are chosen for strength and durability.

Manufactured in the United States of America

10 9 8 7 6 5 4 3 2 1

CONTENTS

| v |

Contents

ACKNOWLEDGMENTS

Marcia Pally, the founder of Feminists for Free Expression, was the first person who encouraged me to write this book when I started planning it in 1995. Others who spurred me on in the early stages are Dr. Sharon Presley of Resources for Independent Thinking; Cathy Young and Rita Simon of the Women's Freedom Network, who invited me to speak on the subject in 1996; Lee Nason; Ann E. Stone of Republicans for Choice; David Boaz and Ed Crane of the Cato Institute; and Walter Olson. I would not have taken on this task without their encouragement.

I particularly thank my agent, Carol Mann, who knew that this was a trade book and was so impressed with my thesis that she couldn't believe it hadn't already been the subject of a book. (I had to bring her the results of three days of library research to convince her.)

Of course, the book could not have been written without the many people whom I talked to and corresponded with, who shared their opinions and experiences. Those whose names I can divulge are Molly Hays, Carol Cunningham, Rebecca Shipman Hurst, Marion Neustadter, Dorothy Lang, Tama Starr, Noreen Storrie, Susan Niederhoffer, Suzanne Riggenbach, Elizabeth Rodenz, Joanne Kelly, Dr. Elsa Bastone, Dr. Lois Copeland, Dr. Richard Sperling, Professor Kingsley R. Browne, Rita Risser, Esq., Aleeza Strubel, Sharon Szymanski, Dick and Irene Riemann, Dr. Anne De Gersdorff, Sally Begley, Eleanor Lord, Virginia Sullivan Finn, Danny Rosenblatt, Jeff Riggenbach, Annelise and Martin Anderson, Lee M. Shulman, David R. Lagasse, Esq., Joyce Shulman, Lou Foritano, and Laura Kroutil.

I also must mention the constant inspiration I have received over the past years from my friends at Feminists for Free Expression. Cathy Crosson of the legal committee first made me aware of the similarity between protective labor legislation and current sexual harassment law in her amicus briefs, but I hasten to add that she does not necessarily agree with the use I have made of the idea. And President Jennifer Maguire and board members Ann Beeson, Mary Dorman, Marjorie Heins, Marcia Pally, Candida Royalle, Catherine Siemann, and Veronica Vera have all, in different ways and at different times, represented to me the importance to the feminism movement of comradeship coupled with a true respect for diversity of thought.

Several people have also provided crucial input at various stages of the preparation of the manuscript. George Wu's Chelsea Cottage restaurant in New York City provided a home away from home while I was writing the book. Christine Kelly typed up interviews; Sharon Presley gave me a great deal of help with the research and also read the drafts of several chapters; the Reverend Lois Rose read and gave helpful comments on a nearly completed manuscript; David Boaz and Darcy Olsen read and commented in detail on the penultimate version.

Finally, my editor at New York University Press, Niko Pfund, has been guide, philosopher, and friend through all the drafts and reorganizations of the book, and the remarkable Ellen Frankel Paul of the Social Philosophy and Policy Center at Bowling Green State University provided really invaluable editorial help at the end. I am deeply grateful to everyone.

What to Do When You Don't
Want to Call the Cops

INTRODUCTION

When people asked me what I was working on during the time I was writing this book, I found that as soon as I said, "Sexual harassment," two or three people elsewhere in the room would gravitate towards me to hear what I had to say. And immediately, the anecdotes would start. But it didn't seem as if everyone was talking about the same thing.

"It's the language at the office I can't stand," said one young woman. "Stockbrokers are the worst," agreed another.

"I couldn't get this one man who worked for me to stop bothering a secretary who wouldn't go out with him," said a male employer. "Sexual notes, cards, phone calls; I even found him crawling on the floor just out of sight of her desk, preparing to jump out and startle her. And he was a friend of mine! I finally had to forbid him to go into the room where she worked."

"Do you know why I was never charged with sexual harassment in all my years of teaching?" asked a former professor. "Because I never had a conference with a female student without leaving the office door wide open."

"Don't you think that the issue of sexual harassment is really a question of manners?" asked a former office colleague of mine.

"Dignity and humor," said the woman president of a construction company. "You can get through any situation with dignity and humor."

"It's part of the litigation explosion," said the author of *The Litigation Explosion*.

"It's the most important issue in the workplace today," said a man who had run one of the divisions of IBM.

"There was this guy who worked for a nonprofit, and he gave his secretary a raise and, when she thanked him, unzipped his fly and took out his penis and said, 'Now, suck me off.' When she said no, he fired her. And this other guy went to the board of trustees on her behalf and said, 'It's him or me. If you don't do right by this woman, I'm going to go public about this.' So they gave her some money and fired him. But the guy who championed her has been paying for it ever since. His career has never been what it could have been." That story came from the head of an advertising agency.

See what I just did? I told a story that may have shocked you, but you more likely thought, "Oh, good, this isn't going to be just one of those academic books—it may even be spicy." But forget the point of the story for a moment. Suppose I told it in the workplace. I used explicit words and described two explicit acts, one that happened and one that was invited. All in the service of criticizing sexual harassment, that's true. But would it have been a harassing story if I told it to you, or you overheard it, in mixed company on the job? Suppose I were a man, and you a woman, and you heard that story when you were in the company of sixty guys and no other woman. Or suppose we were both women in a group of women, having drinks after work and swapping war stories about harassment, and we were overheard by a fellow male employee. Or suppose you were a young man on your first job, and I were your homosexual male boss. Does it matter that it was not a joke but a story with a serious point?

In present-day law, the answer to the questions implied by all these suppositions depends on which court and even which judge decides on it. All of us have heard the stories that might be called "cliches of sexual harassment." They go the rounds and are brought up to bolster an argument, over and over—the graduate student at the University of Nebraska who was asked to remove a picture of his wife in a bikini from his office after two women sharing his office complained to the administration that it harassed them; the sign that has been reported at construction sites, in offices, and in a surgical operating room: "Sexual harassment will not be tolerated. But it will be graded"; the man who was fired for referring to a risqué episode on *Seinfeld* and then sued and got over $2 million. I sat next to a businesswoman at a luncheon, and when I told her the subject of this book, she allowed as how "[t]here is probably more of that going on than anyone is aware of." But she agreed when I added, "Both more and less." One of the points of this book is that much behavior that has been punished, such as telling the story I told earlier, wasn't a harassing act and legally shouldn't be considered one.

But another point of this book is that depending on the circumstances in which you heard the story, you might be more or less uncomfortable. If you were very young or very timid, you might even *feel* harassed, especially if you heard other stories like it from me. In that sense, even if it shouldn't be so in a legal sense, harassment is in the perception of the harassed. The 1993 *Harris v. Forklift* Supreme Court decision said that "conduct that is merely offensive" is not actionable. But no one wants to spend most of his or her time in an environment that is perceived as offensive.

People often don't know what to expect in the workplace. They are told they have rights, but it's not at all clear what those rights are, or how they are to be enforced, or by whom. Do people have a right to voice their opinions? Do other people have a "right" not to be offended? There is a not-so-clearly defined legal area of forbidden conduct on the one hand and an equally undefined area of shifting sensibility on the other. Some courts, although not the Supreme Court, have even adopted a "reasonable woman" standard of what is harassing, rather than the age-old standard of what a "reasonable man" (meaning "reasonable person") would hold. In one case, the court specifically held that the standard might change as time passes—what is considered permissible behavior today might in a few years no longer be acceptable to the "reasonable woman."

So the idea of this book crept up on me, because it was a subject that everyone was discussing and that everyone seemed confused about. Since I began writing, the subject has taken center stage in the media with President Bill Clinton's sex scandals and later with his impeachment and acquittal. This has led to a plethora of articles and even books. How does mine differ? I am focusing not on sexual harassment as a legal problem but on sexual harassment as a problem of expectations and communication, especially in the nontraditional workplace, in which men strikingly outnumber women. Women are entering more and more of these workplaces, as previously all-male occupations are discovering that they need women workers. As I researched this book and became more immersed in the subject, it became increasingly clear to me that the present legally oriented climate, which was supposedly invented to be beneficial to women, is anything but.

In one spectacular 1991 court case, Lois Robinson sued Jacksonville Shipyards, Inc. (JSI), for creating and encouraging "a sexually hostile, intimidating work environment."[1] At the time of the trial she had worked there as a welder for eleven years (1977–1988), one of a very few women employed as skilled craftsworkers: never more than 5 percent of the workforce. (In 1980 she was one of two women working with 958 men in that category—by 1983 there were seven women. It's not clear how many women were there in 1988.) She objected strongly to the remarks the men made and to the fact that they posted nude calendars and photos torn from sex magazines in the work areas. She thought the remarks and photos were sexually harassing, said so, and began a crusade. The men retaliated by escalating the behavior she found offensive.

In an interview with a manager, at which Robinson formally requested an order forbidding "pictures of nude and partially nude women," Barbara Dingle, a union secretary who worked as a mechanic, was asked if she objected to such pictures. She did not. Apparently, other women at the shipyard also didn't feel they were harassed. When Lois Robinson brought suit, the prosecution called K. C. Wagner, an expert on sexual harassment, to analyze workplace harassment in general and to review documents in the case, including depositions from female employees.

Wagner found that the women at JSI evidenced "common coping patterns by individual victims of sexual harassment." She identified five such strategies, including denial, avoidance, and filing a complaint, but also including "telling the harasser to stop" and "engaging in joking or other banter in the language of the workplace in order to defuse the situation." The judge concluded that "Ms. Wagner's testimony provided a credible, sound explanation for the variety of responses to harassing behavior at JSI to which other witnesses testified."

In other words, the fact that some people could deal with offensive remarks and pictures helped prove, in this lawsuit, that the unpleasant behavior was illegal. But in reading the case, I wondered if a different conclusion were possible. Some women said they weren't being harassed. And some women were doing something different about things that they found offensive, and it was working for them. I wanted to know in more detail what they might be doing.

So I started interviewing women I knew who worked in nontraditional workplaces. I concentrated at first on professionals who had become managers, because I thought they would know about harassment from both the worker and the management point of view. None of them saw herself as having had a real problem with harassment in her career or in her company, but all of them had lots of experience with potentially volatile situations.

I heard stories of receiving anonymous hate mail, of being considered typical of all women and being constantly asked, "What do women think about . . . ?" I heard about a situation that became explosive when two employees thought it was funny to pretend they were having an affair when they weren't—but other women thought it was real and got upset. I spoke to a doctor who, when she was an intern, was the "token female" and couldn't get her fellow interns to cover for her. I heard about sexual advances that were ignored, about a secretary who stopped a worker from making remarks she didn't like by saying, "Frankie, how would you like it if someone was talking that way to your daughter?" And above all, I heard repeatedly that even if you think of someone as your enemy, "Always give him the benefit of the doubt." "Always leave him a way out." "Give what you want to get."

At first I thought I was going to write an article based on these interviews; then, a series of articles. Finally, I realized that it had to be a book. Uniquely, this sort of conflict is rarely approached with techniques of conflict resolution, partly because the federal Equal Employment Opportunity Commission (EEOC) considers that management *may not* deal with accusations of sexual harassment by telling people to "work it out" or resolve it, even if that is the way in which the company usually deals with personnel problems. Too many workplaces are becoming places for hostile encounters between men and women workers, and it seems as if the present reliance on regulation and litigation is increasing the hostility.

Women are being encouraged to enter new fields and take their place beside men—but they are also being told they have rights not to be offended that must not be violated, and they should stand up for these rights. So the women go into these new situations with little knowledge of the group dynamics in place before they got there (with little knowledge of the fact that there *are* group dynamics) and wait for something offensive to happen. And then what are they to do? Complain or sue.

Meanwhile, men have been told that women are coming, that they are going to change the workplace for the worse, and that they are going to get preferential treatment. And then, the first inappropriate step they take is reacted to as discrimination.

I submit, this is a prescription for disaster. Nobody has a right not to be offended. But if we are going to put aside the legal model, what are the alternatives?

This book presents a number of them, all to do with making expectations more realistic and with developing strategies—to forestall real conflict and harassment before it starts but also to communicate what you find offensive without escalating the offensive behavior.

Obviously, saying that much of what is causing distress in the workplace can be averted, dealt with, and forestalled doesn't mean people are not doing wrong out there. I certainly do not want to be understood as saying that there really is no problem or that it is all in people's heads. On the contrary, in the Jacksonville Shipyards, for instance, things were so out of control that there were instances of men pinching and fondling women, cornering them with sexual propositions, and exposing themselves or mooning. It had escalated into a truly hostile workplace.

But it does not have to be that way. One woman manager whom I spoke to, an architect who has worked in construction for a number of years, put it this way: "When a woman comes to me with a complaint, I want first of all to make sure that no harm comes to the woman. But I want to make sure that no harm comes to the man, too. Because if a charge of sexual harassment goes into his folder, he may never get another promotion in his entire *life*."

To do no harm, it seems to me, should be the ultimate goal of our policies. We want to resolve conflict, not to make it more polarized. We want everyone protected, which doesn't mean that both sides won't have to change a little. And these are precisely the things that our present policies aren't doing.

This is a book that began with asking a number of women how they handled unpleasant encounters in the workplace, and how they would suggest that others handle them. I then explored hundreds of articles on the general subject of sexual harassment that have been published in various journals in the fields of business, psychology, sociology, and gender studies. I wasn't sure where my research would lead me when I began, but it told me that there was a dynamic to what was going on that had to do with workplace composition and workplace change. When I first envisioned this book, I didn't expect to take much of a position on the law itself; I thought the law was extraneous to those aspects of gender relations in the workplace I was examining. But as the work continued, I found my view of the law became more and more negative, until I became convinced, by the time I reached chapter 13, that major changes to cut back the law are necessary, in the interests of women.

To demonstrate the situation to the reader, the book is organized into three parts, each of which has five chapters. Part 1 is called "The Scope of the Problem" and begins with an overview of the law's demands on business and what businesses have attempted to do to comply. Then I examine the history of sexual harassment law (chapter 2), the research findings relevant to a view that this is an issue of communication (chapter 3), the difficulties and fears that both men and women have with communicating about sexual subjects in general (chapter 4), and a "how to" on communication in general that also introduces the reader to differing cultural assumptions of men and women with regard to business and communication (chapter 5).

Part 2 discusses five areas of "Male Group Culture" that women may overlook or not be aware of and that can make male-dominated workplaces seem harassing to them: language, sexist jokes, visual pornography, the ubiquitousness of competition, and hazing. The point of these examinations is not to explain that these propensities play a role in harassment; on the contrary, it is to explain that male behavior that may seem directed at women in a hostile way may just be treating them as women often say they wish to be treated—like men.

Part 3, "What's to Be Done?" begins by examining steps that companies might take to forestall general sexual harassment and individual woman workers might take to forestall particular instances of it (chapter 11). It then turns, in chapter 12, to the various criticisms that have been made of sexual harassment law, most specifically, of its genesis in discrimination law and of its conflict with the First Amendment. Chapter 13 discusses connections between sexual harassment law and hate-speech codes, which are equally contrary to the spirit of the First Amendment. Chapter 14 discusses management's reliance on workplace training, and the reliance that this training in turn has on present-day law. Finally, chapter 15, "Towards a Feminist Theory of Training," suggests in some detail how businesses might improve their training, and how unions and women's organizations might make courses and training available that would help women not be the passive figures that today's law encourages them to be.

Throughout this discussion, the emphasis is on what women might do to make the new workplace more comfortable for them and (if need be) to protect themselves from insult and offense. The question might rightly be raised, Why give this advice specifically to women? Why not tell *men* to shape up? One answer is that almost all existing training does just that—tells men to change what they are doing and saying. There is no need for my voice to add to that chorus.

But another answer is, while it is certainly true that outside the workplace the responsibility for clear communication is and should be fifty-fifty, in heavily male workplaces it is the woman who is coming into male territory, not vice versa. Therefore, she needs to know how that territory operates; and unless he is interested in pursuing a personal relationship outside of work with her, he has no corresponding need to know her territory. If a part of the way in which male territory operates is offensive to her, it is she who has the burden of communicating her concern. He may have nothing to complain about.

The reader may have guessed that this book is therefore addressed to women. It is also addressed to company managements, who may find useful a new perspective on what may be going on in their companies. Some chapters, especially chapters 2, 12, and 13, which are legal in content (although I hope sufficiently explained to be clear to the nonlegal reader), may have more relevance for the manager than for the woman worker. Other chapters may have more examples and how-to-respond detail than managers feel they need to know. But I hope all this material will seem relevant to my third, ideal reader—the person who is interested in exploring a different take on this area of contemporary life, on how we got into this legal morass, and on how we might conceivably get out of it.

PART I

The Scope of the Problem

CHAPTER ONE

The Starting Point

Paula Corbin, a clerk in a state government office, apparently caught the eye of Arkansas governor Bill Clinton in May 1991. A state trooper invited her to come to the governor's room in the Excelsior Hotel in Little Rock. The governor allegedly asked her to perform an oral sex act, and she refused. Paula Corbin later married a man named Jones, and Clinton was later elected president of the United States.

Jones stayed in her job, went on maternity leave, left her job, was brought to public attention by the *American Spectator*, and decided to bring a sexual harassment suit against the man who ran the organization (the state) that had employed her, and who had put her through what she claimed was a shocking and unpleasant experience. She received support from conservatives but little or none from feminists (the National Organization for Women [NOW] finally issued a press release on June 2, 1997, denouncing the personal attacks against Jones as a "nuts and sluts" strategy) and faced a barrage of publicity and media attention, much of it unpleasant. The case was filed in May 1994. Jones struggled with various sets of lawyers and went through a series of legal motions and countermotions until, almost four years later, on April Fool's Day, 1998, the judge dismissed the case, saying that the alleged conduct didn't constitute sexual harassment. The president's allies were gleeful, and Jones was crushed.

But then, as Clinton's troubles in general worsened and as he came under threat of a possible reversal on appeal, a settlement of $850,000 was reached between the president and Jones. Was this a triumphant end to her travail? The story wasn't over. In the fall of 1997, one of her previous sets of lawyers had filed an $800,000 lien against any proceeds she made from the case. She may not end up with much of anything, barring notoriety and a new look. And this was a sexual harassment lawsuit that *prevailed*—one in which the plaintiff, unlike most such plaintiffs, had enormous support of every kind from conservatives. Were all those years and all that negative attention worth it? Jones told talk-show host Roseanne it was, on a show that aired in February 1999, but Roseanne didn't believe her.

Bringing suit has costs (both monetary and psychological) for the plaintiff. I interviewed Aleeza Strubel of the NOW Legal Defense and Education Fund, which has an intake department and phone lines that are open every morning for women to call with legal problems; it gets about twenty-five hundred calls a year, not all of which deal with sexual harassment. Even if you win your suit or get a settlement, Strubel points out, much of the money will go to the lawyer—that is, if you can get a lawyer. "So many women do not know that in a civil matter, they're not entitled to representation," Strubel says. This means the lawyers in the field can "cherry-pick" clients, so that a woman with no chance for a big settlement has a very hard time getting representation. Also, legal action takes a long time. By the time women come to NOW for advice, "they are a wreck"—often on disability leave, in therapy. Strubel mentioned cases dragging on for as long as six years.

Many women think that their lawyers press them too hard to settle the case, that the lawyers just want the money, while what *they* want is "a day in court," an apology. (Jones turned down a $700,000 settlement in the fall of 1997 because it didn't include an apology. She never did get one.) That criticism of lawyers is wrong, says Strubel. The lawyers know what a difficult, long, drawn-out process a civil suit is. And though a plaintiff may start by not caring about the money, after years of legal fees, she needs it. "When people are offered settlement, I ask them, What have you gone through? How much more are you willing to go through?" she concludes.

Sexual harassment is a major problem in the workplace today. One 1998 article states, "The average judgment in a sexual harassment suit is $250,000, and that doesn't count legal costs or negative publicity."[1] Employers with "deep pockets" often feel threatened by what seems a never-ending game of Russian roulette, as courts in different jurisdictions award large penalties to some employees and nothing to others who seemingly have the same grounds. Some business advisers predict that settling lawsuits may become a major cost of doing business.

Feminists are also concerned. While management wants to do whatever is necessary to avoid suits, feminists want to protect women from being exposed to predatory behavior. From a feminist point of view, the argument from cost is by no means deciding, because it is silent on the issue of justice towards women. Women have long been tormented on the job with demands for sexual favors and hostile remarks disguised in the language of sexual attraction, which often turn into overt actions that could be called assaults. Often, too, women have felt they would lose their jobs if they didn't put up with gross behavior on the part of their office superiors. Don't think Anita Hill, who followed her employer Clarence Thomas from one government job to another even though she was upset at what he discussed; think Senator Robert Packwood, who, when he was accused of routinely physically mauling numerous female colleagues and employees, defended himself by saying that standards of behavior had changed without his noticing.

They have. Until the late 1970s and early 1980s, there was no general discussion of sexual harassment—as Gloria Steinem said, "We didn't even have a word for it. We called it 'life.'" It is an advance in civilization that it is no longer routine for women to expect such behavior as part of earning a living. But it does still exist. The Packwood style of sexual harassment—white-collar harassment in all its forms—is characteristic of work situations where little or no gender mix exists at the top. This type of harassment has flourished wherever men and women are stratified by authority, with women generally holding the vast majority of service jobs and men dominating upper management. It has existed between doctors and nurses and between professors and students. In all these situations, the women are considered more or less replaceable; the men are not. Therefore, the men have had the power to require all sorts of personal services from the women who attend them, from sexual compliance, to picking up dry cleaning, to the often-scorned making of coffee.

Some people see most sexual harassment as involving not offensive *actions* but what men *say* to women—and speech and expression are constitutionally protected by the First Amendment, aren't they? Even if it may not be unconstitutional, isn't interference with workplace speech a form of "political correctness"? Of course, some kinds of speech are really actions, often actions that violate rights. It is sometimes hard to tell where expression ends and action begins, as word turns into gesture, demand, or punishment. The Supreme Court has ruled that nude dancing on stage is a form of "expression" that cannot be banned by governments; but surely, no one takes this to mean that a man exposing himself to a woman in his employment is merely exercising free speech—even if he is governor of Arkansas. Thirty years ago, managers were generally not punished for using their workplace authority to ask for sexual favors on threat of dismissal; today, almost no one agrees that such behavior should be allowed.

But the concern that sexual harassment law not only improperly but unconstitutionally requires companies to forbid speech has a basis, as I examine later in this book. This development has occurred largely because today women report that they are experiencing a new style of sexual harassment, coming not so much from their superiors as from their colleagues and based not so much on the extortion of sexual favors (called, in sexual harassment law, quid pro quo harassment) as on what they perceive to be hostile expression couched in sexual terms. And they are bringing suit.

When the employee wins the suit, the company pays. To avoid such suits, it is becoming more and more routine for companies to require anti-harassment training courses for their employees, especially since the Supreme Court has said that such training can create a defense to a lawsuit. And yes, a growing sense of political correctness has put a number of topics and even certain words out of bounds. An article in the *New York Times* of February 1, 1998, said that the scandal about Bill Clinton and Monica Lewinsky, then just beginning, "seems to have released men and women, at least temporarily, from the careful, sometimes strait-jacketing rules of behavior." "Suddenly," wrote Alex Kuczynski,

> topics that have been off limits in the workplace for years—banished by the fear of causing offense—are out in the open, thanks in part to Linda Tripp, the world's most notorious busybody. Sex—graphic sex—is the

subject du jour in the American office. . . . But the window of opportunity that has let in the earthy banter may not remain open for long.[2]

The view of what sexual harassment is has been polarized, with some people seeing it as a fabricated issue while others think the recent spotlight on it is just the beginning of the attention that the exploitation of women deserves. Members of each side of this argument are sure they know in advance all that anyone who disagrees—by definition, an adherent of the "other side"—has to say. I disagree with both the view that there is no such offense as sexual harassment and the view that any behavior to do with sex that makes someone uncomfortable should be actionable.

Feminism has viewed the law and how it might be of help to women in two different ways. From Elizabeth Cady Stanton and the Seneca Falls Declaration of Sentiments in 1848 to many who urged an Equal Rights Amendment (ERA) in the early 1970s, certain feminists—the individualists—have urged a classical liberal approach to the legal treatment of women: namely, human beings have individual rights. Women are human beings and should have equal rights under the law and equal citizenship, which entails striking down not only the old common-law restrictions on women that existed when the nation's founders declared *all men are equal* but also more recent legal special treatment for women. Another group of feminists, from those who fought for special protective labor legislation for women early in the twentieth century to Catharine MacKinnon (of whose views I present more later), has urged that the differences between men and women mean the law should treat women differently in order to create equality for them. Women, say these feminists, need to be given an equality by the law that they don't otherwise have, whether because of physiological differences or because of a cultural tradition of male dominance.

From the time women won the vote in 1920 until the 1970s, these two factions fought, mainly over protective labor legislation, and the protectionists lost. The ERA advocates were convincing in their argument that mandating special treatment for women in the workplace—by regulating their hours, overtime, and physical stress, as well as by prohibiting certain jobs to them entirely—was "protecting" them out of promotions and better-paying jobs. The protective laws for women were installed bit by bit after such different treatment was first declared constitutional in 1908, in order to improve their working conditions at a time of transition; instead, the laws froze women into lower-echelon occupations. More and more focus on legal solutions and legal intervention turned out not to be in the interest of women. Even though a national ERA was ultimately defeated, the argument was so compelling that in most states a large edifice of differential treatment—including not just workplace restrictions but different prison sentences for men and women and different ages of sexual consent—was dismantled.

Today we live in another time of workplace transition. And lo and behold, another system of legal solution and legal intervention to solve social problems—sexual harassment law—has been installed to improve working conditions for women. Bit by bit, it has expanded in its application. Perhaps we should ask again, Is this legal focus actually helping women? Or are we again missing some elements of what is going on?

The new approach began while ERA advocates were still trying to get the amendment ratified. Suits claiming that "sexual harassment" was a form of workplace discrimination forbidden by Title VII of the Civil Rights Act of 1964 began to be filed in federal courts in the mid-1970s. In 1980, the Equal Employment Opportunity Commission (EEOC) published guidelines on sexual harassment that accepted this view. Since then, thousands of suits have been filed. But it was after the summer of 1986, when the Supreme Court decided *Meritor Savings Bank v. Vinson* in favor of the suing employee and ruled that a firm can at times be liable for a supervisor's actions even when management didn't know about the offending behavior, that companies evidenced widespread concern. In 1988, the magazine *Working Woman* surveyed the directors of personnel, human resources, and equal-opportunity offices at 160 Fortune 500 corporations, all of whom "responded in depth" to its questions. Sexual harassment, said the resulting article, "costs a typical Fortune 500 company with 23,750 employees $6.7 million per year in absenteeism, low productivity and employee turnover. That doesn't include additional millions in possible court costs, executive time and tarnished public image should a case end up in court." One-third of the companies surveyed had already been hit by a lawsuit. Kmart had paid $3.2 million in fines and penalties to settle a single case. Seventy-six percent of the companies surveyed had instituted "written policies banning sexual harassment and another 16 percent include it in their policies against discrimination."[3]

Federal suits brought under Title VII initially allowed winning plaintiffs only compensatory damages such as back pay or legal fees. Private tort actions, brought under state law and claiming such grounds as intentional infliction of emotional distress, assault and battery, or breach of contract, in contrast, had the potential for the plaintiff to collect punitive damages. But the 1991 Civil Rights Act amended Title VII of the 1964 Civil Rights Act to give those bringing harassment suits in federal courts a new right to a jury trial and to punitive damages for financial and emotional harm as well as to compensatory damages.

In 1992, after the Anita Hill–Clarence Thomas confrontation over sexual harassment during the televised Senate Judiciary Committee Supreme Court confirmation hearings, *Working Woman* sent out a new survey, following up on the 1988 Fortune 500 survey. This time the magazine surveyed its readers as well as human-resources executives of corporations and compared the two sets of answers. Almost ten thousand readers (an actual total of 9,680) answered this survey. The summarizing article was written by the same journalist who reported on the 1988 survey.[4]

The 1992 *Working Woman* survey found Fortune 500 executives feeling legally vulnerable, fearing that sexual harassment suits might be "the 'next asbestos.'" *Treasury*, a magazine for financial executives, had predicted that settling such suits over the next five years might cost more than $1 billion, and as a result, some companies were firing accused harassers immediately.[5] Some 81 percent of the companies that *Working Woman* surveyed now had training programs on sexual harassment in place (up from 60 percent in 1988).

More than 60 percent of *Working Woman*'s reader respondents acknowledged that they had been harassed, but only one-quarter of these had reported the harassment. Only 15 percent of the readers said they were not sure what sexual harassment was—54 percent said they knew what the legal definition was, and 30 percent knew "by intuition."[6] (However, the survey questions didn't ask respondents to give a definition so that answers could be compared for consistency.) Half the readers said that harassment was not an issue of sex but "the desire to bully and humiliate," and almost half said that they had worked with "chronic harassers."[7] Trying to ignore the problem was the most common tactic used to combat harassment, but the article said that "a firm 'No' can work better than reporting the problem. One out of three women who protested got the harasser to stop, compared with one out of four who tried to ignore or avoid the harasser."[8]

The surveyed executives who feared an increase in suits turned out to be right. The combination of the Anita Hill–Clarence Thomas confrontation and the amendment of Title VII in the 1991 Civil Rights Act resulted in a sharp spike in the number of official complaints. Less than a year after Thomas's confirmation hearings, inquiries sent to the EEOC had increased by 150 percent and charges filed by 23 percent.[9] After continuing to increase for a few years, the complaints, according to official EEOC figures, leveled off. By March 1998 the *New York Times* reported, "Complaints filed with the Equal Employment Opportunity Commission, as a prelude to bringing suit, have more than doubled since the 1991 amendment, to 15,889 cases last year."[10]

But according to a March 1998 article in *Time* magazine, the law has become so "jumbled" that it is hard to predict the outcome of any case. "Since 1991, juries have returned well over 500 verdicts on sexual harassment—decisions that often contradict one another and send mixed signals about how we should behave anytime we meet a coworker we'd like to see after five."[11]

Of course, the etiquette of dating is not the issue for company managers who feel their company is in jeopardy. As a reaction to the fact that many of these jury trials have cost companies money, employers continue to tighten the restrictions on workplace behavior.

In February 1998, the EEOC negotiated a settlement of nearly $10 million from Astra U.S.A., which was paid to a number of employees whose charges ranged from being subjected to a hostile environment to having been fondled and asked for sex by supervisors, including the former company president. The *Time* article reported, "Companies have responded to the legal morass with wildly varying policies. Some ignore the issue, and others, particularly those burned with lawsuits, even ban interoffice dating."[12]

Such a ban may seem far-fetched, but not to some feminists. In a widely reprinted 1991 article on sexual harassment, law professor Susan Estrich made this statement about the legal requirement that sexual advances be "unwelcome" in order to be found harassing:

> The strongest justification for the welcomeness doctrine is that the rule ensures that consensual workplace sex does not provide the basis for a civil action. The more radical response to this argument is that there is no such thing as truly "welcome" sex between a male boss and a female employee who needs her job.[13]

Many vocal feminists have supported this view and have persuaded company human-resources experts of its validity. Although early in 1998, after President Clinton got into trouble, leading feminist theorist Catharine MacKinnon[14] and *Ms.* magazine founder Gloria Steinem[15] separately went on record with the view that whatever had occurred between him and White House intern Monica Lewinsky was clearly consensual, the view in the world of sexual harassment consultants at the time was, as *Time* quoted, "if Clinton were president of a Fortune 500 company instead of the country, he'd probably be toast."[16] There is no indication that puritan tendencies in management will be reversed in the near future.

Worry over sexual harassment seems well on the way to turning the workplace into a nightmare for employees of both sexes, as well as for employers. Each group has its own perspective, and the stakes, if you make a mistake, are very high. The woman, perhaps young and new at her job and feeling uncomfortable and uncertain, is told by much feminist culture, as well as by what the EEOC requires management to do, to "stand up for her rights" through punitive confrontation: that is, to report any incident and demand an investigation, and to expect the accused to suffer management reprisal under her potential threat of lawsuit. She may feel expected to be ready to sue or to threaten to sue at the drop of a hat, no matter what the cost to her may be.

The man has heard horror stories about people losing their jobs in "zero-tolerance" workplaces because of complaints women have brought about words they have overheard, jokes everyone else has laughed at, or nonsexual touching that caused unintentional offense. He may have been told in a training session, "When in doubt, don't do or say it."

The company, of course, stands to lose large sums of money if a lawsuit can show that its harassment policy is inadequate or that someone is secretly behaving badly in ways the court decides should have been known by management.

Linguist Deborah Tannen, who specializes in analyzing communications problems, tells us that men and women don't understand each other's fears in this area. Women, she points out, fear assault from a man they can't escape, whereas men fear being victimized by a false charge. Each group tends to dismiss the fears of the other and even to find them insulting. Men think that women's fears mean they are saying all men are potential rapists, whereas women think that men are charging all women with being manipulative liars.

> In fact, it is far more common for women to be physically assaulted or sexually harassed than for them to bring false charges, but these realities do not change the power each fear holds for the individuals who identify with one party or the other.
> . . . In other words, each group tends to dismiss the other's deep fears as unlikely to occur. Their own fears, however, thrive on the awareness of possibility.[17]

A good example of how polarizing sexual harassment legal investigations can be is the situation that existed in a Mitsubishi plant in Normal, Illinois, in the summer of 1996. Twenty-nine women had filed complaints with the EEOC in 1994, which led to a lengthy investigation and an EEOC suit on April 9, 1996, charging that women at the plant had been "subject to groping, sexual graffiti, and abusive comments while management took little or no disciplinary action." The company, in turn, in late April subsidized a march on the EEOC office in Chicago by almost three thousand workers; it posted sign-up sheets for the march in the plant and also warned employees that, because of the charges, massive job losses might result. Mitsubishi even installed phone banks at the plant to enable workers to call their legislators to protest the EEOC actions.[18]

The fifteen women suing who were still working at the plant claimed to have received death threats from fellow workers ("Die, bitch, you'll be sorry" was one that appeared in a locker), and graffiti in the plant suggested "hunting" women who caused job losses. The case was finally settled in the summer of 1998, when Mitsubishi agreed to pay $34 million.

This case, according to *Business Week*, was "one of the largest sexual harassment cases ever," so it is hardly typical. A 1998 telephone survey of community opinion in the area around the Illinois Mitsubishi plant found that, while half the respondents thought the women's claims legitimate, only about one in three would find for them in a jury trial. Gender differences were not as important as might be expected. "It is not men in general, but men employed in traditional male lines of work, men who think women ask for it and/or define plaintiffs as golddiggers, and men who claim no prior knowledge of someone who has been harassed that tend to discount such charges. Conversely, it is not women *per se*, but younger, single, and divorced women who know someone who has been harassed that are likely to accept . . . such charges." Despite the complications introduced by the fact that the company had a Japanese management with misogynistic views and encouraged after-hours partying, doesn't the following recipe sound like many other blue-collar work sites? These findings, say the authors of the 1998 community survey,

> can be used to infer the conditions under which harassment is most likely to occur. First, hire a small percentage of young, single women and scatter them through a cavernous, sprawling work setting. Second, fill that cavernous work setting primarily with men, some of whom harbor Neanderthal-like attitudes, such as feeling strongly that women who want high-wage manufacturing jobs are asking for harassment. Third, throw in an indecisive, indifferent, or complicitous circle of foremen and managers. Do all of these things and you have, as demonstrated elsewhere . . . the makings of a postmodern morality play.[19]

The resulting "postmodern morality play" is called "hostile environment" sexual harassment. It raises two important questions: Why does the environment become so hostile in some workplaces? What should be done about it? The answers many contemporary experts on the subject give are simple: American culture is deeply misogynist, and the cure for this behavior is lawsuits or the threat of lawsuits. Only the possibility of legal penalty will scare companies into taking proper action. (If the expert is advising the company, the advice varies a little: it is, *be scared*. Avoid the likely lawsuit by instituting an objective set of rules and a management training program; make it a habit to take action at once; get any troublemaker [read, suspected harasser] out of the organization quickly.)

This climate of advice may help explain the startling cases of first-grade students being charged with sexual harassment for kissing girls in class—schools are, among other things, businesses. If the schools go on record early as taking such incidents seriously and punitively, then they build up a record that will defend them against damages if students do something worse in the eighth grade.

Both the expert contention that hostility stems from a deep misogyny in American culture and the accompanying assumption that the primary cure for hostility is legal action against behavior defined as misogynistic are wrongheaded. Two things have happened in the American workplace that are helping to create the problem, and they have nothing to do with general misogyny. The first is that more and more women are starting to work in high-paying, nontraditional jobs that have previously been male enclaves—jobs in the construction trades, engineering, police and fire departments, commodities trading—as well as flooding professions such as law and medicine in which they used to be a small minority.

The second factor is that American society now widely proscribes "sexual harassment," but we have no generally accepted definition of what sexual harassment *is*. As with obscenity, we're supposed to know it when we see it. Women are told, in books and articles and courses, that the final definition is their *feelings*: anything that makes them uncomfortable is illegal sexual harassment and therefore potentially actionable. A public-service ad on New York City television epitomized this approach. A man tells a woman that she should buy some new clothes and make more of her appearance—"After all, it's your job we're talking about." "No," she replies, "it's sexual harassment we're talking about—and I don't have to take it!" An announcement of how to get information on bringing suit then flashes across the screen.

If hostility is related to social changes that have little to do with misogyny, shouldn't we rethink the idea that the cure for hostility is to scare, by invoking serious legal consequences, purportedly misogynistic company managements into taking proper action to curtail their equally misogynistic male employees? The issue has been framed as the indignity of vulnerable employees (usually women) having to put up with upsetting behavior. Certainly, no one in management or the workforce wants a tinderbox workplace. The question can be reworded as: How can we defuse the situation?

Playing the misogyny card requires the assumption that workplace hostility is entirely on the part of males. But a closer examination shows us it is not. In fact, as we shall see, the hostility between men and women is not unidirectional. Many men are faced with new and unfamiliar competition from women on the job. Many women are working with an overwhelming majority of men for the first time. Both men and women are faced with the amorphous concept "sexual harassment," which encourages women to classify male behavior they don't like as hostile and illegal. At the same time, it encourages men to feel put upon and unfairly challenged to live up to an unstated code. When you read the court cases of truly egregious harassment—mooning, group groping of a woman in sight of a supervisor who does nothing to stop it, threatening messages in women's lockers and lunch boxes—you begin to suspect a climate of hostility that existing practices and policies may have helped create and may even continue to foster.

The polarizing hostility brewing in the workplace comes from both sides, male and female. While men may want to keep their old-boy territory from being invaded, women are sometimes vocal about their scorn for all things masculine and may take advantage of the fact that they have a favored position under some interpretations of sexual harassment law. There are reported cases in which women have said to men, essentially, "Nyah, nyah. I can talk dirty to you, but I'll take you to court if you talk dirty to me." A woman whom a 1990 Iowa court found engaged in "raw sexual banter" nevertheless won her suit because she later served notice that such banter was "offensive and unacceptable."[20] Another judge indicated that a plaintiff who had initiated some of the sexual speech she later complained about might have prevailed if she had been able to pinpoint a moment at which she had clearly told her co-workers to stop.[21] And yet a third case was overturned by an appellate court and remanded back to trial court in order to find out whether or not the plaintiff had welcomed the particular conduct about which she was suing, in the light of evidence that she had used foul language and "sexual innuendo" with others in the workplace. (She was a flight attendant who had grabbed one pilot by the genitals as an invitation.)[22]

Encouraging or even allowing such hostility to run rampant only further fragments people, most of whom in their secret hearts would rather work together.

We live in a period of cultural change. Hostility is often an indication of fear of danger, in both the macho man and the shrill woman. However, we have two typical reactions to perceived danger: we have fight but also flight, which in a civilized environment can include the avoidance that was so prevalent among the readers of *Working Woman*. Women especially, while moving into jobs they haven't held before, while challenging old stereotypes of what they can and cannot do, and while showing their ability to be astronauts, construction workers, neurosurgeons, and fighter pilots, still may have been brought up to be deferential to men. Habits of avoiding conflict rather than answering back, of maintaining harmonious relations at all cost, may not always serve them well in these new worlds they are entering. They know very well how to excel in job performance; they sometimes are not as sure of how to make clear the way in which they want to be treated. Rather than attempt to protect themselves verbally, they may turn to law or management to protect them, often with a sense of relief. But the purpose of the law is to protect citizens from extreme situations, not to be a substitute for self-assertion in daily life.

Ultimately, relying on authority does not meet the real challenge that the new workplace holds for women—the challenge of breaking down the stereotypes with which the entering woman may be confronted and winning the respect and acceptance of skeptical male colleagues. Doing an excellent job of work while remaining an outsider will not completely meet that challenge.

I am concerned that when women feel their first and only recourse in dealing with offensive behavior is an appeal to authority, they are giving up the possibility of acting on their own behalf, which in most cases actually turns out to be more satisfactory and empowering. After all, acting from strength doesn't consist of saying, "I'll get my Big Brother to beat you up."

CHAPTER TWO

What Sexual Harassment Is and Isn't

History and the Law

Chapter 1 was a kind of snapshot of the existing concern over sexual harassment—management wants to do something to confront the specter of lawsuits; feminists want to better the ways in which women are treated in the workplace, particularly with regard to their sexual treatment by men; and both of these priorities have an impact on employee relations. This whole area is primarily dealt with today as a legal issue, so it is worthwhile to take a fairly exhaustive look at what the law in this area is and how it has evolved.

There are two main kinds of law: judge-made law and statutory law, that is, laws passed by legislators. (In the United States we also have constitutional law, in which Supreme Court judges interpret and apply our Constitution.) *Statutory law* defines what is illegal in advance and sets forth the punishment or range of punishment for transgression. The idea is to give notice of what may not be done—it is in this context that the saying "Ignorance of the law is no excuse" arose. What you may not do is written down, and if you don't know it, you should. The law says you may not assault anyone, may not commit armed robbery, may not drive drunk, may not buy or sell drugs. All these offenses are carefully defined, with different punishments for different degrees of offense.

But a great deal of the law of the United States, both state and federal, has been *judge-made law*—either law that interprets what the statutes mean or law embodied in decisions in which the courts function to resolve a specific dispute in the light of general principles that everyone accepts, in accordance with how similar cases have been decided in the past. Judges decide if the facts in a particular case fall within those principles or not. This kind of law is more a process of discovering what the law *is* than one of inventing needed laws that will then be written down. Constitutional law is also a kind of judge-made law, but one resting on the written Constitution, not on unwritten principles.

In all the states of the United States except Louisiana, the basic law of the land was originally judge-made—British Common Law, which was written down only in records of court decisions and relied heavily on precedent. However, common law always is preempted by statutory law, just as state law is preempted by federal law; so as legislators continue to pass laws, courts increasingly have less leeway to operate in this manner, even though judges still influence the law by interpreting the statutes. And of course, the ultimate source of "what the law is" is the Supreme Court, whose justices interpret how the general principles of the Constitution should apply not only to disputes but to legislation itself.

Statutory law is hammered out in legislatures and often reflects compromise. The laws of the United States that Congress passes are usually subject to discussion and debate, during which those who support the law and those who oppose it say what they expect the law to cover, what pitfalls opponents fear if it passes, and how supporters interpret all its possible shades of meaning. These discussions are part of the record and are considered a statute's "legislative history," which elaborates and elucidates the meaning of the wording of the statute in case of later dispute.

The statute from which our present sexual harassment law derives is the Civil Rights Act of 1964. A great many issues were debated during its history, but what sexual harassment *is* was not one of them. Not only was sexual harassment not considered by Congress at the time, but the very parameters of sex discrimination itself were not discussed, since including "sex" in Title VII of the act as one of the grounds on which employers may not discriminate was added as an amendment the day before the vote—some say, as a "joke" to help defeat the entire bill. The concept of gender discrimination in Title VII of the Civil

Rights Act (to say nothing of the notion of sexual harassment later de-
rived from it) therefore has no legislative history.

Included in the 1964 legislation was a new federal agency, the
Equal Employment Opportunity Commission (EEOC). Like all federal agencies, it was invested with the power to interpret and adminis-
ter the application of the law: in the area that interests us, Title VII's
statement is that an employer may not "discriminate against any individual with respect to his compensation, terms, conditions, or privileges of employment because of such individual's race, color, religion,
sex, or national origin."[1] Originally the Department of Justice enforced this ban, but the Equal Employment Opportunity Act of 1972
transferred enforcement power to the EEOC. Ultimately, the EEOC
was empowered to bring a civil suit against employers that had not
complied with Title VII. And, says legal scholar Walter Olson, one
original function of the agency was to lessen the possibility of employees bringing individual lawsuits by allowing "no 'private right of action' to bypass the agency's vital screening and conciliation function."
It was only after the EEOC had examined an employee's claim and
tried to mediate the dispute that it would sometimes give the employee a letter saying that the individual was entitled to bring suit on
his or her own.

> Individual workers who felt discriminated against had to file complaints
> with the EEOC and submit to a lengthy "conciliation" process in which
> the commission staff would try to resolve the problem. If it failed,
> workers might eventually be allowed to sue on their own behalf, but a
> number of provisions in the law discouraged any idea that such resort
> would mean easy money.

Olson lists among these provisions: no right to a jury trial, no re-
covery of more than two years' back pay if an employee had been
wrongfully fired, no punitive damages, and even a provision that
judges might award attorney fees to the "prevailing party," so that if
an employee brought a weak case and lost, that employee might have
to pay the attorneys on both sides of the case.

> In an extraordinary binge of judicial activism over the decade that fol-
> lowed, however, the U.S. Supreme Court knocked down one of these

obstacles after another, with the consistent effect of turning bias claims from objects of conciliation into objects of high-stakes litigation.[2]

So, although there is no legislative history concerning sexual harassment, a growing judge-made federal policy about the right to sue developed, by which the Court made it easier and more monetarily attractive for individuals to sue for job discrimination. "EEOC conciliation was soon reduced to a paperwork turnstile; the key was to get the agency to sign off and issue a 'right-to-sue' letter, so the real action could begin."[3]

Still, the idea of *sexual* harassment suits under Title VII became viable only gradually. The first step was accepting the idea of *racial* harassment. In 1971, the Fifth Circuit recognized for the first time that a racially hostile environment in a workplace was a violation of Title VII. The decision said that the phrase "terms, conditions, or privileges of employment" in Title VII should be interpreted widely to include within its scope "the practice of creating a working environment heavily charged with ethnic or racial discrimination."[4] As early as 1971 also, a suit was filed against the Western Electric Company of New Jersey, claiming that the firing of a woman engineer, Kyriaki Cleo Kyriazi, was discriminatory "and that prior to her firing she was sexually ridiculed and harassed by her male co-workers. The case evolved into a more than ten-year battle on behalf of a class of women at Western Electric. Eventually, it brought an $8.5 million judgment as well as separate fines against five bosses who had harassed Kyriazi."[5]

The term *sexual harassment* wasn't coined until 1975, when Carmita Wood, a laboratory assistant at Cornell University, asked for help from feminist activist friends after she resigned from her job because of sexual pressure from her supervisor and found her subsequent application for unemployment insurance denied. A conference in Ithaca, New York, was organized in the spring of 1975, sponsored by Cornell's Human Affairs Program and a just-formed organization, Working Women United, later to become part of the Working Women's Institute, "which opened in 1971 in Manhattan to promote awareness of the discrimination and harassment of working women."[6] Cases similar to Wood's were presented, the term was coined, and the general problem of sexual harassment was formally born. The definition of sexual harassment announced as a result of this conference was

> any sexual attention on the job which makes a woman uncomfortable, affects her ability to do her work, or interferes with her employment opportunities. It includes degrading attitudes, looks, touches, innuendos, gestures, and direct propositions. It can come from supervisors, co-workers, clients, and customers.[7]

Notice that this definition applied to women only, unlike the legal guidelines that were to come, and that no overt connection was made with the sex discrimination proscribed by the 1964 Civil Rights Act—that also was to come. At the time, the main recourse women felt they had was to quit their jobs, and the presenting issue of the conference was: If the job atmosphere has been made so insupportable that a woman feels forced to leave, shouldn't she be entitled to unemployment insurance?

A year earlier, in 1974, a young lawyer named Catharine MacKinnon had begun work on a manuscript that would be called *Sexual Harassment of Working Women* when published in 1979. Her working hypothesis was that sexual harassment at work was a kind of sex discrimination that was forbidden by the 1964 Civil Rights Act. In 1975, MacKinnon began circulating her manuscript to colleagues,[8] but the new theory that sexual conduct could violate Title VII of the Civil Rights Act and constitute sexual discrimination did not at first catch on in the courts. MacKinnon's early definition was "the unwanted imposition of sexual requirements in the context of a relationship of unequal power."[9] Her thesis was that two forms of workplace sexual harassment existed: quid pro quo harassment, in which a supervisor demands sexual favors from a woman in exchange for a job or a promotion, and what would later be called hostile environment harassment, when co-workers' or supervisors' harassing actions of a sexual nature make the workplace unbearable for a woman.

In 1975, an Arizona district court dismissed the complaint of two women that they had been discriminated against at the company Bausch and Lomb because they had been subjected to verbal and physical advances by their supervisor, Leon Price. The court explained that it was indeed unlawful under Title VII for employers "to discriminate because of an individual's sex with respect to hiring, discharging, classification or compensation of individuals . . . to discriminate against individuals with respect to job assignment or transfer, hours of employment, or 'fringe benefits,'" but that

> such discriminatory practices were employer designed and oriented. . . . Mr. Price was satisfying a personal urge. Certainly no employer policy is here involved; rather than the company being benefitted in any way by the conduct of Price, it is obvious it can only be damaged by the very nature of the acts complained of.[10]

The court also considered that allowing such grounds for suit could not have been intended by those who passed the Civil Rights Act because

> an outgrowth of holding such activity to be actionable under Title VII would be a potential federal lawsuit every time any employee made amorous or sexually oriented advances towards another. The only sure way an employer could avoid such charges would be to have employees who were asexual.[11]

But other courts were soon to rule that quid pro quo sexual harassment was not merely a "personal urge"; it was a manager's act that improperly exercised the power, delegated by the employer, to hire, fire, and promote based on sexual behavior rather than job performance. Since the employer had delegated the power, the employer was liable. In 1976, Catharine MacKinnon was one of the lawyers on the first federal court case that recognized sexual harassment as a violation of Title VII. A federal district court for the District of Columbia held that Diane Williams, a public information specialist at the Department of Justice who was dismissed after she turned down her supervisor's sexual advances, had been harassed "based on sex" within the meaning of Title VII.[12] Other cases soon followed.

From then on, MacKinnon's theory prevailed. In 1977, she was one of the lawyers who brought the first case that extended the argument to education and established that a harassed student can sue her university.[13] MacKinnon quickly moved from being a behind-the-scenes influence, to winning cases, to publishing *Sexual Harassment of*

Working Women through Yale University Press in 1979, to having the EEOC, in 1980, adopt her legal view that sexual harassment is a form of sexual discrimination that is a violation of Title VII. The EEOC guidelines also adopted MacKinnon's division of harassment into two categories: quid pro quo harassment that was linked to an economic benefit, and hostile environment harassment, which MacKinnon had referred to as "condition-of-work harassment."

Moreover, MacKinnon wrote the plaintiff's brief and was co-counsel when the first sexual harassment case, *Meritor Savings Bank v. Vinson*,[14] appeared before the Supreme Court in 1986. The Court unanimously upheld the new theory, in an opinion written by Justice William Rehnquist.

Lower courts, even though they had found the quid pro quo argument persuasive, had more difficulty accepting the hostile environment argument, although some had done so. In the *Meritor* case, the plaintiff was able to use the accusation of unwelcome sexual involvement with a supervisor that had been successful in quid pro quo cases. But (perhaps because she had not suffered any economic damage, which most such cases involved) she used it peripherally, as behavior that had created a hostile environment. In *Meritor*, Mechelle Vinson claimed that her employer and supervisor, Sidney Taylor, vice president of the bank, had made demands on her for sex to which she had submitted over a period of several years, during which time she had been promoted from trainee to teller, to head teller, to assistant branch manager. In her fourth year of employment, according to her testimony, she informed him that she was taking indefinite sick leave, and she was discharged for excessive use of sick leave two months later.

Taylor denied the sexual relationship, and the bank denied knowledge of it. A district court held that if there was a sexual relationship, it was voluntary and the bank hadn't been notified, so it, as employer, wasn't liable; and since Vinson had suffered no economic damage, no actionable harassment had taken place. The D.C. Circuit of the U.S. Court of Appeals reversed this decision and held that harassment could take place if an offensive work environment had been created, even without economic damage to the plaintiff. It also held "that an employer is strictly liable for a hostile environment created by a supervisor's sexual advances, even though," in Justice Rehnquist's words, "the employer neither knew nor reasonably could have known of the alleged misconduct."[15] When the bank appealed to the Supreme Court, the Court upheld the main decision of the appellate court, citing previous racial harassment decisions and the EEOC guidelines. It did not issue a definitive ruling on employer liability in a case of hostile environment created by a supervisor, however, even though strict liability—meaning that the employer was always liable if the plaintiff prevailed—was the general rule in Title VII cases. Instead, the Court decided that the issue of liability should not be an automatic one but should be decided on a case-by-case basis.[16]

The Court also disagreed with the court of appeals that testimony about Vinson's dress and manner was not relevant, holding that it was relevant to whether or not Taylor's advances were "welcome," and that the gist or heart of sexual harassment cases was welcomeness. It otherwise affirmed the court of appeals' reversal of the district court's decision.

This was a major victory for MacKinnon, because it established the validity of hostile environment harassment as the basis for suit in the highest court in the land. *Meritor* decided that sexual harassment could occur in the absence of economic damage to the plaintiff.

The next sexual harassment case that the Court decided, *Harris v. Forklift Systems, Inc.*, in 1993, held that severe psychological damage also was not necessary in establishing a hostile environment. Justice Sandra Day O'Connor summarized the point this way in the unanimous opinion: "Title VII comes into play before the harassing conduct leads to a nervous breakdown."[17] The Court expanded on its *Meritor* decision, trying to draw a line between "an offensive utterance" that would not be actionable and frequent, severe, and humiliating conduct that "unreasonably interferes with an employee's work performance."

Meritor also had held that the bank's anti-discrimination policy was inadequate to avoid liability. This was to have a strong effect on what companies did in the future to protect themselves. The reasoning behind the determination of inadequacy was that the policy didn't specifically mention sexual harassment as a forbidden activity, and that it required employees to report instances of discrimination to their immediate supervisors—in the case of Vinson, the offending Taylor. In 1988, the EEOC issued a "Policy Guidance on Sexual Harassment," which counseled that employers could avoid hostile environment charges "by implementing a strong policy against sexual harassment and maintaining an effective complaint procedure. When employees know that recourse is available, they cannot reasonably believe that a harassing work environment is authorized or condoned by an employer."[18]

Sexual harassment law is still in flux. This is an area of the law that judges continue to shape, both at the bottom of the legal system and at the top. District courts vary widely as to what they consider harassing behavior. Some have strict standards requiring targeted, repeated behavior that often has some physical component; others find for plaintiffs on the basis of one or two jokes or remarks. When Judge Susan Webber Wright dismissed Paula Jones's lawsuit for sexual harassment against the President of the United States, law professor Eugene Volokh contrasted the fact that Judge Wright had held that, as a matter of law, exposing oneself to an employee and asking her for sexual services wasn't harassment with a very different decision in a New Jersey court:

> Not all judges are so forgiving, however. Six weeks ago, the New Jersey Supreme Court held that a single epithet said by a supervisor to a subordinate could be harassment, if a jury so finds. Indecent exposure, of course, is a crime, while epithets are not. Presumably, then, if one of the New Jersey justices had sat in Judge Wright's seat, the Jones decision would have gone the other way.[19]

Courts differ on other points. Up until March 4, 1998, one extremely controversial issue was that of same-sex harassment. The District of Columbia Circuit Court had held it was a Title VII offense; others had held it was not. State courts in California had allowed such litigation under the California Fair Employment and Housing Act, which bans discrimination on the basis of sex both in the workplace and in housing.

But on March 4, in its third unanimous decision on sexual harassment—this one written by Justice Antonin Scalia—the Supreme Court held that Joseph Oncale, who had not been allowed to bring suit in Louisiana for sexual harassment against an oil company and the members of its oil-rig crew who "had singled him out for crude sex play, unwanted touching and threats of rape,"[20] should be allowed to bring charges of same-sex sexual harassment in the state's courts. The decision overturned a Fifth Circuit decision that the Civil Rights Act does not apply to same-sex harassment, with Scalia saying, "We see no justification in the statutory language or our precedents for a categorical rule excluding same-sex harassment claims from the coverage of Title VII."[21] Legal authorities agreed that the decision was not intended to outlaw harassment because of sexual preference (which is not a federally protected category), but beyond that, opinions varied as to what it meant. According to Linda Greenhouse of the *New York Times*, it "offered relatively little guidance about what must be proved to win a sexual harassment case against someone of the same sex."[22] The controversy over how to interpret this decision had not been resolved by the time this book went to press.

Although district courts in different circuits may disagree widely in their interpretations of what is legal and what is not, on the appellate level a fairly narrow definition of hostile environment sexual harassment is emerging. According to Rita Risser of the Fair Measures Management Law Consulting Group, federal courts of appeals applied a standard to such cases decided between November 1993 (when *Harris v. Forklift Systems, Inc.*, was decided) and November 1996 that "almost always involves physical abuse, from crotch grabbing to pinning women against walls to stalking to rape."[23] In early 1999, Risser produced an updated version of this study, which applied the same analysis to the ensuing appellate cases through the end of 1998 that dealt with the definition of sexual harassment. The revision summarized a total of sixty-two cases from late 1993 through 1998. Twenty-eight of these cases claimed sexual harassment on the basis of verbal comments only; of these, only eleven found sexual harassment. And she pointed out that none of those cases punished isolated or sporadic remarks:

> Every case held that verbal comments alone are not sexual harassment, unless they are directed at the particular person on a repeated, almost daily basis, and they are one or more of the following: physically threatening, slanderous (publicly implying a lack of chastity), humiliating (degrading one in front of others), or discriminatory (personal questions, propositions, slurs).[24]

One case illustrating discriminatory verbal behavior that was held to be sexual harassment is that of a woman doctor in St. Louis Hospital whose department head not only made "constant gender comments" but refused to refer to her (or indeed, to any woman doctor) as "Doctor" in front of patients.[25]

The last Supreme Court decisions in 1998 did not repudiate this trend but instead added an interesting twist—the definition of harassing behavior may be growing narrower, but the liability of management has increased. On June 26, 1998, the very last day of term, the Supreme Court decided a pair of cases, *Faragher v. City of Boca Raton* and *Burlington Industries, Inc. v. Ellerth*, that distinguished not between speech and action but between the consequences of the actions of supervisor and employee. These cases were intended to clarify employer liability for supervisor hostile environment harassment, an issue that had been left open by the Court's *Meritor* decision. Both the *Burlington* decision (written by Justice Anthony Kennedy) and the *Boca Raton* decision (written by Justice David Souter) incorporated a list of identical rules, as follows:

> An employer is subject to vicarious liability to a victimized employee for an actionable hostile environment created by a supervisor with immediate (or successively higher) authority over the employee. When no tangible employment action is taken, a defending employer may raise an affirmative defense to liability or damages, subject to proof by a preponderance of the evidence.
>
> The defense comprises two necessary elements: (a) that the employer exercised reasonable care to prevent and correct promptly any sexually harassing behavior, and (b) that the plaintiff employee unreasonably failed to take advantage of any preventive or corrective opportunities provided by the employer or to avoid harm otherwise.
>
> While proof that an employer had promulgated an anti-harassment policy with complaint procedure is not necessary in every instance as a matter of law, the need for a stated policy suitable to the employment circumstances may appropriately be addressed in any case when litigating the first element of the defense. And while proof that an employee failed to fulfill the corresponding obligation of reasonable care to avoid harm is not limited to showing any unreasonable failure to use any complaint procedure provided by the employer, a demonstration of such failure will normally suffice to satisfy the employer's burden under the second element of the defense. No affirmative defense is available, however, when a supervisor's harassment culminates

in a tangible employment action, such as discharge, demotion or undesirable reassignment.[26]

The *Meritor* decision decided not to adopt a rule of "strict liability" in hostile environment cases. These *Burlington* and *Boca Raton* cases say they are adopting a rule of "vicarious liability." The differences between the two terms (both of which originate in common law) are very slight, particularly in these cases. *Strict liability* is liability that does not depend on negligence. *Vicarious liability* imputes the negligence of one person to another, often sought when courts want to find a defendant with money.[27] Liability in harassment cases involving supervisors is "strict" in that it depends on a rule rather than on what specifically happened; it is also "vicarious" in that the harasser is considered to be acting as the company's agent and so the company is always liable. Until these decisions, companies were held liable for hostile environment actions only if they knew or should have known what was going on, and that was decided on a case-by-case basis. Now companies are liable when supervisors are involved.

In other words, the Court held that the employer is always liable for a supervisor's "hostile environment" actions as well as quid pro quo actions. The only defense is in the event that the supervisor exercised no punitive job action and management can show both that it had a good (and well-publicized and circulated) sexual harassment policy and that the employee didn't use it.

The new rules were hailed by the mainstream media and by some representatives of business, because now at least there seemed a clearcut defense to harassment charges—having an anti-harassment policy in place that is enforced. Linda Greenhouse wrote that the rules "cut through a thicket of confusing and contradictory lower-court rulings that had grown up in the 12 years since the Justices first ruled that sexual harassment was a form of employment discrimination."[28] However, Anita Blair of the Independent Women's Forum objected in an op-ed piece in the *Wall Street Journal* that "the *Ellerth* and *Faragher* cases give plaintiffs more ways to reach wealthier defendants" and predicted more suits against employers by plaintiffs deciding to "try their luck."[29] And *The Economist* ran an analysis that said not only had the new rulings "made it easier for plaintiffs to sue by putting the burden of proof squarely on employers, and failing to say what is a reasonable anti-harassment policy," but they had "left employers with no defense at all against a supervisor who misuses his authority to penalize a subordinate for resisting his advances."[30]

So, where do these decisions leave relations between peers in the workplace? Don't bet on freedom from liability for employers. Company liability in the case of co-worker harassment is still case by case. But if the atmosphere is such that the employer knew or should have known what was going on, or if the employer doesn't have a strict policy and deal stringently with "offenders," he (or she) is still liable. The general trend towards clarification does not mean that lower courts and state courts are not being and will not continue to be creative in their views of what is harassing. But the legal hierarchy *is* a hierarchy. Rulings of appellate courts are binding on the courts below them, and every federal court is bound by the Supreme Court. If the appellate courts are now specifically discussing the definition of sexual harassment in narrower terms and knocking down what I called the creative approaches of lower courts on appeal, then we can look forward to the evolution of a more limited—and predictable—view of what constitutes sexual harassment. This, such experts in employment law as Rita Risser have said, is what employers can expect from the legal system— always provided that they recognize the possibility of losing in a lower court and budget for an appeal at the start of any sexual harassment case.[31]

For an employee to take legal steps under the post-*Harris* trend would mean, of course, abandoning much of the early definition that came out of the 1975 Cornell conference. The bottom line seems to be that it is still true that no one can tell for sure what sexual harassment is, but it can no longer be defined as sex between unequals or as "anything that makes you uncomfortable." And the importance of "degrading attitudes, looks, touches, innuendos, gestures, and direct propositions" depends in large part on whether they are repeated and how often, and whether they come from a supervisor. Direct propositions need to be tied to quid pro quo to be actionable, unless they are uttered almost daily. Despite the increased employer liability endorsed by the Supreme Court, the trend in the courts is towards a much narrower interpretation of what behavior is culpable. Also, as this law evolves through judicial decisions, many in legal circles are having reservations about its underlying reasoning (to be dealt with more fully later). Suffice it for now to say that many decisions have been criticized as conflicting with established First Amendment law, and there is also criticism of the uneasy fit between the offense of sexual harassment and discrimination law.

Up to now, this chapter has dealt with the legal definition of sexual harassment rather than with how that definition is perceived in the workplace. But the lay definition can be hopelessly at odds with the courts' perception. Since behavior that is distressing in this way must be tied to job discrimination, and since, under Title VII, it is only the employer who can be sued for discrimination, the legal issue becomes: How is the employer involved?

Employers and employees may not be aware of this. Compliance manuals, government departments concerned with discrimination, and consultants continue to dispense material implying that seemingly innocent words are discriminatory. Columnist Robyn E. Blumner quotes a U.S. Department of Labor pamphlet, *Sexual Harassment—Know Your Rights*, that gives these examples of sexual harassment: "1. Someone said something sexual about how you look. 2. Someone made sexual jokes or said sexual things that you didn't like. 3. Someone showed you or put up pornographic pictures."[32] And the EEOC Guidelines on Sexual Harassment (adopted November 1980 and revised in 1990) remain confusing. At least one lawyer has remarked, "The EEOC accepts claims for conduct that clearly is not illegal."[33]

Media reports sometimes add to the confusion. It is not generally known, for instance, that one of the main reasons Paula Jones's lawsuit was dismissed is that she had missed the filing deadline for a sexual harassment suit and so actually sued under another section of the civil rights laws that didn't quite fit her complaint.[34]

However, the Paula Jones lawsuit and President Clinton's putative problems with what were presented to the public as other instances of sexual harassment, with Monica Lewinsky, Kathleen Willey, and others, in 1997 and early 1998 did contribute in a positive way to the honing of the popular definition of sexual harassment. A number of prominent feminists who came publicly to President Clinton's defense—particularly regarding the possibility that he had sex with women who worked for him—made excellent points (some of which did seem to contradict previously held positions) that may have served to further refine the definition for the general public.

Wendy Kaminer: Paula Jones has been trashed unfairly by some feminists simply because she is a working-class person. But I think that if you take all of her charges at face value—and I do—that they do not amount to a serious claim of sexual harassment. . . . Harassment is still very much a problem. It's a form of discrimination. The trouble is that the more subtle forms . . . the cases involving persistent derogatory remarks or the hostile-climate cases, are hard to deal with. They pit free-speech rights against equality rights, and I usually tend to err on the side of protecting free speech.[35]

Catharine MacKinnon: The courts are clear, if others are not, that working women cannot sue for having mutual sexual interactions. Sex under conditions of extreme inequality can be coerced and exploitative; sexual compliance can be coerced. But sex cannot be harassment at work by law unless the woman or man really didn't want to have it. Sex between unequals is sometimes prohibited outright, but not usually at work or in sexual harassment codes. Schools sometimes use disciplinary rules, the military uses anti-fraternization policies, and mental hospitals and prisons use criminal law, all to forbid sex between hierarchical unequals. These provisions work like statutory rape laws: because of power differences, sex with students, recruits, or inmates is prohibited, no matter who wants what. This is not sexual harassment law at work.[36]

Susan Estrich: Sometimes I find myself explaining to young women that if they don't like something a man is doing they have a responsibility to say no, and to cool their jets a little bit about *Playboy.*[37]

And from the always-quotable Gloria Steinem:

Commentators might stop puzzling over the President's favorable poll ratings, especially among women, if they understood the common-sense guideline that came out of the women's movement 30 years ago: no means no; yes means yes. It's the basis of sexual harassment law. . . . The truth is that even if the allegations are true, the President is not guilty of sexual harassment. . . . In other words, President Clinton took "no" for an answer. . . . As reported, Monica Lewinsky's case illustrates the rest of the equation: "Yes means yes."[38]

Management interprets what seems to be going on in the law with the goal of protecting itself. The trend in management, therefore, may be towards more and more legalistic rules that curtail worker freedom, so that the company may be protected from suit under that increased employer liability. The 1998 Supreme Court *Burlington* and *Boca Raton* decisions made the law more predictable, which is why so many people hailed them, but they also exposed the hazard for workers whose behavior can lead to an assumption of company discrimination: if management is going to be held responsible for the negative consequences of individual behavior, it can hardly be blamed for taking over more and more control of greater and greater areas of that same individual behavior.

CHAPTER THREE

It May Not Be a
Legal Problem

No one wants lawsuits. But how much of a threat are they? Let's look again at the figures I mentioned in chapter 1.

Approximately 15,500 complaints are now being filed each year with the EEOC. These do not all go to trial: some are settled out of court; others are dropped before trial; still others the EEOC finds to be without merit. In fact, in one fairly typical three-year period, from November 1993 to November 1996, federal trial courts decided only 376 cases. Even if we posit a higher number of state cases *not* brought under Title VII (there were 229 state appellate court decisions during the same period, which would imply perhaps 600 state trials), the total is surprisingly small when you consider that American workplaces employ tens of millions of workers.[1]

So although most employers, workers, and members of the media may assume that sexual harassment is an important legal issue, the legal action is minuscule. Yet it's clearly a matter of concern. In fact, there is a large body of lesser-known sociological research that presents a different picture.[2] Looking at this research leads one to the conclusion that much of what we call sexual harassment is based on reactions to changes in the demographics of the workplace, which lead to clashes in expectations and to misunderstandings of communication styles. Therefore, countering sexual harassment and making the workplace more user-friendly isn't primarily a legal problem. Changes in workplace population mixes may, in fact, turn out to be more effective in lessening perceptions of sexual harassment than any amount of punitive regulation.

If we adopt a more limited view of the scope of the law and its curative powers, what do we find we actually know about workplace relations? Perhaps the most important finding for the purposes of this book is the work of contemporary linguists that elaborates on the fact that people of different cultures have difficulty communicating because of their different patterns of speech and habits of relating: fast/slow, direct/indirect, formal/playfully insulting, deferential/take-charge, and so forth. The work of linguist Deborah Tannen has applied this body of research to the communication between men and women and made many identifications about the cross-cultural nature of that communication which can illuminate problems that arise between men and women in the workplace (of which much more later, when we examine communication itself more closely).

The next area of research that tells us a lot is in the area of group composition. It is a fact that the ratio of men to women in the workplace makes an enormous difference in how they behave towards each other.

A seminal work here is Rosabeth Moss Kanter's 1977 book *Men and Women of the Corporation* (reissued, tellingly, in 1993). Kanter found, in studying personnel behavior within a large corporation, that factors such as opportunity for advancement, power and powerlessness, and relative numbers produce what had been assumed to be gender-based behavior. "Indeed," she writes, "the problems of women in managerial roles (a preference for male bosses, an image of women's controlling style) spring into focus as problems of powerlessness, not sex."[3]

Populations within a group relate to one another in different ways depending on their proportions. When a uniform group (e.g., a workforce consisting of white males) adds a few members of another group, the members of the dominant group will have stereotypical expectations of what the new members can and cannot do, and the token members of the new group will react in certain ways. Kanter identifies four group types: *uniform* (100:0), *skewed* (with a few "tokens" of another racial, national, or gender type—perhaps up to 85:15), *tilted* (majority/minority, ending somewhere near 65:35), and *balanced* (60:40 to 50:50). She shows how the behavior and the impact of the "other" in terms of social expectation change with the proportional numbers.

The token is highly visible; his or her differences from the dominants are exaggerated; and the token is stereotyped as an example of his or her group. These factors keep the token with less opportunity to advance—the token feels pressure to conform, finds it hard to be credible, is excluded from informal networks, is isolated and peripheral— which in turn creates what Kanter calls "self-perpetuating, self-sealing systems, with links that can be broken only from outside."[4]

The structural difficulties of the token change as group proportions change, and they diminish as the ratio approaches balance and the person is increasingly accepted and judged as an individual rather than as a representative of an outside group. This analysis of tokenism explains the early but isolated successes of outstanding women in unusual professions in the 1920s and 1930s: despite being treated as a stereotype, there are ways in which a token has an easier time than does the minority member of a skewed or tilted group. Visibility can be an asset as long as the token is no threat to the dominant group; she is an exception to the rule that her kind doesn't really belong. But add a few more tokens and they

> can create even more problems—backlash, resistance, complaints of "reverse discrimination." Research shows that dissatisfaction and tension are greatest in groups in which there are several women or minorities, but not enough to fully balance the numbers or create a routine expectation of diversity.[5]

When gender is the difference between the token and the dominant group, the token is saddled with a sex-role stereotype. All women are caring and nurturing. All men are natural leaders and good with tools. Or perhaps, women are good for just one thing, and all men want only that one thing. It depends on your stereotype. A lot of work has been done to explore the concept of "sex-role spillover," defined as "the carryover into the workplace of gender-based expectations for behavior that are irrelevant or inappropriate to work." This occurs "whenever the sex-ratio at work is skewed—in either direction."[6] But it occurs in two different ways.

In all-male workplaces into which a few women have penetrated, male culture defines the workplace roles. Entering women are "'role deviates' who are treated differently from other (male) work-role occupants; they are aware of the differential treatment, and they think it is directed at them as individual women rather than as work-role occupants." The men, according to this thesis, having previously interacted with women only as sex objects and family members, treat women in the workplace according to "sex roles" rather than "work roles"—sex roles being defined as "a set of expectations about the behavior of men and women," and work roles being "a set of expectations about behavior on the job."[7]

When the sex ratio is skewed the other way and the workplace or the occupation is woman dominated, with only a few male bosses, the job itself is sexualized. Waitresses and receptionists expect to be flirted with—it's part of the job. This is because "a high percentage of one sex in an occupation leads to the expectation that people in that occupation should behave in a manner consistent with the sex-role of the numerically dominant sex."[8]

This concept explains why the lone woman—or the lone man—in a workplace is often overtly viewed as a sex object: the sex role is predominant to the viewer. Some years ago, a popular television commercial featured an office full of women drooling over a shirtless male construction worker drinking a Diet Coke outside their window. If it had featured a similarly scantily dressed woman up on a catwalk being whistled at by a phalanx of men, it clearly would not have been taken as amusing. The humor here was rooted in inversion of traditional gender roles.

Interestingly, although women in male-dominated workplaces have tended to report more sexual harassment than those in female-dominated workplaces (who expect sexual banter and report that "it comes with the job"), women in sexually integrated workplaces not only uniformly said that sexual harassment was not a problem at work but also found employee dating widely acceptable. This suggests that sex-role problems tend to disappear as the sex ratio becomes more balanced. The figure 30 percent has been widely bandied about as the point at which sex-role spillover begins to be minimized and women become treated primarily as co-workers rather than as symbols of Woman, although a woman who specializes in training programs tells me that in her experience in blue-collar settings, progress requires "almost 50 percent down at the plant."

But very often, what women encounter when they enter previously all-male jobs is protection and paternalism, not sexual hostility. A group of 331 women who joined with 1,700 men to replace strikers in a utility plant[9] indicated that paternalism was the main effect of sex-role spillover, "much more common than hostility or harassment,"[10] which only 19 percent of the women found to be a problem. The women also complained of a sexual division of labor through which they were given less-desirable jobs, perhaps due to an assumption that they couldn't handle more challenging ones. But this study concludes that the reported reactions to these women "failed to dampen women's interest in returning to plant jobs." The authors say this finding so "flies in the face of commonsense"[11] that they checked their data several times to be sure they were accurate, because "women in overwhelmingly male work settings may have to put up with short-term harassment to prove themselves and long-term harassment as a reminder that they do not belong." The authors never found an explanation for their results. Clearly, in some way the benefits of plant jobs outweighed the reported disadvantages to the women in this study. The findings may well generalize to other workplaces, as the levels of harassment reported in this study were said to be "only slightly below"[12] those reported in other studies of women in blue-collar jobs.

Extreme harassment is not the norm, and acceptance can accompany familiarity. A survey of conditions in two steel plants reported that women "experienced sexual harassment, that male employees did not teach them jobs that they taught other men, and that they were assigned to menial tasks. Furthermore, both men and women perceived that there were some physically demanding jobs that supervisors did not assign to women."[13] At the same time, the male employees in these plants "felt that the participation of women in the workforce had no negative effect on cooperation, morale, ability to do the work, and productivity." But the male supervisors in these plants "reported that women in the workforce had a mildly negative effect on cost, productivity, and workplace relations." However, in a study of attitudes towards women doing blue-collar civilian jobs for the U.S.

Navy that interviewed both male workers and supervisors, it was the male workers, not the supervisors, who viewed males more favorably, "at least partially due to stereotypes regarding women's inability to perform certain tasks . . . and/or the strain of working with persons of the opposite sex." In this study, the hypothesis of which was an expectation that both groups would treat women differently and have negative attitudes towards them, supervisors "who had previously worked with women tended to have higher expectations of women" and treated them in ways not statistically significantly different from how they treated men.

So we have a research picture of gender communication differences, stereotyping in skewed work populations, sex-role spillover, and indications that familiarity with diversity will, in time, breed acceptance. The picture is being complicated by anger.

Hostility—anger—is created in an individual when that individual feels that rights are being violated. Men workers, women workers, and management all have different agendas when it comes to the bundle of behaviors subsumed under the title "sexual harassment." And in different ways for members of different groups, the ways in which those agendas have been implemented create this kind of anger. A reporter looking into how men were feeling about sexual harassment in 1995 began by interviewing Stephen Paskoff, who runs sensitivity-training sessions for companies:

> "When men see women doing stuff that would get them in trouble, they get very very mad," said Mr. Paskoff, a lawyer who has both prosecuted and defended sexual harassment cases and now runs a training firm in Atlanta. "The degree of anger about this, and the way the issue has been positioned as a political cause—so one group thinks it has special rights and the other group feels frustrated—is going to spill over."[14]

Some of the legal remedies for discrimination help deepen this reaction. Apart from being on the receiving end of sexist cracks and derogatory stereotypes from women, many men, especially in workplaces that have been all-male enclaves, have been specifically informed that the only reason women are being hired is to satisfy legal affirmative-action requirements. Construction workers know that there are quotas for hiring women[15] and sometimes have worked with women who have passed the licensing exams but have been hired without the experience that makes it safe for them to be put on dangerous jobs. So in a sort of governmental featherbedding, at some sites such women may be reporting to work without assignment but still getting paid the same as everyone else, because no one wants to be their mentor, and at the same time no one wants to risk legal action by firing them.

One manager of blue-collar workers whom I interviewed told me that some of her workers have been informed through the grapevine that not only will the women not be qualified to do the work but they will be promoted over the heads of the men who were there before them. This perception of unfairness is reinforced when specific experiences seem to confirm it.

In one instance, a young, black, female army veteran, Kimberley, who worked as a driver in a university maintenance system, was recruited to be on a search committee looking for a management system operator in heating, ventilating and air-conditioning, which everyone in the company referred to as HVAC. One of the reasons she was on the search committee was that minority participation was a requirement, and she was one of the relatively few African Americans on that workforce. The job to be filled was a highly technical position: running the HVAC equipment by computer. Kimberley could use a computer, as she had proved when she worked from time to time as acting supervisor of the drivers, computerizing the driving schedules.

The manager of the HVAC group was the chair of the search committee and was so impressed with Kimberley's energy and intelligence that he decided to hire her for the job as a trainee. Union rules required that the job vacancy be posted in case someone more qualified wanted it, but after two months, Kimberley was the only applicant, even though the head of maintenance had recommended it to two other people. So Kimberley was to work in the energy-management systems as energy-management supervisor-operator intern.

HVAC was a small, tight-knit group, at the time all male, all white, even all Irish—men who had worked together in isolation in a sub-basement for a long time. When Kimberley came into this group, there were immediate complaints. The men complained that she was incompetent; she didn't know what she was doing (which, said the head of maintenance, was true; she was only a trainee). They assumed that she got the job because of preferential treatment. Even when they were told that wasn't true—that she had been the only applicant—the hostility continued. The real issue was that her presence changed things. She wanted the room warm, while the guy she was paired with wanted it cool. She had to be told how to do things. Not only that, but she got to take over the ladies' room, which the men had previously used in addition to their own toilet.

The ladies' room became a battleground. First, the men urinated on the walls and the floor in Kimberley's absence. In response to this, a lock was put on the door and she was given a key, which further annoyed the men—"Why should she have her own key? What happens if my wife comes to visit me at work?" (This had never happened, but in the event, there was a bathroom upstairs.) Then the lock was jammed shut—not with a key broken in it, which could have happened by accident, but with a sliver of glass. Finally, one of the workers (who had a terminal illness) spent what was reported as "two hours" cussing Kimberley out in front of the entire work group, using every racial and sexual epithet he could think of.

She chose to refuse to take it seriously, saying, "He's crazy; he's dying." Just as she was beginning to impress her colleagues with her resilience, she injured her back and was out for two weeks. Since the job required constant presence, her colleagues had to cover for her and work longer shift hours, so the resentment of her built again.

The men expected incompetence from an African American woman, and every change that Kimberley brought into their closed group was interpreted in that light. Would it have helped the situation if the affirmative action officer had pulled them off the job for a sensitivity training session, as she wanted to do? As the head of maintenance pointed out to the officer, Kimberley's cohorts would interpret that as punishment and would end up making things harder for her. Kimberley eventually transferred to another unit, and the HVAC crew regained control of their territory.

A combination of misinformation, bad experiences, and backlash towards affirmative action can predispose men to greet the arrival of women with hostility. A reflexive hostility towards feminists plays a significant role as well. An example is this diatribe that spilled out of one man when he came across the Feminists for Free Expression web site:

> You cannot possibly imagine what it's like for the average American man to work in the "modern" office environment, under constant psychic and administrative threat based upon the interpretation of harassment by any female present. In the past 30 years feminism has expanded the use of "offense" to cover any word, gesture, or situation with which they are challenged, gainsaid, or find disagreement. Of course, if men in the workplace find the words or actions of females objectionable, that's another matter. . . .
>
> A couple of years ago I worked in a public-sector setting in which front-office discussion of the various and unending deficits of males were [*sic*] a common occurrence. No problem there, though. As usual, the guys just crept around with their heads down and pretended not to hear, or be injured by, these attacks. Had the situation been reversed though, immediate complaints, filings, and repercussions would have ensued, believe me—I have seen it firsthand, and I have experienced it. One of these liberated women—liberated not to equal opportunity but to protection from personal and cultural responsibility—liked to parade around with her coffee mug, which contained a "humorous" male-hating slogan. These are quite popular, by the way, as are calendars containing male-demeaning "jokes." It's always a one-way street, however. It's only harassment if women say it is.
>
> . . . I've worked in all kinds of settings in both the public and private sector, and I haven't seen anything by any man that is even close to harassment (which doesn't mean, by the way, that it doesn't occur—but if it were as common as women claim it is, I'd at least have encountered it by now). What I've seen instead is the use of policies and enforcement procedures propagated by feminism used to bludgeon men at random and with impunity. "Feminists for Free Expression"?—you've got to be kidding. You're the ones who have turned the American workplace into a truly hostile environment. Feminism has turned media, academia, and the workplace into environments hostile to anything like "free expression" from men, into ideological fiefdoms in which men must grovel and apologize every time they burp, and now you're coming down on the side of "free expression"? Forgive my incredulity and earned cynicism. I supported feminism when it meant equal opportunity, and I supported sexual harassment codes when they stood against coercion by persons in power to elicit sex. But the fact is that feminism in the past

30 years in America has been in the forefront of censorship and repression, not only in the context of sexual harassment, but across the cultural spectrum. The policies you've championed have spread a cancer of injustice and pain through American men that you cannot comprehend, because your eyes and hearts have only been open to the sufferings—real and fabricated—of your sisters.[16]

Training experts echo the perception that men feel unreasonable restriction. One writes, "The most frequent comment men make at the start of my harassment seminars is that they are afraid to say anything. They believe they can be sued for off-hand remarks, compliments, and casual conversation."[17] But many employers will punish or even fire employees on stringent or even capricious grounds, even though the law as to what will prevail in a lawsuit may be changing. The courts and the EEOC hold that "prompt action" towards harassment is required of employers to show good faith, so it is not surprising that some men may be concerned—and angry.

Women are also made angry by their own expectations. Just as the grapevine has encouraged men to feel that workplace *rules* violate their rights, women are encouraged to expect that the workplace *climate* will violate their rights. Training courses may tell them they are too slow to understand that jokes and leers and even compliments should be interpreted as sexually harassing. A common form of sociological study is to describe fictional office interactions to students in college and ask them to rate the intensity of the "harassment" described. Some feminist spokespersons publicly deplore the permissiveness of young women towards male behavior; feminist groups sometimes encourage women to think of themselves as constant victims of male aggression. In general, women are encouraged in many ways to feel that they are underhired, underutilized, underpromoted, and denigrated by "the patriarchy" in the workplace. This view is so pervasive that even Wendy Shalit, who identifies herself as a conservative, put it this way in *National Review*:

At every turn one hears conservatives hopefully proclaiming the "death of feminism" but they couldn't be more wrong. Feminism is not only alive and well, it lives precisely on what conservatives have forgotten.

. . . Women who identify with feminism will continue to do so not because they hate men, but because they feel mistreated by them. From vulgarity on the streets to transient husbands at home, our culture is not kind to women. As long as conservatives ignore this reality and remain incapable of addressing it, the personal will remain political.[18]

My own view is that although there may be some truth to this observation, one shouldn't create for oneself a prior expectation of bad treatment. It is not empowering.

Sexual harassment law puts this perception of mistreatment into a context of rights violations, thereby *making* the personal political. Especially because it seems to be harder for women than for men to express anger,[19] it can be easier to support what one sees as an abstract principle through impersonal channels than to make a person-to-person statement of outrage. If complaints about men's behavior are based on the earlier, nonlegal definition of sexual harassment as whatever makes you uncomfortable (a definition still widely in use), you have a potential collision between men and women, both of whom feel their rights are being violated and both of whom feel justified in their reactions—and both of whom have, at least in part, been given misleading information.

Managers, of course, can be angry too—at their employees for putting their businesses at risk in the way in which they are dealing with one another, and at the state and federal government for fostering policies that, in their minds, require inefficiency.

So if you are starting your work life, no matter which sex you are, you can expect some diffuse anger and suspicion: a hot button that is there to be pushed. The differing viewpoints of men and women on the issue can make for a volatile mix. As one (female) manager of blue-collar workers said:

Actual cases of out-of-the-blue discrimination are very few and far between. Usually what happens is some man acts inappropriately because of disorganization, ignorance, attraction, malice of a nondiscriminatory nature, etc., and the woman assumes that it is discrimination. Overreaction on her part may then escalate the situation and polarize the parties away from a satisfactory resolution.

Add to the mix the innumerable surveys—by popular magazines, by sociologists and social psychologists, and by government agencies— that have asked women if they have been sexually harassed. These have resulted in statistics that are essentially meaningless. The pattern among such surveys is to offer a broad range of categories, beginning with something as innocuous as leers or complimentary remarks and escalating to sexual assault and attempted rape. The results are quantified and then published as statistics on sexual harassment. One study of women graduates of a technical college which reported that over 75 percent had experienced "some sexual harassment" had as its most frequently experienced category "nonabusive verbal commentaries (i.e. personal remarks regarding clothing, body, or love life)" but also included physical assault.[20] This mix of apples and oranges implies no coherent definition of sexual harassment: but what the studies do show is that a large number of women are offended by men's behavior in the workplace.

What else research suggests about the contemporary workplace is complex, but we can draw some general conclusions. In sex-ratio analysis, sexual harassment becomes simply one reaction of dominant males, who have enjoyed a uniform population, to the influx of women into their territory, changing the population ratio to skewed and, later, tilted. "Threatened members of dominant groups sometimes express their discontent at shifting numbers by harassing the newcomers or trying to put them into their traditional subservient place. . . . The more women, it seems, the more potential for harassment, and the more it handicaps the women and distracts them from their tasks."[21] (This last does not persist as the ratio of women to men approaches balance.) If a woman is entering a male-dominated field, she can expect to encounter, at least initially, some sex-role spillover, as well as some latent anger and erroneous expectations of what she can and cannot do. This can all add up to strikingly differential treatment. But a lack of experience and false expectations, even anger, are nonmalicious. It could be a potentially career-ending mistake to assume that these reactions must indicate prejudice or job discrimination. If the field is female dominated, the spillover effect will be different, but a similar false conclusion may have an equally negative effect on a new worker with a feminist consciousness.

In both situations, the answer is the same for the neophyte worker. (The answer for management will be dealt with in forthcoming chapters.) Know what to expect, and take the time to observe before you act. Knowledge is one kind of power, so it is most important for the worker to identify what is going on. With that knowledge, it becomes possible to move towards taking control of your immediate situation.

Here again, social science research provides useful information. We have been looking at what is; let us look at what can best be done about it, by someone who feels uncomfortable and offended.

The person who has problems entering a group is the person who feels different. Since, generally, the work role in most workplaces is the male sex role, many if not most neophyte male workers will find no difficulty fitting into the job. For the uncertain woman or the man who is different enough for some other reason to feel he is a target for harassment, information from various studies discussed here can help.

Communication with those you have problems with is not just one of several useful tools—it is by far the best tool, as was indicated by the 1992 *Working Woman* survey. A more formal study of members of a university faculty, which examined how targets themselves reported their satisfaction with the outcome of various responses to sexual harassment, found that what most often led to a satisfactory outcome was talking to the harasser, but without relying on aggressive responses such as threats or verbal attacks. The researchers had expected that some form of "calling the cops" would have created the most satisfaction but found that it wasn't so—neither formal nor informal complaints gave a reported feeling of resolution in the way that direct communication did.[22]

Other studies have found that assertiveness can be especially effective when the target is not only non-aggressive but actually makes an effort to maintain a positive relationship with the harasser and not put him down. This is often called "facework."[23] In the preface to her 1984 book *Powerbase*, Marilyn Moats Kennedy comments on the general importance and difficulty of making such efforts in the office.

The hardest choices will always be those that involve trading off your desire to get even or to tell someone your "honest" opinion or to show off with your need to build and maintain relationships with the patently unlikeable. To make these choices will test your real desire to be powerful.[24]

(In her book discussing Internet interactions, Wendy Grossman quotes what she calls a "well-known Net saying": "Never wrestle with a pig. You both get dirty, and the pig likes it.")[25]

Unfortunately, as satisfactory as assertive communication combined with facework may be, it is not the usual response of choice. One analysis of ten studies of responses to harassing situations in different environments found that the most frequent response was avoidance, even though "evidence from research and women's narratives suggests strongly that the personal impact of harassment is related not only to its severity but to her ability to respond in an effective or assertive manner."[26]

The moral is: Don't rush to give away power to co-workers or management—or the law. At times a person may need the law, but invoking it as a first response to a new and difficult interpersonal situation surrenders the responsibility of being able to make things happen. That's the opposite of how careers are prepared for or implemented. Rather, the first response to a new and uncomfortable situation, after identifying as much as possible what is going on, should be to look at all your options and to be prepared to say clearly and without hostility what makes you uncomfortable.

CHAPTER FOUR

A Failure to Communicate

But communication doesn't seem to be that easy. Why is it so hard for many women to say what they want and don't want, clearly and assertively, when faced with sexual behavior they find obnoxious? Why is it hard for men to change their ways?

The difficulty is that we are communicating about sex, and that puts a number of issues on the table: perhaps including hostility, to be sure, but also self-esteem, assumptions (not always well founded) about human nature and gender relationships, ritual ways of dealing with others, expectations about new situations, and characteristic ways that men and women have of communicating.

We like to think the whole area of sex involves instinctive knowledge, but it doesn't. Sexual harassment isn't the crossing of an invisible line that everyone understands. Some communications labeled "sexual harassment" have to do with wanting sexual relations with fellow workers. Of these, some are exploitive in nature, and some are seeking relationships that might have a future. Other such communications may signal an attempt to throw the target off balance, either as a strategy to advance one's own power in the workplace or in the hope that somehow the *status quo ante* of an all-male workplace may result. Still others may be simply the result of not knowing how to behave in a new situation. As with any communications, the more accurate one's understanding of what is being communicated, the better off one is. Unchecked assumptions can undermine such understanding.

Take just those communications that are actually seeking some sort of personal relationship. Unspoken generalizations can affect one's perception of what is happening. On the one hand, women who assume that all men are predatory and most of them don't know what women want will react with suspicion and hostility to whatever they perceive as male advances. If, on the other hand, certain men assume that women don't know what they want and won't say what they mean, these men will keep pressing their advances, no matter what response they get. Many men who subject women to unwanted attentions do so from an internalized conviction that women like men who are aggressive and persistent. The more she refuses politely, the more he sees this as an incentive to redouble his efforts. And many women feel it would be rude to say no clearly.

The whole hypothesized exchange takes place in what Deborah Tannen calls "metamessages":

> Information conveyed by the meaning of words is the message. What is communicated about relationships—attitudes towards each other, the occasion, and what we are saying—is the metamessage. And it's metamessages that we react to most strongly. If someone says "I'm not angry," and his jaw is set hard and his words seem to be squeezed out in a hiss, you won't believe the message that he's not angry; you'll believe the metamessage conveyed by the way he said it—that he is.[1]

Some people (particularly, according to Tannen, American men) pride themselves on focusing as much as possible on the information level of conversations and ignore their own metamessages or those of others. (Sex, however, is a large area of exception. Men often assume metamessages about sexual receptivity from a woman's dress or manner that the woman may not intend to be sending at all.) Different people and different cultures have different standards of what is polite or appropriate. Some value indirectness and think that direct statements and questions are not only rude but probably have hidden meanings. Volume, pace, rising or falling intonations—all may convey unintended messages. "The adage, 'Do unto others as you would have others do unto you,'" writes Tannen,

> may be the source of a lot of anguish and misunderstanding if the doer and the done unto have different styles. . . . The ways we show our involvement and considerateness in talk seem self-evidently appropriate. And in interpreting what others say, we assume they mean what we would mean if we said the same thing in the same way. If we don't think about differences in conversational style, we see no reason to question this.[2]

Add to this Tannen's contention that men and women have such different life experiences that their communication is almost always cross-cultural, and you have a recipe for misunderstanding. Even more basically, we all know how hard it is to communicate about anything to do with sex itself. Here, the stereotypes run rampant. Entangled in what we do to express our desire for love is women's fear of male violence and men's fear of female manipulation. And the reason sexual harassment is such an explosive issue for both sexes is that, at bottom, it dredges up these deeply embedded fears and assumptions of both men and women concerning rape—fears and assumptions that permeate not only cultural myths and images but the very structure of the part of our Western legal system to do with rape.

Consider: We know that some people enjoy rough sex. How, then, can we know what is and is not rape? As Susan Estrich put it in an influential 1991 law journal article, "If nonconsent is essential to rape (and no amount of force or physical struggle is inherently inconsistent with lawful sex), and if no sometimes means yes, and if men are supposed to be aggressive in any event, how is a man to know when he has crossed the line? And how are we to avoid unjust convictions?"[3] Her answer is that we should return to the common-law tradition of *mens rea,* or the mental state of the accused. What did the defendant know or intend about consent? A mistake about consent, she postulates, ought to be "reasonable" in order to be exculpatory—negligently not thinking about it, ignoring explicit statements, or assuming that any woman who wears a flattering dress would want to have sex with him won't do.

Instead of doing this, says Estrich, our judicial system is so "intent upon protecting against unjust conviction"[4] that rather than requiring the man to prove why he thought he had consent in circumstances where it would not be reasonable to think so, it requires the woman to prove her *lack* of consent, generally by showing either that she fought back or that the "force" with which she was confronted was both so immediate and so overwhelming as to "reasonably" preclude any show of resistance. By using this standard, she tells us, convictions were reversed of a man who seized a woman at gunpoint and told her he was a notorious train robber and later had intercourse with her (*Mills v. United States,* 1897); of a man who confronted a former lover with whom he'd been violent in the past, took her to a friend's house after telling her he was going to "fix her face," and proceeded to have intercourse with her there although she said she didn't want to (*State v. Alston*, 1984); and of a violent father, who had in the past threatened his children at gunpoint and frequently beaten his wife and his son, when his fifteen-year-old daughter submitted to him sexually after he became angry (*State v. Lester*, 1984).

This "fight back" standard of nonconsent, says Estrich, is that of a boy in a schoolyard. How can you expect a woman who has been beaten repeatedly in a relationship to fight back when cornered again?

> She wouldn't fight; she might cry. Hers is the reaction of "sissies" in playground fights. Hers is the reaction of people who have already been beaten, or who never had the power to fight in the first instance. Hers is, from my reading, the most common reaction of women to rape. . . . That a woman feels genuinely afraid, that a man has created the situation that she finds frightening, even that he has done it intentionally in order to secure sexual satisfaction, may not be enough to constitute the necessary force or even implicit threat of force which earns bodily integrity any protection under the law of rape.[5]

Here we see why some feminists feel that such laws are a male construct that pay credence to the male fear of unjust conviction while ignoring the female fear of sexual assault. Juries, however, often do sympathize with such female fears. In the cases cited by Estrich, the lower-court juries all convicted the men accused; it was appellate-court judges who reversed these convictions by applying the arcane rules of what legally constituted "force" and "consent."

The ordinary person might tend to assume that the presence of force demonstrates lack of consent, and that sexual intercourse despite expressed lack of consent proves the presence of force. In fact, as Estrich discusses, the legal system differentiates between force and lack of consent and requires both to be present. Thus, in the absence of physical force (proved by bruises on the victim and the marks of her resistance on the accused), the *threat* of force must be shown to have been enough to inspire "reasonable" fear.

Being alone and out of earshot with a stranger much larger than the woman has been held as "simply not enough to have created a reasonable fear of harm so as to preclude resistance and be 'the equivalent of force' . . . even though the intercourse may have occurred without the actual consent and against the actual will of the alleged victim."[6] That was in a 1979 case with which Estrich was familiar when she wrote her 1991 article. But her argument has continued to be applicable in ensuing years. In 1993, another judge stated that saying no throughout the encounter

> is not relevant to the use of force. . . . In *Commonwealth v. Mlinarich*, this Court sustained the reversal of a defendant's conviction of rape where the alleged victim, a minor, repeatedly stated that she did not want to engage in sexual intercourse but offered no physical resistance and was compelled to engage in sexual intercourse under threat of being recommitted to a juvenile detention center. . . . [W]here there is a lack of consent, but no showing of either physical force, a threat of physical force, or psychological coercion, the "forcible compulsion" requirement . . . is not met.[7]

The better the parties involved know each other, the more proof of force is legally needed. Even though by 1991 all but two states had removed the "marital exemption" to rape laws, which had traditionally shielded husbands from prosecution for rape of their wives,[8] the standard of proof required in such cases is so high as to still make conviction rare, as was confirmed to me by a New York City human resources expert in early 1999. In one South Carolina case, the jury saw a videotape made by a husband corroborating a wife's testimony

> "that her husband dragged her by the throat into a bedroom, tied her hands and legs with rope and a belt, put duct tape on her eyes and mouth, and dressed her in stockings and a garter belt. He then had intercourse with her, sexually assaulted her with foreign objects, and threatened her with a knife which he ran around her breast and her stomach. . . . Her muffled screams could hardly be heard through the duct tape. At trial, the wife claimed her cries were of pain, and that none of these activities were consensual." The husband testified that "when his wife said no to sex, he did not think she was serious; he knew she meant yes," because, he alleged, she liked rough sex. He had tied her up before. Because South Carolina law permitted testimony about a plaintiff wife's past sexual history but not about that of a defendant, the

wife's former husband was allowed to testify that "she enjoyed violent, abusive treatment" but testimony from the husband's former wife about being assaulted and raped by him was excluded. Despite testimony that it was shown that the couple had planned to separate on the night of the alleged rape and that the husband left his wife tied up alone at the end of the incident, to painfully work her way loose from her bonds and flee naked to a neighbor's house for help, the jurors acquitted the defendant and said there was not enough evidence to convict.[9]

For our purposes here, the important point is that the courts often construe lack of resistance as an indication of consent. So even when (as in all the cases mentioned except the last) the court agrees that the sex took place against the will of the victim and that the victim said she didn't want it, proof of that is not enough to prove rape.

How is this relevant to sexual harassment? Rape, of course, is a crime, and what criminals do and assume is no guide to attitudes in the society in general. Or is there perhaps at least a continuum of assumptions? After all, jurors sometimes sympathize with accused rapists. And the controversy over when sexual intercourse during a social engagement is "date rape" sometimes exposes a similar sympathy for the accused perpetrator on the part of police and district attorneys who advise the victim against pressing charges. The implicit assumption of the defense in many of these cases seems to be that the woman may have been ambivalent and giving out mixed signals, so the man can't be blamed for choosing to respond to the signals he wanted. The metamessages were confused. What police and jury acceptance of such an argument indicates, in turn, is a general cultural acceptance of a deep lack of communication between men and women about sex.

Feminist Lois Pineau has suggested that date-rape cases in particular involve mythical general assumptions about sexuality that underlie the notion of "consent" in contemporary rape and sexual assault laws. The myths are that women will try to hide their sexual desire, that a woman's pleasure is created by overwhelming male insistence, and, above all, a belief in "incommunicative male prowess, a conception of sexual pleasure that springs from wordless interchanges, and of sexual success that occurs in a place of meaningful silence." These myths add up to the assumption "that a raped female experiences sexual pleasure [which] implies that the person who rapes her knows how to cause that pleasure independently of any information she might convey on that point." It is but a short step from here to the "she asked for it" defense to a rape charge—sexually provocative attire or behavior implies a contractual offer that, unlike any other contractual offer, cannot be withdrawn, especially since it is often culturally assumed that "no means yes." In other words, the jury's assumption sometimes seems to be that an exchange offered by the woman's clothing or demeanor was just what took place—a pleasurable experience for both parties, even though one party forced it on the other. (Such a view of the right to enforce a contract does not actually apply in contract law.)[10]

We know that plaintiffs in rape cases deny that such forced sex is pleasurable to them. Could there be such a widespread lack of communication about sex that men would generally assume as facts some reactions that women would generally repudiate? Not all men believe in Pineau's rape myths, of course; but certainly, lack of communication does exist. We know that many couples go to therapists in order to improve their communication about sex. Many other couples never communicate verbally about the subject. Nancy Friday, in her 1973 examination of women's sexual fantasies, *My Secret Garden* (reissued in 1998), found that when she began asking couples she knew to talk about women's sexual fantasies, the men uniformly seemed so bothered that women might have fantasies that didn't involve them that they denied any such possibility.[11] When she advertised for input from strangers, the letters she received "marked the turning point" in her attitude towards the book, because so many of them were from women who said they had fantasies but had never before been able to tell them to "a living soul."[12]

Similarly, in the 1976 *Hite Report*, an analysis of the responses of three thousand women to a detailed questionnaire about sexual experiences, woman after woman reported a lack of meaningful communication about sex: "Men I know seem to lose momentum while I . . . make verbal suggestions."[13] "They wanted to make me happy according to *their* conception of what ought to do it . . . and acted as if it was damned impertinent of me to suggest that my responses weren't programmed exactly like those of mythical women in the classics of porn" (p. 316). "Most didn't seem to be aware that what brought them to climax was not what brought me to climax" (p. 318). "Men differ, but most do not seem to understand a woman's body" (p. 320). "Men don't seem to have much imagination about sex. They don't readily accept new ideas or suggestions" (p. 322). Hite went so far as to conclude that

> the pattern of sexual relations predominant in our culture . . . has institutionalized out any expression of women's sexual feelings except for those that support male sexual needs. Many women expressed their frustration about this. . . . So women are put in the position of asking for something "special," some "extra" stimulation, or they must somehow try to subliminally send messages to a partner who often is not even aware that he should be listening. (Pp. 384–385)

Admittedly, this report was published in the 1970s; but is there less ignorance today? What research into women's sexuality has been conducted since then? A 1998 article by Gina Kolata in a *New York Times* section on "Women's Health" quotes several scientists on how 1970s studies on women's sexuality "are still state of the art" and tells us that

> suddenly, drug-company scientists, wondering whether Viagra or something like it can enhance sex for women, are asking academic scientists what is known about women's sexual responses. The answer is not much. . . . No one disputes the evidence that many women are unhappy with their sex lives. Dr. Sandra R. Leiblum . . . noted that "every survey invariably finds that many more women than men complain of sexual difficulties." Dr. Leiblum cited a major survey in the United States that found a third of women respondents—but only a sixth of the men—saying they are uninterested in sex. One-fifth of the women—but only one-tenth of the men—said sex gave them no pleasure.[14]

Wrong assumptions about women's view of sex and sexual responses seem implicit in our culture—widespread enough still to be embodied in the legal notions about "consent" in rape cases and about "welcomeness" in sexual harassment cases. The evidence indicates that many men may assume no particular need for special communication about sex between individual men and women—that just as what pleases a man can be experienced as automatic and instinctive, the same actions will automatically and instinctively please the woman involved. It also indicates an unknown number of women out there who don't try very hard to communicate but who, even in supposedly consensual sexual episodes, just let sex happen, without experiencing very much pleasure in the occurrence.

If these women and men assume that such experiences are all there is, there emerges from the assumptions of feminists such as Catharine MacKinnon (that there is a continuum of dominance and submission in all sexual relations that makes marriage similar to prostitution and heterosex similar to rape) what I see as an interesting partial truth. Let's reframe what they say this way. Women who are not consulted as to what gives them pleasure "let it happen" in marriage, let it happen in consensual relations on dates, let it happen when they are paid for it (but say that nothing could have given them more pleasure), are seen letting it happen in much of pornography. When a woman lets it happen under the threats of a stranger rapist—how indeed is a man, or a juror, to tell the difference between all of these socially "normal" interactions and the time when a women really didn't want to let it happen but was frightened out of her mind? This, of course, is not a picture of Everywoman, even to MacKinnon; but polls and sexologists (and popular art forms) tell us it exists enough to be readily recognizable.

Ever since the publication of Alfred Kinsey's research on women in 1953[15] and of Masters and Johnson's books in 1966 and 1970,[16] a growing number of therapists and sexologists have spent their professional lives getting people to talk about these things. "Sexologists," Pineau tells us,

> are unanimous, moreover, in holding that mutual sexual enjoyment requires an atmosphere of comfort and communication, a minimum of pressure, and an ongoing check-up on one's partner's state. . . . [T]he way to achieve sexual pleasure, at any time at all, let alone with a casual acquaintance, decidedly does not involve overriding the other person's express reservations and providing them with just any kind of sexual stimulus.[17]

Assumptions in society—myths, if you like—about sexual relations and what they mean to the men and women involved are sufficiently widespread to be institutionalized in our laws and customs and accepted without question by many people, at least as other people's experience if not their own—including, of course, by many women. (Contemporary sexual harassment research also confirms this.) Pineau's interesting suggestion about doing away with the "problem" of date rape is that the law should adopt a new standard of "communicative sexuality" that assumes what is wanted in a sexual encounter is mutual enjoyment and accepts the sexological research that tells us the only way to achieve that is by inquiring as to one's partner's preferences.

> On the old model of aggressive seduction we sought evidence of resistance. But on the new model of communicative sexuality what we want is evidence of an ongoing positive and encouraging response on the part of the plaintiff. . . . [T]he communicative nature of an encounter is much easier to establish than the occurrence of an episodic act of resistance. . . . For one thing, it requires that a fairly long, yet consistent story be told. . . . Secondly, in making noncommunicative sex the primary indicator of coercive sex it provides us with a criterion for distinguishing consensual sadomasochism from brutality. For even if a couple agree to sadomasochistic sex, bondage and whippings and the rest of it, the court has a right to require that there be a system of signals whereby each partner can convey to the other whether she has had enough.[18]

Some of the most egregious aspects of rape law have been changed over the past decades. Rape shield laws in most states forbid inquiry into the victim's past sexual history to indicate that she may have invited the attack. But leaving aside the question of whether Pineau's conclusion could in fact be implemented, it is clear that communicative sex is hardly the standard of consent.

If encounters labeled as sexual harassment evoke deep concerns parallel to those that both women and men have about rape and rape charges, and if examining the issues raised in the area of rape brings to light subterranean myths and lack of communication about sex, what does this mean? Women in both instances fear the possibility of violence and compulsion. Men fear manipulation in general from the woman who may bring a totally false charge, but they also fear the witch-woman, *la belle dame sans merci*, who will enchant them and later change her mind and turn cold and vindictive after one has reacted positively to her. Don't forget the importance of sexual metamessages. I have heard men seriously ask in training sessions how they can do something about women's provocative dress, saying that they feel harassed by it because they sometimes can't help but be attracted. One woman engineer I spoke to told me with great disgust that she had encountered women who wore skirts when they were up on a cat-walk on construction sites, and they had to know that the men standing below could look up their skirts. Nevertheless, they took great umbrage at any ensuing wolf whistles.

Women in revealing clothing rarely intend to be making a sexual offer and are insulted at the suggestion, but perhaps they should see that a woman who habitually wears revealing dress can be reacted to as giving the same message as the man who leers at every woman and calls her "darling." I think it possible that both men and women sometimes resent someone who they think is putting sex on the table, so to speak, as a general, indiscriminate offer. It's not flattering to be viewed as one of a crowd.

This is not to say in any way that women "ask" for assault. Rather, both men and women can fear the power that the other sex has to make them behave against their will: men, to compel compliance by their strength, and women, to compel sexual awareness and involuntary response by their looks and manner. Apart from these fears that both sexes invoke, is there a connection between rape and sexual harassment, in terms of personality factors, causal factors, or anything else?

There is a connection, and this is how it works. Particularly in light of any perception that they are pitched economically against each other, men and women can see their "cultural" differences and miscommunications as immutable (and culpable) gender differences. One of the ways in which some men react to this view is with sexual hostility, of the "can't live with them, can't live without them" variety. Promiscuous, sexually exploitive men exist on every level of our society. Some have a disregard of women's feelings in a sexual situation that is equivalent to condoning rape.[19]

In the 1980s, Neil Malamuth conducted an extensive series of studies on rape which concluded that a majority of the college-age men he surveyed in North American universities would rape if they could get away with it; at least, they said they would. He correlated this finding with other factors to construct a scale that would predictably measure which men held beliefs that made them highly likely to rape, or at least to self-report that they would rape.[20] This Likelihood of Rape (LR) scale is now recognized and in use by psychologists and discussed in textbooks.

In 1987, John Pryor compiled a Likelihood of Sexual Harassment (LSH) scale, modeled on Malamuth's LR scale. He published a report on studies of this LSH scale which found not only that it could predictably profile those likely to sexually harass but that it correlated with the LR scale. In fact, the LR scale turned out to be the single best predictor of men who would score high on the LSH scale. According to Pryor, these high scorers have a number of beliefs in common:

> The profile of a person who is likely to initiate severe sexually harassing behavior...is one that emphasizes sexual and social male dominance. . . . The relationship of LSH to the acceptance of rape myths shows a tendency to believe women accept and even enjoy male sexual dominance even when it means physical coercion. These belief structures seem to contribute to the likelihood of sexual harassment and to the likelihood of rape. . . . These beliefs in male dominance also seem coupled with a basic insensitivity to other's perspectives.[21]

Pryor's studies also found that high LSH men tend to dominate women rather than to try to seduce or manipulate them; that they are authoritarian, "describe themselves in socially undesirable masculine terms or masculine terms that strongly differentiate them from stereotypical femininity"; and, interestingly, that they have negative feelings about sex in general. He speculated that such men may have less sexual experience and less sexual knowledge than others less likely to harass. He and two other researchers published a study in 1993 that showed the LSH scale could be used to predict who in a group of men would harass a woman in a situation that would appear to disguise harassing motives. The variable was the behavior of a man who introduced the male subject to a young woman whom he was to train in a task and then evaluate. When the introducer treated the woman in a sexist rather than a professional way, high scorers on the LSH scale were almost three times as likely as low scorers to harass the woman, with both words and touches. "Psychologically speaking," the authors wrote, "sexual harassment seems to involve a fusion of ideas about power and sexuality."[22]

The LSH subjects in Pryor's studies were what you might call hard-core sexual harassers: people whose personalities are authoritarian and rigid, who tend to think in gender stereotypes, and who have so little awareness of the perspectives of others that they don't try to seduce or manipulate, as other annoyers might do—they just come on.

How can we use this information? Sensitivity training and reasonable arguments are not likely to reach such men; assertiveness will, and so will a general sense of what the people around them consider acceptable. For real-life examples of how the way in which women behave makes a difference with such men, we might turn to the court-martial of Sergeant Delmar Gaither Simpson at the U.S. Army's Aberdeen Proving Ground in 1997. A drill sergeant in command of a number of women, Simpson was convicted of raping six of them. As reported in the *New York Times*,

> The testimony of some of Sergeant Simpson's rape victims was fraught with ambiguity. One said that she had encouraged his attention; another testified that she found him attractive; some did not overtly resist. One 21-year-old former trainee from Illinois, whom Sergeant Simpson was convicted of raping five times, acknowledged that she believed these were essentially appointments to have sex and that Sergeant Simpson did not force her to have sex with him. . . . Another victim, a 23-year-old former trainee from Wyoming, whom Sergeant Simpson was convicted of raping eight times, testified that before the first encounter, he asked if he could touch her. "I said, 'I guess.' I was thinking in my head, 'Is there a right or wrong answer to this question?'"[23]

Lest this sound as if Sergeant Simpson were an essentially courtly gentleman, unfairly caught in the toils of a military system that defines fraternization as rape, but who wouldn't harass a soul, the women who refused him included one twenty-year-old trainee who, when he put his hand down her sweatpants as they passed on a stair, "grabbed his hand, told him to stop it and moved on. . . . He never bothered her again."[24] Even in this extreme situation, women who were clear about what they didn't want were able to prevail and protect themselves, while women who were deferential and unsure ended up being victimized.

We see again that assertiveness pays off. We cannot expect communication in the workplace always to be easy, especially when, as at Aberdeen, power imbalances are involved and exploited. We cannot rely on superficial standards of decorum and politeness and ignore underlying issues; we may need to pay more attention to what has *not* been said. If we look at the complex of issues involved in sexual harassment as problems of expectations and communications, both workers and managers can make the workplace less hostile. But first, it helps to understand more about communication itself.

Men and women don't communicate easily about sex. To men inclined to be sexually exploitive, this lack of communication is an asset, enabling them to deceive themselves and others about the nature of their behavior. To men and women seeking satisfying relationships, lack of communication is a frustrating barrier. And to the extent that inability to communicate in this area is based on fear, it can only be positive for the fear to be identified, examined, understood, and, as much as possible, overcome.

CHAPTER FIVE

How to Communicate
Your Concerns

Workers and managers alike can benefit by becoming more aware of how misunderstood any communication can be, even when we are sure we know exactly what was said and how it was intended. What Deborah Tannen calls "the liability of conversations we thought were about one thing coming back at us, refracted through someone else's mind, as if they were about something else entirely"[1] is an experience all of us have had too often, and we may need to go to the experts to understand more clearly why it occurs. When we speak of sexual harassment, we are generally referring to unwelcome behavior of some sort, to which a person has reacted negatively. Men and women alike will be well served by examining why much that may seem offensive to women seems normal to men.

In the words of the Gilbert and Sullivan song (from *H.M.S. Pinafore*), "things are seldom what they seem," especially when communication is what linguists call "cross-cultural." Much male behavior that makes certain women so uncomfortable that they interpret it as harassment may be intended to treat the woman like one of the guys. Seemingly hostile behavior may not be specifically directed at these women in a discriminatory way at all. And because all bonding within a group implies an out-group, generalized male stereotypes of women do exist, and women have to understand and deal with them.

Women have to do most of this work because, as we have seen, the workplaces they usually want to be in are predominantly male, and the unexamined medium in which the workers exist is male culture. Men get together, in the workplace and in gathering places outside work and do what they learned to do while they were growing up, behaving in ways that feel totally natural. What happens when women enter these all-male enclaves? Obviously, the more exclusively male a workplace has been, the more the workplace culture will be male. A woman entering it does well to inform herself about contemporary male culture.

Betty Lehan Harragan's 1977 book *Games Mother Never Taught You*[2] analyzes the ways in which what she calls "the game of corporate politics" is based on the male models of military life and team sports. Women, Harragan writes, "have stumbled onto a playing field where the rules of participation are rigidly enforced and the criteria for success are known to all but them."[3] She, like Tannen, sees much communication between men and women as cross-cultural.

Women, Harragan says, often don't understand that the hierarchical organizational structure of business is military, including which jobs are in the chain of command and which are merely peripheral (e.g., secretarial jobs). They do not understand that it is always the rank that gets the credit. Nor do they realize that the everyday operations of business follow rules that derive from sports, especially football, and involve such things as knowing your position on the team, never reacting emotionally to a setback, and supporting your boss (coach) in public and never going over his head.

Boys learn these rules, says Harragan, in childhood from team sports, at the same time that most girls are playing games that involve taking turns, such as jacks and jump rope, or perhaps learning sports that are primarily solitary exercises in skill (e.g., horseback riding, fencing, golf, diving, ice-skating, tennis). True, more and more girls have been taking part in team sports since Title IX of the Civil Rights Act required funding parity for them in schools receiving federal funds. However, most young women entering the workplace don't have extensive team sports experience behind them. What the boys learn is not just the rules of the game but the enjoyment of male camaraderie. And this is what they carry over to the workplace.

How do men experience this camaraderie? To a large extent, by competing with each other. Harragan points out, "In the male culture, competition is the reward. Competition is the fun. Competition is what makes it all worthwhile."[4]

If you are a woman who comes into a workplace expecting to take turns, to concentrate on your job and do it well, to make friends by using your self-deprecating sense of humor (which you don't expect anyone to take literally), it can be a shock to have colleagues who tease and make fun of you and compete by trying to steal the credit from you for that well-done job. Add some rough sexual language on their part, and you may start believing they are out to get you. Why are they communicating this way?

Because it seems natural to them. And only an unexpected response from those whom they deal with will make them question what they are doing. For women trying to make clear the limits and expectations they have, it is extremely important to be sure you know what you have said to someone whose behavior or language offends you. One thing women can learn from Tannen's research is that the indirectness many people (not just women) feel is the polite way of communicating reactions and preferences does not always make intentions clear.

Therefore, patterns in interactions between people must be conscious, in order to see when they aren't working. A person whose natural style is to communicate a desire by asking what the other person might want needs, first of all, to be aware of feeling uncomfortable in situations where things are spelled out, and then to resolve that sometimes such spelling out must be done. The other person in the conversation may take a question at face value, not as a hint.

A woman who is distressed at what she sees as pressure to date a colleague but, because she wants to spare his feelings, makes up a reason why she doesn't want to socialize with him *right now* may not really be communicating. If the invitations continue, she will need to spell out what she means, even in ways that seem overexplicit or unnecessary to her. If she doesn't realize this, her next step may be a desperate one: what the *Working Woman* 1992 survey called "threats or verbal abuse" on her part, which can make both parties feel unhappy. One good rule is: Even if it's not your normal style to do so, if you see a conflict of values or interpretation, make your awareness of the conflict explicit.

Psychologists who specialize in communication have several concepts that are relevant here. One is *non-accusative communication*. It entails communicating the *feelings that you have* in response to another's behavior, rather than focusing on what you assume to be the *negative intent* of that behavior. This is often called "taking responsibility for your feelings" or "owning your feelings," as it presents your feelings as your personal reactions, rather than accusing the other person of eliciting inevitable reflex reactions by his or her bad behavior. An example of non-accusative communication would be to say, "I really don't like it when you call me 'dearie'; it makes me very uncomfortable" rather than "Don't come onto me all the time!" Another important aspect of this technique is that it specifically describes the behavior you are reacting to, rather than making a generalized statement about its evil. This gives the other person detailed information of what you want changed.

Too often women who are aware of sexual harassment as a political issue are so aware of the law and the literature that they start with the assumption that anyone who offends them should know better. Using terms such as *inappropriate* immediately communicates this attitude, and also communicates that these women think they are speaking from a superior position, which can be a red flag to competitive men. This kind of accusative language doesn't help resolve anything—the other person is getting the metamessage that he needs to protect his status, and you haven't said exactly what should not have been done, leaving him free to interpret your complaint in whatever way he wishes or feels is to his advantage.

Along with speaking specifically and non-accusatively, it is important to listen. The communication technique called *mirroring* can be helpful here. When the person being addressed responds, instead of answering the content (or the metamessage) right away, the speaker gives back to the other person a paraphrase of what he or she said, in different words, and continues the conversation only when it is confirmed that what was meant has been understood. Then the speaker can answer *that*. Look at this example, from one handbook on sexual harassment, of how a manager ("You" in the example) might deal with a man whose female supervisor propositioned and apparently threatened him:

You: You think you have a way to stop her from hurting your job?

Dick: You bet I do, Steve. And don't try to stop me. I want her fired!

You: I hear you saying that there's no way to settle this thing between you and Linda. You want to see her punished.

Dick: She'd better be. I didn't ask her to bed. She asked me.

You: You haven't done anything in this situation to lead her to misconstrue your feelings?

Dick: I knew you'd ask that, Steve. You're on her side. I got along great with Linda until she decided I'd be a good bed partner. I'm not taking any blame for this.

You: Dick, I'm not taking Linda's side here. I'm just trying to understand what happened. You say that you and Linda got along well until this business started?

Dick: Sure, we did. We've always kidded around a lot. But it never meant anything. A few weeks ago, though, I noticed she was starting to come on pretty strong. I didn't pay much attention. But last week she asked me to fly to Memphis with her to close the Reginald deal. She said we could have a lot of fun while we were there, especially if we saved the company some money and shared a hotel room. I said, no thanks, I wasn't interested. Then Wednesday she tried again. Would I like to come home with her after work—she'd like to see if I was as good in bed as she thought I was. That's quite a challenge, but I'm not going to jeopardize my marriage for Linda. Well, I jeopardized my job instead. When I said no, she told me I'd better think it over, otherwise she'd see to it that I didn't get the Monroe account.

You: So things have really come to a head between the two of you. And you say that until a few weeks ago you didn't have any problems with her?

Dick: Everything was fine. I don't know where in hell she got the idea that I'd go to bed with her.

You: Nothing you've done in the past would have given her that impression?

Dick: No way! Oh, we kidded around a lot, but that's all it was—kidding.

You: She should have known that the kidding between you didn't mean anything.

Dick: Of course. It was all in fun. I suppose she might have gotten the wrong idea, but that's her problem.

You: If she misread you, she's got to take responsibility; is that what you're saying?

Dick: Yes. Oh, I guess maybe I could have backed off when we'd tease each other, but I thought it was all in fun.

You: Sounds like Linda took it differently, Dick.

Dick: You're right. I guess she thought I was encouraging her. But how was I supposed to know that?

You: It wasn't easy to put yourself in Linda's place and see how she interpreted your conversation.

Dick: Yeah, but maybe I shouldn't have assumed she was teasing. I guess I could have let her know earlier where I was coming from.

You: If you'd cleared the air awhile back, maybe she wouldn't have come on so strong these past two weeks.

Dick: You know, you're right, Steve. Maybe Linda thought I was serious and decided it was time to be serious too. It must have been a shock to her when I said no. I'll bet that's why she lashed out at me like that. But hell, Steve, that's still no excuse. She had no right to do that.

You: I agree, Dick. Linda can't threaten your work because you won't go to bed with her. But you have to take some responsibility also. If you didn't let her know where you stood, it's not surprising that she decided to escalate the game. I'd like to talk to Linda. I'm sure we need to take some action on this. But let's move one step at a time and see where we're going. I'll get back to you tomorrow afternoon, and we'll talk some more then. In the meantime, think about what we've talked about and maybe tomorrow we can figure out the best way to handle this.

Dick: Thanks, Steve. I appreciate your help.[5]

Although I generally have followed the pattern of casting the harasser as a man and the harassed as a woman in this book, it is useful every now and then to break that pattern, as this example does, lest we fall into the trap of making it an unbreakable stereotype. Notice how, step by step, without criticizing or confronting Dick, by repeating points Dick has made and asking clarifying questions, the manager elicits more of the story and, in the process, not only defuses some of the anger but brings out a possible explanation of Linda's behavior that casts her in a potentially less culpable light.

Dick assumed Linda knew he was teasing. Often what we assume about people we are dealing with is even less conscious. One of the values of social science research is that it can discover discrepancies between stereotypical assumptions and what is actually the case. When these assumptions are acted on, they can sometimes cause offense when none is meant, or they can operate subconsciously to cause escalating misunderstanding.

Barbara Gutek wrote a book applying the sex-role spillover theory that I discussed in chapter 3 (where the behavior considered normal at work is the usual behavior of the dominant sex—and however they behave, members of the other sex are seen in their sex-role stereotypes) to a study she conducted in California of 827 working women and 405 working men.[6] She discovered a number of gender differences in assumptions about sexual behavior in the workplace, including the fascinating finding of a huge gender gap, of which *neither men nor women were aware*, as to whether or not sexual propositions in the workplace are flattering to women (as former *Cosmopolitan* magazine editor Helen Gurley Brown has suggested over the years). Most men are flattered, and both sexes assume this. But most women are not; yet they assume, as men do, that other women are. Gutek finds this result "astounding" and calls it "a classic case of a group endorsing a stereotype about itself."[7] She compares it to welfare recipients who think that, as a class, other welfare recipients are cheats, although they themselves are not.

Therefore, Gutek suggests, one policy that it might be important for management to employ in order to lessen the perception of sexual harassment in the workplace would be to inform men publicly that although it may be assumed women like and even expect sexual comments, they in fact do not. "Tell men," Gutek writes,

> that women are insulted by sexual advances and overtures. . . . They may be understandably concerned that when their sexuality is noticed, their work is not. When men make sexual comments, they are noticed as insults because they draw attention away from work. Men do not have this problem.[8]

In other words, saying a woman is a decorative asset to the workplace implies that her job performance is secondary and may not even be noticed. Perhaps she was hired to be decorative. But men are assumed to be serious workers; any personal attractiveness they may have on top of that is icing on the cake, so to speak.

Not only do men talk about sex more than women do and use it to express a variety of feelings (positive and negative), but they tend to sexualize situations that have no overt sexual meanings, just because they involve men and women. That is, Gutek found, "men were more likely than women to label several sexually ambiguous interactions between the sexes as sexual." Examples given were making business calls together, escorting a female colleague to a social function, or lunching with a woman client to discuss her investments. Men would say these were "dates" but also would consider them normal work behavior. This may be another area of potential misunderstanding between men and women—encounters that one person (usually the man) might see as escalating a relationship the other might think of as entirely business-like until some overt move, perhaps even a quid pro quo demand as in the fictional case of Dick and Linda, suddenly makes the situation one of harassment.

The example of Dick and Linda makes it clear that although it may be statistically usual for the man to be the one interested in escalating the relationship, we are not biologically programmed for it to be so. However, the statistical probabilities are still useful. The authors of a study of responses to such scenarios concluded that "one form of intervention may be for women to realize that some of their friendly intentions might be misinterpreted as sexual by men."[9] Women who have experienced situations in which something seems to happen "out of the blue" after a long and seemingly friendly relationship often blame themselves, whereas men, as illustrated in Dick and Linda's scenario, do not. Information as to male–female differences, again, can be helpful here to encourage women to tune in earlier to misapprehensions.

Unfortunately, dealing with sexual harassment, like dealing with other kinds of human relations, cannot be reduced to formulas or lists of dos and don'ts. It would be easier, perhaps, to be able to say, "This is the line you mustn't cross." In fact, many men, with their concerns about what they can and can't say, seem to be asking for such a list. ("If you'd just tell us what to do, we'd be glad to do it.")

There is a fundamental don't, of course—for men: Don't touch a woman in any way if she has asked you not to. And there is a fundamental do—for women: Articulate, in a non-accusative way, what really bothers you, and do it early and in private. A 1998 advice column by Michelle Cottle in the *New York Times* spelled out how wrong it can be to act otherwise. A writer with a new boss who was "verbally abusive to the point of using an obscene term to describe me in front of my colleagues" wanted to know if the boss could be sued and had already reported the incident to the department head. The letter didn't state that it was written by a woman, but it seems likely—a man whose boss described him as a "prick" would be unlikely to think it serious verbal abuse. Cottle advised: (1) Don't sue. (2) Is this characteristic behavior, or could it be the result of short-term personal problems? (3) "After sizing up the situation, confront your tormentor privately (and quickly, since you've spoken to the department head)." (4) Reporting him should have been a last resort. Now you have to make an impersonal case and try to get witnesses. (5) Maybe you have poisoned the atmosphere so much that you should transfer or move on. "If you thought your boss was unpleasant to begin with, just wait until he learns that you've squealed."[10] This is a classic analysis of what can go wrong with the stand-up-for-your-rights approach, and why it doesn't work.

When you speak in private with the person with whom you have problems, also don't label the behavior or language "sexual harassment": as I discussed in chapter 2 on the law, it may not be anything that is legally actionable, but if it offends, you have a right to speak on that basis. As Rita Risser explained to me, "Ground zero is, here is the stuff that is illegal, which most people are not going to do, here is the company policy that sets a higher standard, and then there are our own values. . . . So what we talk about is, if that is my value, then I need to tell you that, and if one of our values is to respect others, then we will work out a negotiation. You won't compliment me, or only do it once a month instead of once a week. Whatever."[11]

We've seen that studies tell us that communication about your concerns is the most potentially useful strategy; at a time when the law seems to be retreating from the punishment of simple offensiveness, it may be the only one. Now that the law will not act against behavior that merely makes women uncomfortable, women will have to do it themselves. Too many handbooks on sexual harassment spend too much time telling people how to complain to authorities or bring suit.

An alternate and more useful view is implied in the facework approach, which suggests that every businesswoman has more than one task: she has to pay attention to diverting the sexual overtures she may receive, as well as to her real job. In a 1998 interview, Helen Gurley Brown (whose approach some women may find a bit old-fashioned) responded that the best way to respond to harassment is "with a sense of humor and flattery, flattery, flattery." Say to him, she goes on, "You're fabulous and so attractive and have lots of women, but I don't like it when you rub up close to me."[12] *Games Mother Never Taught You* suggests less effusively that the real challenge for a businesswoman is to develop "expertise in blocking these passes while maintaining a pleasant, friendly, unsullied work relationship with the man (men) involved. . . . Tact and diplomacy are the skills required."[13] Harragan suggests several tactics, including the following:

If surrounded with men who pressure you, sign up for a karate course and talk about it—never to threaten them, of course, but to protect yourself from assault in the streets.

Act like an enthusiastic drinker but never get drunk. If he gets drunk, don't kid him the next day; "Pretend you weren't there."

And one suggestion I'm particularly fond of: When you have a necessary tête-à-tête with a superior who asks you to talk about yourself— tell him your career plans.

Some women may feel it's unfair that they should have to do anything, because they feel men shouldn't be making passes in the first place. But we live in a culture that accepts a great deal of public sexual explicitness. While everyone is placing strictures on the workplace, the people who work there are spending their leisure time in mixed company enjoying movies, magazines, and TV shows that are raunchy beyond belief. Couples listen to and laugh together at situations and jokes that could get them fired if repeated in the office. Add to that the fact that we spend most of our time in the workplace, and according to a number of surveys, a majority of us have met the people we marry there. There is no way a universal rule sanitizing the workplace could be adopted. And short of that, there is no way we can expect other people to read minds so perfectly that they will know without being told what behavior and what words will be considered charming and funny and what is beyond the pale.

A different but complementary view is expressed by some young women today. They don't respond to sexual talk in the workplace, but not because they dislike what is said to them; it leaves them indifferent, so they see no need to change anyone's behavior. Instead, they ignore. Celia Farber lived for years through a harrowing and lengthy sexual harassment suit, in which she was a witness, brought against the rock magazine *Spin*, where she once worked. The allegation was that the *Spin* environment was so sexualized that only women having affairs with management men were promoted. Farber, who was attacked as a witness because she had had such an affair, remembered only one sexual remark directed at her during the eleven years she worked there—one of the targets of the suit said to her, "Nice ass, Celia." She doesn't now remember how she felt. "And this is the axis around which the whole thing revolves—the idea, the insistence that there is only one proper response to such a comment. The real power, surely, resides in not reacting. Yes, yes, I can see, it's not right, it's inappropriate, men should learn that they can't talk that way. Fine. But women should learn the art of staying cool, of not reacting, because it offers the ultimate reward—you get to get *back to work*. He said 'Nice ass.' So what?"

As for the office atmosphere, Farber saw it differently, too. "There were 'toxic people,' yes, jerks, yes. Are jerks illegal? Hungover, caffeinated, stressed-out, people with borderline personalities. Who else would be available to edit a rock magazine?"[14]

The real lesson to be learned is that women should do whatever makes them feel comfortable, not what they feel they owe to other women. Sexism exists and we need to recognize it, but no one is under obligation to act against one's own interests, as long as we are acting out of knowledge and not out of feelings of inadequacy. Let's go back to the concept of sex-role spillover. Very few workplaces are truly integrated by gender—most are skewed to be predominantly male or predominantly female. The woman executive for whom Betty Harragan wrote *Games Mother Never Taught You* years ago is still in a predominantly male environment (of other executives), so she is constantly perceived as a *woman* performing her job. Somewhat in the same way that Samuel Johnson was amazed by a woman preacher, whom he compared to a dog walking on its hind legs, men in such a situation can be constantly amazed at the prowess of a token woman: the surprise, as Johnson said, is not that it was done well but that it was done at all. Some men, perhaps most men, as the studies show us, do not immediately think of sex objects when they think of a woman's role; they most often think of mothers, daughters, caretakers, and they react protectively. But those who may be harassers think of relationships with women as, first and foremost, sexual.

In a predominantly female workplace with male bosses, since sex-role spillover causes everyone to perceive the workplace itself as sexualized and to accept flirtation and banter as part of the job, generalized banter can segue into predation. Barbara Gutek and Bruce Morasch interviewed one industrial cleaning woman who considered that, "although she was expected to sleep with the foreman to avoid getting a rough assignment, she was not sexually harassed because *all* the workers were expected to do the same. It was part of the job."[15]

In any workplace, the feedback that the harasser gets from the target can be all-important. As in the situation with Dick and Linda, propositions rarely come out of the blue—the move is made after a series of what one person may consider trial balloons but the target may dismiss as harmless kidding. Even in the raunchiest workplaces, some people never feel harassed and are not subjected to unwanted propositions—or if they are, like Celia Farber they can deflect them so skillfully that they pass in the blink of an eye and are not repeated. So another very important step in any encounter that offends is to analyze one's own feedback behavior—not just what you said but how it might have been misunderstood. What metamessages were you sending? Could your manner be interpreted as flirtatious? Did you laugh at a joke you hated in order to be polite? If you give a person you are dealing with contradictory feedback—your words say one thing but your demeanor says another—you can expect that person to pick the alternative he wants to believe.

Managers need to be concerned with all these aspects of communication, too—being aware of different styles and the possibility of misunderstanding, speaking non-accusatively, mirroring what the person you are speaking to has said. The feedback managers give can be crucial, because they are representing the behavior the company expects in the way they treat both parties to complaints. The mirroring technique is particularly important for managers bent on conflict resolution, because it can draw out each person's side of the story. The mirroring technique can lead a harasser to move from total denial of the accusation to admitting some behavior that helped create the situation, to accepting as a brilliant insight the manager's mirroring of what the harasser had just said himself.

The *Meritor* Supreme Court decision has had one unintended negative consequence—it has discouraged companies (and their professional advisers) from putting their sexual harassment policies in a wider context. Since the Meritor Savings Bank was specifically chastised for including sexual harassment in a general anti-discrimination policy rather than separating it out, a trend towards such inclusion was invalidated. Some companies are now compensating for this by pairing their policy on sexual harassment with a separate policy on general harassment and distributing both together in orientation materials.

Why does sexual harassment exist in some workplaces and not in others? We know that some factors that affect it change when workplace sex ratios change. Theories of sex-role spillover don't explain why sexual harassment exists but do explain differences in reporting it—it is noticed more in predominantly male workplaces and tolerated more in workforces that are skewed in the other direction.[16] Sexual harassment handbooks discuss areas in the system that can provide opportunities for harassment[17] and even organizational sanction for it. But many people think the basic personality of a company, including its attitude towards personnel, is made at the top.

If the company fosters general civility and respect for others, it will have accessible managers and will probably have instituted grievance procedures long ago, before court rulings made it all but obligatory. If management isn't concerned about generally humiliating behavior, about harassment of other employees regarding race, religion, sex, or national origin, tolerance of gross sexual harassment will probably prevail too. Such a general attitude can ruin intracompany relations and should never be tolerated by management. There is a virtue in broadening required civility at work that we should not lose sight of by narrowing our focus too slavishly on legal consequences.

Rita Risser makes a similar suggestion:

> [N]ow is the time to refine your sexual harassment policy so that it is in the spirit of your organization's values rather than written to the letter of the law. The law requires you to prohibit severe or pervasive physical, physically threatening, humiliating or degrading conduct directed against individuals based on their sex. But your policy should go beyond that. . . .
>
> Personnel policies, corporate values, statements, and training can increase awareness, but respect won't become the culture unless it starts at the top and infuses the organization.[18]

We put a spotlight on sexual harassment because it is one aspect of human interaction at work that has been made liable to civil suit and civil damages, and sometimes it has even been artificially exalted as *the* major problem in business. But other offensive and potentially damaging interactions in the workplace have no similar legal identity. Forget about sexual harassment for a moment. What about bosses who get their kicks from employee humiliation? What about people who advance solely by taking credit for the work of subordinates? What about people whose personal habits and hygiene make sharing an office with them an ordeal? We know people like this exist and have to be dealt with, but we don't have specific labels for their offenses.

We live in an imperfect world full of imperfect people, and we have to learn ways to lessen their impact on us. No matter what the legal climate, the same is true for dealing with sex—and sexual hostility—at work.

This, then, is the general sexual harassment problem presented to the business world. To recapitulate, sexual harassment brings the specter of expense to businesses in two ways: personnel costs, as employees lose time and efficiency when they feel harassed, and the possibility of a lawsuit. It is defined as a violation of discrimination law, which has the consequence of making employers almost uniquely the target of suits (which, in turn, ensures that managements often want to control more and more areas of workplace behavior).

But there are really surprisingly few lawsuits. And if we take our attention away from legal liability and legal definitions and look at what research tells us, we discover several things:

1. Men and women often don't understand each other. People of different cultures have different habitual patterns of speech and ways of relating and communicating. So do men and women— in this respect, their communication is often cross-cultural.

2. Men and women have different expectations about how to behave on the job. Populations within a group relate to one another in different ways depending on their proportions, and only when different populations approach a balanced ratio within a group do minority members receive treatment as individuals rather than as stereotypes. When populations are specifically sexually skewed, the stereotypes concern sex roles—therefore, sexual harassment is most acutely perceived in previously all-male workplaces.

3. Women expect more harassment than exists and often don't deal with it when it does occur in the way that would be most personally satisfactory—saying assertively and without hostility that it makes them uncomfortable and they would like it to stop. Surveys of the extent of sexual harassment in workplaces generally overreport it because of the wide range of behaviors included in the definition. Women entering blue-collar jobs experience more paternalism than sexual harassment; many women who say they have been sexually harassed also report that they took no action or took useless action. And women who spoke firmly and assertively to those who harassed them report a satisfactory conclusion to the event more often than do women who took any other action, including lodging a formal complaint or bringing suit.

I conclude that the most fruitful approach to sexual harassment in the workplace is to view it primarily as an issue of communication and expectations and to focus both on enhancing the knowledge and the ability of vulnerable workers to communicate successfully and on management's communication of the importance of respect for others generally in the workplace.

Such a conclusion is reinforced by the work that has been done on predicting and analyzing the attitudes of men who might be called hard-core harassers (as opposed to men whose communications are misunderstood or those reacting to changes in workplace populations). This area of research finds that such men accept deeply entrenched myths about rape and sexuality and are not subject to indoctrination or persuasion (e.g., sensitivity training sessions) but will often modify their behavior in response to assertiveness and to group stigma.

The current emphasis on punishment (either by lawsuit or by management punishing worker behavior, as the law requires in order for companies to have a defense to a suit) has created a workplace characterized by polarization and anger. I submit that a general atmosphere of sharing knowledge and communication skills can do much to lessen workplace malaise. To explicate this point further, I turn next to a discussion of some facts of male group culture on which women do not generally focus. Then we will go to the big questions: Why, with all the attention paid to it, hasn't sexual harassment been eradicated? How serious are the growing criticisms of the law itself, and should it be changed? And finally, what goes on in training programs, and how might they be improved?

PART II

Male Group Culture

CHAPTER SIX

Sticks and Stones

The world that men create for themselves together is a world of shared action rather than shared inner life. Doing things together is the key. It's often surprising to women that men will consider as friends other men whom they know little or nothing about, just because they play golf or bowl or fish or even follow a certain sport. There is a kind of common-denominator aspect to much of this—using simplified language such as swear words, joking, whistling at women or pictures of women, and indulging in teasing or horseplay all tend to emphasize broad similarities among men and minimize individual differences. The idea that we are all guys together and that's all we need to know is in many ways very positive, as it searches for commonalities that transcend class and education. It can also, of course, isolate and exclude the person whose differences are hard to overlook—the religious fundamentalist, the effeminate gay, the woman.

Women don't understand or even expect a number of facets of this male group culture; some, because they are at times purposely concealed from women. Let's face it, they are ways of excluding women, or at least of celebrating women's absence. When a woman comes into a workplace, especially one with few women there before her, and encounters some of these aspects of male group culture, it is very easy for her to assume that the behaviors are targeted at her, as a woman. But they are not especially aimed at the newcomer because she is a woman if they were routine before she got there.

However, even if we hold that the simple expression of opinions that others may find offensive or the general possession of sexually explicit materials should not be taken as sexual harassment in the legal sense, many women consider negative opinions about women and sexually explicit words and visual materials to be so offensive as to be harassing per se, no matter what the First Amendment says. This is the crux of many of the encounters that can lead to hostility in the workplace, particularly when women go into workplaces that previously have been all male. Some of these behaviors may be First Amendment protected—some are not. But it is a shame for a woman to let them poison the atmosphere of a challenging workplace for her, so that she feels her only choices are to quit or to sue. Better to begin by understanding how the workplace got to be this way. Patterns that undoubtedly started as a subconscious way of finding common denominators, so that the largest number of workers could feel convivial and included, can function to exclude instead when tokens first enter the group.

The most basic and least complicated issue is "bad" language. *Men alone together use vulgar language that they are sure women won't like.* We all know this. Remember the Watergate tapes? R. W. Apple Jr. said in his introduction to the book *The White House Transcripts* that the reason President Richard Nixon submitted "edited, bowdlerized transcripts" to the House Judiciary Committee was that "Mr. Nixon was unwilling to give the committee the tapes themselves, which were full of the kind of coarse language many men like to use among themselves ('shit' was the mildest of the deleted expletives)."[1]

The in-group intensifies its togetherness by denigrating the out-group. The out-group routinely used to include those of different ethnic, religious, or racial backgrounds; today, that is not routine. Today, the safest remaining out-group is women. Harragan described male-culture language in the late 1970s this way:

> The dominant theme in the male-culture language—and the business lexicon—is sexist pornography. Obscenity is the popular vernacular. This is the lewd, lusty language of the military conqueror, the male locker room, the stag party, the sales meeting, the company convention, the board room, the executive think-tank. The presence of the disparaged object, woman, inhibits men's freedom to "talk dirty" when together, and thus becomes an insuperable barrier to their communications.[2]

This has changed a bit, but it hasn't disappeared completely from many workplaces. Of course, the words that can produce a shock when said in public have changed over the years. Some years before World War II, Ben Hecht and Charles MacArthur's Broadway play about the newspaper business, *The Front Page*, produced a sensation with its last line: "The sonofabitch stole my watch!" When World War II ended and a spate of realistic war books came out—Norman Mailer's *The Naked and the Dead* and James Jones's *From Here to Eternity*, among many others— the publishing industry, not used to printing obscenities, was faced with dialogue in which every other word seemed unprintable. But since these books recounted the adventures of a largely all-male society, to avoid the language was to misrepresent reality. The first solution, to hint at the offending word, as in "f--k," is still used by some newspapers. But all those hyphens were distracting.

Today, the hyphens are often absent, but some communities are still trying to stamp out offensive language—often in the name of protecting children rather than women. One current concern is the language used by rock musicians. A number of people (usually, but not always, male) have been arrested for wearing rock-band T-shirts that offended sensibilities. In April 1998, one twenty-year-old woman, Venus Starlett Dust Morgan, was arraigned for violating a Kentucky anti-harassment statute because she wore a Marilyn Manson T-shirt with "I am the God of Fuck" on its back to a Benton, Kentucky, community celebration. The statute forbade "an offensively coarse utterance, gesture or display" with "intent to harass, annoy or alarm." When questioned by the Associated Press, Morgan seemed to feel unfairly singled out. "They told me I couldn't wear it because it had a curse word. . . . I can understand it, but I'm offended by their shirts sometimes too. . . . There were shirts that say 'Join the Klan,' and there were black people here."[3]

While state statutes that criminalize the use of bad language in front of women today are struck down as discriminatory and based on obsolete stereotypes,[4] workplace women are offended at men's use of the word *pussy* (or as in the first episode of the new version of television's series *Fantasy Island*, *wussy*) to connote weakness. In 1993, a columnist at the *Boston Globe* was threatened with a fine by his editor for calling another male staffer "pussy-whipped" by his female boss—a woman who wasn't present but simply overheard the men talking complained that the use of the term harassed her.[5]

Our society in general has become much more accepting with regard to what can be presented in plays and books and even motion pictures. But for some people, swearing in mixed company in the workplace remains an issue. A man in Minnesota, Roger Dorma, went so far as to file a lawsuit for harassment against a female co-worker, Debra Stromberg, in the Stroh's brewery in St. Paul, charging among other things that she invited him to have intercourse by saying, "Fuck you." In a 1993 article in the *Village Voice* about the case, the different views of what transpired were described this way:

> Stromberg does admit to one of Dorma's charges. She concurs that, like many employees in the plant and brewery, she routinely said "fuck you" to her coworkers. They disagree, though, in their interpretations of the time-honored phrase. Stromberg and Stroh's describe it as everyday, nonsexual workplace banter. Dorma cites it as an integral part of a pattern of sexual behavior, testifying that "a common, decent woman does not say 'fuck you' repeatedly to different people." To him, the meaning of "fuck you" changes with the gender of the speaker.[6]

One management consultant whom I interviewed told me of the first woman vice president of a particular company, who wanted to commission a training program that would instruct the other executives (and the chief executive officer) that it was "inappropriate" to swear in front of her. The consultant (herself a woman) suggested gently, "If the message they get is we can't let off a little steam by swearing, are they going to say, okay, we won't swear anymore? Or are they going to say, we won't hire any more women?" She also suggested the executive take the worst offender aside and ask him personally to modify his language, but in general, "fight the battle of getting women to be VPs, instead. When you hit a critical mass, the swearing you dislike is going to stop, or it will tone down."

Sexist language doesn't have to be obscene to be offensive. Ever since military women's branches were ended in favor of gender integration in 1973, the armed services have been forced to question some assumptions that had never been questioned before. Among them is the widespread use of anti-female language. The armed forces had, for instance, a long tradition of insulting their trainees by calling them "girls." A 1996 *New York Times* article concluded,

Pentagon reformers are fighting an entrenched male culture that has historically devalued, if not degraded women. Less than 10 years ago, Marine Corps drill instructors still led training runs with chants like this: "One, two, three, four. Every night we pray for war. Five, six, seven, eight. Rape, kill, mutilate."[7]

Carol Burke, an educator who taught at the U.S. Naval Academy for seven years, suggested in a 1992 *New Republic* article that socially questionable language—not just swear words but anti-female language—has been traditionally used in armed forces training to create a sense of "celebration of a new life as a member of the group."[8] She discussed the importance of drilling to misogynistic marching chants, "a kind of early white version of rap music" (several of which she quotes), as a part of this celebratory male bonding and even feels that chants with a sadomasochistic view of women ("My girl's a paraplegic. Making love is so strategic. I'll do most anything to keep her alive.") increased after women were admitted to the academy.[9]

The midshipmen clearly had no compunction about what they said in front of female colleagues. There is often the distinct possibility that when the presence of women is seen as a threat to the traditions of a place of work, the use of questionable language escalates. A study of "The Frequency, Sources, and Correlates of Sexual Harassment among Women in Traditional Male Occupations" found that of seven different categories suggested by the authors as forms of sexual harassment, the second most common were "verbal abuse" and "leering," and that they came from peers rather than supervisors.[10]

Although lawsuits have alleged that an atmosphere of rough language is by itself abusive, Rita Risser's analysis of appellate-court cases between 1993 and 1996 labeled it a "surprising finding" that

> the cases consistently held that casual non-directed swearing, including frequent use of the f-word, is not sexual harassment. As one court said, profanity and vulgarity are not hostile or abusive. The only court that ruled specifically on the word "bitch" said it was not gender related but instead showed personal animosity, just like "bastard" and "asshole."[11]

Risser also said in an interview, however, that slander, derogatory slurs ("whore," "slut"), and humiliation ("a potentially true statement about somebody that is highly personal and degrading") are verbal behaviors that can still be actionable. And she added,

> I make a special distinction between sexual harassment and gender harassment, and the courts do too. If you say women are only good for one thing, or women will never make it in sales—it doesn't take a lot of that before it becomes illegal. And in the racial harassment area, there have been a number of cases where just one slur was enough to be illegal harassment.[12]

So swearing *in front of* someone is different from swearing *at* them. Although swearing in the presence of a person may be generated by hostility, it should not be considered abusive as such. But no manager should passively encourage the use of degrading language directed at another worker. A better strategy is an attitude that sets a wide context of respect for others, in which male–female encounters become instances. Barbara Gutek, for instance, says in her recommendations to management that sexual harassment issues and considerations should be included in the definition of *professionalism.* "If an employee uses racial or sexual slurs in discussing a colleague we generally consider that unprofessional conduct. Discouraging such slurs allows the potential victims the freedom to work in a nonthreatening environment."[13]

A 1997 article about initiations at West Point details how the new superintendent of the academy, General Daniel W. Christman, intended to maintain toughness and continue weeding out those who can't make it "while reining in hazing and sexual harassment."[14] Restraining swearing is part of this.

> This summer, the superintendent showed each upper class the scene from the movie "Full Metal Jacket" when Sergeant Hartman kicks, punches and chokes recruits while hollering every known vulgarity. "This is exactly what I do not want," General Christman told them. During Beast [a six-week basic training program], when he caught two upperclassmen shouting at new cadets ("What the hell are you doing?" they kept yelling), the three-star general pulled aside the unit's senior cadet. "I said: 'I don't like what I'm hearing. It's inconsistent with what I'm trying to instill.'"[15]

One telephone company manager agrees that swearing and bad language directed at someone can be experienced as harassing regardless of the recipient's gender. She says she would take offenders aside and say that their language wasn't "professional" or "effective." If what they said was particularly raw, she would tell them that they sounded like longshoremen. That had an effect, she says, "because engineers don't like to be compared to longshoremen."

Another example I heard was of an electrician who was so concerned about a job he considered unsafe that he went over his supervisor's head to higher management. Higher management agreed with the electrician and canceled the assignment without informing the supervisor. The supervisor was so livid that he swore at the electrician by name over the public-address system. In this instance, too, the manager took the supervisor aside, telling him, "You have to be careful not to degrade your workers."

Managers have to tread a fine line between protecting the sensitivity of workers and fine-tuning other people's speech to such an extent that they create an authoritarian atmosphere. The University of Wisconsin set up a committee of faculty, students, and academic staff in 1997 to rewrite their faculty speech code. But the faculty senate found that by the fall of 1998, the committee had become deeply divided. A substantial minority—seven out of seventeen—wanted faculty members to be disciplined only when students could prove the teacher had an intent to harm that had succeeded, rather than just for "offensive teaching methods" or derogatory comments. (The example of an offensive teaching method given in the committee proposal occurred before there was any speech code, when an agriculture professor used a *Playboy* centerfold to illustrate cuts of meat.) But an interesting phenomenon in the debate is that all three student members of the committee, representing those to be protected by the code, were among the dissenters. They were the openly gay president of the senior class, a white woman, and an Asian American woman.[16]

In contrast, what can happen when management totally ignores or is indifferent to interworker hostility was graphically illustrated by conditions at the Miller Brewing Company plant in Fulton, New York, as described in a 1993 article in the *New York Times*:

> For almost a decade, through last year, many black and female employees at the plant in Fulton, a small industrial town north of Syracuse in central New York, say they were targets of racial epithets or sexual comments over the speaker system or were harassed by other means, such as messages written on restroom walls, obscene drawings and prominently placed items, like a noose, that spoke of overt hostility.[17]

The article went on to quote Lawrence Kunin, general counsel to the New York State Division of Human Rights, as saying that "sometimes a company 'has established a culture, without realizing that it's discriminatory.'" The company had been unable to catch the perpetrators, but a spokesman stated to the *Times* that at issue were twelve or fourteen pager messages over a decade, out of literally millions of messages. However, several employees had filed discrimination complaints, enough evidence was presented to the United States Attorney in New York to spark an FBI civil rights investigation, and one African American man, who began at the suggestion of his supervisor to keep a log of derogatory racial and sexual references to himself and others, logged at least two dozen such in the space of three months. Another listed twenty-one personal instances of offensive pages or messages to his beeper over a period of seven months—each one of which had been duly reported through channels.

The old saying "Sticks and stones may break my bones, but words will never hurt me" is clearly not always true. When a situation escalates out of control in this way, the targeted worker is literally a victim of mob action, and he or she can do little or nothing except quit or, possibly, bring suit. At that point, the matter is and should be in management's hands. But when a woman faces general rough language as a part of the workplace environment, what then? Generally, it's not really directed at her, except perhaps as a representative of Sex Objects Unlimited.

In a white-collar environment, the woman may find that male co-workers seem to expect her to be totally sheltered, as Harragan describes:

> Relatively successful women frequently report an inexplicable, disquieting, and extremely irritating experience in business meetings. Everytime the word "damn" or "hell" escapes a man's lips in a business setting, he

immediately turns to apologize abjectly to any woman present. . . . One woman executive told me that a male colleague interrupted himself fourteen times in ten minutes and finally turned to her in anger and said, "Dammit, you'll just have to get used to this talk if you think you're going to be in business!" She hadn't said a word! . . .

. . . What's happening is these mild words (once daring "swear-words" to the boy-child) are setting off a triggering mechanism in the men's heads. They are terrified that they might inadvertently slip into the male pornographic communications argot. Such an accident might suggest that she is "accepted" as an equal "with the boys" by being clued in to the secret codes.[18]

But if being clued in would mean acceptance, should she use the language herself? Opinions differ. Harragan goes on to suggest that a woman can use this male concern to control discussions with male colleagues who are not good at nonsexist language. But she advises women never to "use the typical male expressions which derogate her own sex," comparing the situation to that of a foreign diplomat who knows the language of the host country perfectly but never reveals that fact.

Lee Nason, who is in the maintenance department of the University of Massachusetts, thinks it's important in a blue-collar situation to let the men know that you are not vulnerable to vulgarity. But she also says it's very important never to direct such language at another person.

And Deborah Tannen concurs that, at least for some men, things in some occupations haven't changed much since Betty Harragan's day. At the end of a discussion of the different ways different women responded to sexual conversations, Tannen concludes:

Some women report that they simply join in when men "talk dirty," but that may cause problems they did not foresee. An airline pilot told me that if a woman pilot joins a crew, the talk changes; pilots who normally exchange plenty of talk he would call "dirty" clean up their act. But if a woman pilot chooses to talk that way herself, he said, she gets "a bad reputation."[19]

Perhaps the bottom line is that it depends on the kind of work and workplace you are in. Sex-role spillover theory would seem to indicate that men with conventional or traditional opinions about women—men such as Roger Dorma at Stroh's—find it easier to protect women from foul language than to accept this as an area in which a woman proves her equality by matching them epithet for epithet. Men in less-conventional occupations may not even notice, one way or the other. And some men are impressed.

I heard one anecdote from a surgeon about a woman operating with colleagues, one of whom deliberately touched her breast as they were working. "Scalpel," she ordered. Then she grabbed the other doctor's hand, held the scalpel above it, and said, "Do that again and I'll cut your fucking fingers off." After that, said the surgeon who recounted this, everyone thought she was wonderful—but of course, it was for the assertiveness of the action she took more than for the specific language she used.

A language problem that some women find even more troublesome is the seemingly friendly use of endearments. An article in *Savvy* magazine in 1988 that interviewed a number of successful women (including a real estate lawyer) on subtle sexism said men use endearments to emphasize a woman's different status:

> Equally subversive [to women's desire to be accepted as colleagues]—but harder to combat because they are so subtle—are exclusion and condescension, as the real estate lawyer knows all too well. "[Male lawyers] use 'dear' and 'honey' as a put down—to intimate that you are not their peer." It's a subtle game, and one that's nearly impossible to win. "If you make a stink and say, 'I'm not your dear,' they think it's getting to you and that you'll miss the substance and just look at the form, which is that they're calling you dear. Also, if your client is in the room, you don't want your client to think, 'She's wasting my time fighting over an appellation.'"[20]

In her memoir *Walking Out on the Boys*, neurosurgeon Frances K. Conley quotes from an article she once wrote in which she indicated that she didn't want to be treated like other women who hadn't accomplished what she had:

> I find myself unwilling to be called "hon" or "honey" with the same degree of sweet condescension used by this department for all women—nurses, secretaries, administrative assistants, female medical students.[21]

She also recounts an occasion in which she was performing a brain-tumor operation, with a male junior resident assisting, when Dr. Gerald Silverberg (who was later to be made head of the neurosurgery department of the Stanford University Medical School, where she worked) "walked into the room and loudly asked, 'How's it going, honey?'" The result of this, according to Conley's book, was that the assisting resident became recalcitrant, and it took her five minutes to reestablish control of the operating field. She recounts that the incident made her "return to my early days as a surgeon and ask myself, for what seemed like the millionth time, 'Is a honey, especially *this* honey, good enough and talented enough to be doing this operation?'"[22]

This anecdote, told by the first woman to be granted tenure in neurosurgery at an American university medical school, indicates not only the effect such endearments can have on both genders but also the devastating impact that isolation can have on a person who is a token. Conley, who resigned in 1991 to publicly oppose Silverberg's appointment and was later persuaded to return, by her own admission knew little or nothing about feminism when she made her stand to protest medical school sexism and sexual harassment. She had no community and didn't know what, if anything, to expect in the way of supporters.

How can one keep from being worn down by the subtle sexism of seemingly friendly endearments? This is a problem many women (but almost no men) face. To react effectively, it's important to remonstrate with the offender in private, not in public. As the analysis in *Savvy* magazine's example seems to demonstrate, there is often no right way to complain in front of others. However, if the people involved are more or less equals, a woman can sometimes make a point in public by endearing a man right back. Years ago, I had a job that entailed escorting celebrities to media interviews and took a visiting South African novelist of color to a radio show. He was mortally offended to be handed a script of the questions he would be asked, in which the interviewer called him by his first name; the novelist assumed the interviewer did this because he was black. He said to me, "I will just say with great dignity, 'Yes, *Mister* Smith.'" To which I answered, "No, you won't. He calls you Peter; then you call *him* by his first name." Similarly, if a man calls you "honey" in a conference, one might consider calling him "dearie" or "cutie-pie." (I wouldn't suggest trying this on the chairman of the board, however.) It's been my experience that many men call women "dear" or "darling" because they haven't bothered to remember their names; it could be possible in such a case to retort sweetly, "If you've forgotten, I'm Angela, Richard."

But of course, the real trick is to find a way not to let it get to you. A woman might do well to vent her annoyance by role-playing with a friend the outrageous retorts she'd like to give—and then the friend could role-play firing her. As the management consultant suggested to the executive who hated swearing, concentrate on a goal that will change the workplace more fundamentally. It's perhaps especially important to challenge any thinking that, like Frances Conley's, allows the language of others to eat away at one's self-confidence. A man who continues to address women only by endearments either is a man hopelessly behind the times, in which case he deserves everyone's pity and will soon be gone, or the endearments (especially if he doesn't stop when asked nicely in private) are a sign that the woman is a threat to *him*, and not the other way around. A woman in this situation may even find, once she's thought it out, that the issue no longer bothers her, and she can afford to be generous.

CHAPTER SEVEN

Seeing Sex as Dirty

As I sum up later in this chapter, jokes are often considered to be the glue that holds disparate people in a workplace together. A large part of male culture involves joking around, building on what are assumed to be common male values and views, and mentioning the unmentionable in order to demythologize it. Part of this often involves denigrating their own sexual urges—and the women who inspire them. What happens when a woman comes into this atmosphere? Although the preceding chapter ended with the possibility of a woman feeling generous about language she dislikes, it's harder to be generous when the group to which you belong is attacked, and that's how you may feel when you're the butt of a joke. Jokes about our group can reduce us to stereotypes.

Men tell dirty and anti-female jokes among themselves. Women can overhear these or be told them (maliciously or otherwise) and conclude that it's certain, not just possible, that they are being excluded in a hostile way. All the goodwill in the world to find common denominators that extend past the barriers of race, ethnicity, and class in order to get along doesn't make it any easier to run full tilt into a barrier of gender. Dirty jokes are in one sense an extension of the behavior discussed in the previous chapter, but because their content is often explicitly misogynistic—a big step beyond mere offensive words and phrases—they can be much harder for women to take. This fact makes the very writing of this chapter difficult; I find myself unwilling to quote specific examples of the jokes I have heard, even to concretize what I am talking about.

A friend of mine who has been invited to outings held by San Francisco's prestigious, exclusive, all-male Bohemian Club says he never heard a racist joke there but has heard plenty of anti-female ones. An interesting analysis of the dynamics of some such jokes appeared in a column by Maureen Dowd in the *New York Times* that dealt with a joke Senator John McCain told at a Republican fund-raiser in June 1998. The joke (which Dowd doesn't quote but calls "a junky, misogynistic crack masquerading as humor") apparently targeted Chelsea Clinton, Hillary Rodham Clinton, and Janet Reno. McCain wrote a letter of apology to the president about his wife and daughter. Janet Reno, perhaps because as a political appointee she should expect to put up with insults and cracks, didn't get one.

Reflecting on other offensive cracks politicians make about women, Dowd asks, "Why do they keep doing it?"—and got an expert's answer:

> "They can't stop," says Alan Dundes, a folklorist and expert in the anthropology of humor at Berkeley. "It's part of the male arsenal of weapons to make your way in the world. If McCain is worried about being too liberal for his colleagues, this is one way of indicating that he's one of the Republican boys—attacking the Democratic President by attacking his women. Since ancient times, you get at your male opponent by violating his women. If the women's honor is lost, the man's honor is lost. McCain was in the military. He knows you conquer enemies by feminizing the men and putting down the women."[1]

Some supposedly joking sexual remarks seem (at least to women) to be a way in which men express sexual hostility towards women. In my own experience, a man I worked with for several years and who seemed nonsexist and encouraging about the work and careers of his women colleagues made a misogynistic crack about women in general in the presence of a male friend of mine—who later repeated it to me. This wasn't, like Senator McCain's joke about the Clinton women and Janet Reno, an attack on women who are supposedly a rival's property. It was much more generalized—Us against Them.

Does this mean that my co-worker was really incapable of appreciating the work women did and that his collaboration with them was all a ruse? I don't think so. Rather, it exemplified another way of automatically signaling a bonding against an out-group. (The man who told me about it didn't react as expected—he was shocked.) Perhaps part of the bonding unique to the division by gender is mutual resentment of a shared dependency and need. The cadence calls and songs Carol Burke quoted in her *New Republic* article that have to do with having sex with comatose women and cutting women in half with chain saws exude generalized hostility against women but seem also to show negativity towards the men themselves, for being sexually dependent on women and unable to keep from responding to them.

In a male-dominated workplace, one can expect this form of bonding, whatever its genesis, to exist. Further, because the kind of sex-role spillover that can be predicted in such a workplace emphasizes the sex-object role of women, a climate of acceptance of sexist jokes may also exist.

In a white-collar, upper-management workplace setting, such jokes likely would not routinely involve mayhem and rape. In the early 1990s, magazines aimed at businesswomen were full of advice on how to handle sexist remarks and jokes. Adele Scheele, a career strategist and columnist for the magazine *Working Woman*, wrote in a 1992 column:

> When I recently asked a group of businesswomen whether they like the jokes men tell at work and whether they ever repeat them to their friends, every single one of them said no to both questions. What's the solution? Some women ignore them, recognizing that the jokes really won't damage their careers. Other try to turn the tables on the men and tell equally scatological jokes. Or they simply excuse themselves from the room and hope the men get the message. Whatever you choose to do, don't lecture. You'll only come off as humorless and defensive.[2]

The last remark about lecturing is particularly applicable. One woman I interviewed made an excellent general point: "You can't come into a workplace saying, 'I can do any job a man can do, and I want you to accept me just as you would a man,' and then add, '*But*, I want you to treat me like a lady.'" How, then, to indicate displeasure? It seems to me that, just as it is acceptable to groan at bad puns, you can groan at a joke that seems to you vulgar and tasteless, without either coming across as lecturing or, at the other extreme, trying to be "one of the boys" at the expense of your own standards.

The supposed solution of invoking authorities to stop certain kinds of jokes will always be particularly tricky. (Can't you take a joke?) One woman who was associate director of a nonprofit organization lost a suit in which she complained that her gay male supervisor made her workplace hostile by making "gossipy conversation" about homosexuality.[3] In the blue-collar world, where women, for instance, are only about 2 percent of unionized construction workers, the male group culture may be especially hard to deal with. If you joke back, you may hit a nerve. A manual for women in nontraditional employment available from the NOW Legal Defense and Education Fund points out that a job will ultimately be enjoyable only if a woman finds ways to get along with her co-workers, saying delicately that "the atmosphere [in the blue-collar world] is not as refined as an office setting." The manual further advises, "A sense of humor, a layer of thick skin, and a confident attitude can usually prevent petty annoyances from growing into serious problems." For instance, one worker bought a cowbell and hung it around the neck of a man who mooed at her to tease her about her weight.[4]

Another example of dealing with a sexist joke comes from a construction worker who, on her first job, was the only female in a group of thirty workers going in a hoist to the eighteenth floor of a building under construction. Some men standing near her started questioning the crane operator about what he had done the night before. One of them in particular egged him on into a boastful, explicit, and in her view totally fabricated, joking account of sexual exploits with a twelve-year-old girl. He was being set up; he didn't know a woman was in the hoist.

When he saw her, he was mortified and apologized profusely. She just said, "You weren't the problem," knowing he had been set up. Both recognized that the guys who instigated the story were only half-directing it at her, and he concluded that a dirty trick had been played on him. He continued to apologize every time he saw her, but when time passed and it became clear that she wasn't reporting the incident as harassment, he and his buddies became her supporters and champions in the workplace, and her handling of the incident gained her a number of friends.

Some women in blue-collar situations feel entirely comfortable in a joke-telling culture. One young woman whom I interviewed, who had been a drafter at several engineering companies (including the Ken-

nedy Space Center and General Dynamics), reported that she had
worked closely with a small group in which she was the only woman
and

> I could tell jokes with the best of them; I could take their dirty jokes in
> stride. Then I would say, okay, guys, take your other grotty stories and
> go somewhere else—I have had enough. They respected me for that.
> We all respected each other. I saw other women who were so prim and
> proper that the guys would try to antagonize them. I would tell the
> guys, come on you guys, you know she doesn't want to hear that stuff.
> Plus, you don't want to get in trouble, do you? There is a fine line. And,
> in fact, I would sit there and tell them, hey, be careful, don't tell these
> jokes to any female that is out there. They may not take it in good taste
> like I do. The guys would say, really, Suzanne? So they would take my
> advice also. This happened everywhere that I worked. Everywhere.

In any workplace it's important to have, or if necessary, to seek out,
allies. This is particularly true for a person who feels beleaguered. A
person who feels herself (or himself) the target of unwelcome sexual
remarks and jokes needs to look at the situation realistically in order to
identify possible allies. In the hoist example given above, since the storyteller was a target along with the woman, he was a natural ally. In
other companies, the situation between the actors can be different.
Often the storyteller is trying to make a woman the target for the entire group; in such a case, the onlookers are the ones the woman wants
to get on her side. In general, the issue is one of reinforcement theory—that is, behavior that is rewarded will be repeated. So identify the
reaction the harasser wants to get, and don't give it to him.

Kenneth Cooper, an expert in conflict management who wrote a
book about sexual harassment called *Stop It Now!* has identified several
ways of responding to offensive, targeted, sexually suggestive comments or jokes that would take the fun out of the situation for the storyteller.[5] Five of his ten strategies are passive and five active. The passive ones primarily withhold from the harasser the reward that would
come if the target were visibly flustered or upset. They are named the
Buddha (who totally ignores the harassment), the Lawyer (who responds to every remark literally, not noticing any double entendres),
the Adult (who says clearly and without hostility exactly what she

feels), the Idiot (who doesn't get the punchline and asks to have it re-peated several times), and the Hyena (who laughs at the efforts of the harasser, not at the joke).

The active strategies are meant to be more punitive. They are the Backboard (whatever is said is used as ammunition for a negative reply), the Judge (rating the harassment on its style or skill, like an Olympic Games judge), the Psychologist (each incident is taken as an example of the terrible psychological and emotional problems of the harasser), the Scoreboard (who keeps track of the number of harassing incidents by the day and sets quotas for the week, instead of respond-ing to the content), and the Surgeon (who verbally cuts the heart out of the offender with a devastating remark).

In general, as Cooper himself says, not everyone will feel equally comfortable with all strategies, but they certainly serve to spark the imagination as to the many choices out there for someone who feels she is the target of unpleasant jokes. All these strategies are meant to be used in public (except, I would say, for the Adult), as the impact on the audience and the audience's understanding of what is going on make up a key part of the intended effect on the offender. The great advantage of considering such strategies is that they remind the target she can choose a strategy and take the initiative, rather than being at the mercy of a would-be harasser. Many of them wrest the initiative from the harasser by turning the target into the jokester.

However, a couple of caveats. As the last strategy, the Surgeon, il-lustrates, some of these responses are tit for tat, hostility for hostility, and would probably not serve to defuse an unpleasant workplace at-mosphere. The escalation of activities that can genuinely hurt others in the workplace, even if they are initiated in retaliation, will not help create a positive climate. And there is a potential danger in turning yourself into a comic for a group whose behavior you want to change. Group members may enjoy the show so much that you end up rein-forcing the very behavior you want to discourage.

Managers in particular should concentrate any suggestions they might make about how to respond on the areas of assertiveness and communication and leave exercises in one-upmanship strictly to the individual. A policy that might turn a person with a problem into a cornered rat is not a productive office-sponsored policy. A far better tack for a manager to take would be that of one woman president of a company that works in construction, who stopped an employee from his continual teasing of a secretary. "You should only tease people who can tease you back," she said. "Otherwise, they feel oppressed."

A great deal of behavior that is considered to be sexual harassment by its targets is defended by the harasser's explaining away what happened as "a joke." A common tendency is to discount such a defense as self-serving and to assume that if something hurt, it was intended to. However, it is clear, as I said at the beginning of this chapter, that some joking relationships can be a creative way to bond people with differences together, by introducing taboo subjects and dismissing them. "Indeed, surveys of humor indicate that sexual and ethnic matters are frequently the foundation for humor in the workplace. . . . [A] joking relationship may be the only framework wherein social dysfunction, conflicts, and anxieties caused by differences can be expressed openly."[6]

It's not only men who do this. Although the confrontational use of insulting jokes is widely recognized as part of American male culture, there are ethnic cultures in which women do it too. Women from Italian American, Greek, Japanese, and African American backgrounds "use insults or arguments to create and display closeness." The ethnic background of the female drafter who didn't mind dirty jokes, for instance, is Greek. Sometimes women from these cultures find they get along better with most men than with most women; they may find to their surprise that they alienate women from other backgrounds by their joking insults and argumentative habits.[7]

Such individual differences and differences in background go far towards explaining the varying reactions that women in the same workplace may have to language, jokes, and insults. If an approach fits into their cultural expectations and patterns, they can take it in stride. This is just another way in which individuality makes it hard to predict what will or won't be found offensive at work.

The conclusion is that jokes are not only an inescapable part of male culture but a valuable part of keeping the wheels of working together greased. If it is possible for people who feel like targets to respond to jokes creatively in a joking way (with cowbells or Olympic scores for artistry and technique), that may be the best way to communicate displeasure without communicating dislike. Because that's the key. When it occurs, a joke is an indirect mode of communication, and the joker is saying in the name of camaraderie, "Let me entertain you." What he thinks is entertaining may, of course, still be offensive, but doing anything that is tantamount to calling him a swine in public is not only insulting (which may be okay) but humiliating (which is not). You really don't want to humiliate those you have to work with. If the joke is truly offensive, so that it seems impossible to respond to it in kind, perhaps that is the moment when the target needs to take most seriously the exhortation to communicate any direct objection in private.

CHAPTER EIGHT

Pictures That Embarrass

Men enjoy, or at least tolerate, displays of visual pornography. It is generally accepted that men enjoy pictures of naked or near-naked women, and a market for depictions of explicit sexual relations has long existed. Of course, *pornography* is one of those terms that has no precise definition; it has been applied to the swimsuit issue of *Sports Illustrated* and to *Playboy* centerfolds, as well as to stag films and explicit pictures of genitalia. There's a sliding scale here, as to what men will want to display and as to what women will object to. In the Lois Robinson court case in Florida, involving charges of sexual harassment in the Jacksonville Shipyards by a woman welder who had been battling for years to get sexually explicit pictures of women taken down from the walls of offices and common areas,[1] much of the argument revolved around calendars, some of which were decidedly raunchy. But the interesting thing is how embedded the calendars were in the male culture; they were, in effect, perks of the job. These calendars were traditional gifts to the shipyard from suppliers and other business connections. The shipyard officials, in turn, would give them to workers, who then posted them in the workplace. This was apparently standard operating procedure for a company whose blue-collar workforce was overwhelmingly male—in 1986, there were 546 male welders and 6 female ones at the Jacksonville Shipyards.

Pornography is one fact of male group culture about which there has been a specific public outcry. Two government commissions have investigated the subject. The first was the 1970 U.S. Commission on Obscenity and Pornography set up by President Richard Nixon, which reported that it found no link between pornography and delinquency, crime, or anti-social behavior. The second was set up in President

Ronald Reagan's administration, the 1986 Attorney General's Commission on Pornography (the so-called Meese Commission), which recommended some restrictions on sexually explicit material despite the fact that social scientists still could not find a conclusive causal link between pornography and sexually aggressive behavior.

The suppression of pornography is an issue that some feminists have made their own. In the 1970s, a number of feminist organizations began to protest the violence in some pornography as encouraging violence against women. The idea escalated into a call to legally ban all pornography, loosely defined, on somewhat the same basis that loosely defined sexual harassment has been banned—as a threat to women that violates their rights. Perhaps not so coincidentally, one of the leaders of the anti-pornography crusade has been Catharine MacKinnon, whose work is responsible for the contemporary development of sexual harassment law.

The behavior labeled as sexual harassment includes more than expression, but banning pornography clearly raises free-speech considerations. Because of this, it is a subject that split contemporary feminism in the mid-1980s and is still controversial. The controversy has mainly revolved around freedom-of-speech issues versus women's equality issues: Does the existence and circulation of pornography pose a danger to women that would justify legally suppressing it? Those in favor of the suppression of porn say it doesn't just cause violence against women—it *is* violence against women, it is action, not expression. Those in the other camp say that, on the contrary, people want to ban porn because they find that it embodies a political position they don't like: ideas about women, women's place in society, and the way in which women should be viewed by men. This camp holds that, following our First Amendment traditions, the remedy for ideas embodied in expression you don't care for should be counterspeech espousing ideas you prefer.

First Amendment analysis distinguishes between government interference with expression without regard to what it says (as in regulating the "time, place, and manner" of a parade or a demonstration) and banning material because of its content or viewpoint. A long line of First Amendment cases says that no particular viewpoint on a topic—

in this instance, on how women should be perceived and depicted—
may be either promoted or outlawed by government action.

How does this affect the issue of pornography in the workplace?
One employment-law and First Amendment expert, Kingsley Browne
of Wayne State University, points out that the argument of expression-as-action is the very argument used in support of sexual harassment law. Some years ago, the City of Indianapolis passed an anti-pornography ordinance that provided for civil suits against creators or
distributors of explicit sexual material that degraded women in any of
a number of listed ways. It defended this ordinance (which Catharine
MacKinnon had drafted in part) by saying that, among other things,
pornography leads to discrimination in the workplace. The city held
that the ordinance would reduce the tendency of men to view women
as sexual objects, "a tendency that leads to both unacceptable attitudes and discrimination in the workplace and away from it." This argument was rejected by the Seventh Circuit Court of Appeals because
it distinguished between sexually explicit materials on the basis of the
view of women they projected—clearly an argument banning materials with a specific viewpoint.[2] (Sexually explicit material that promoted women's equality would not have been punished by the ordinance.)

Legal experts like Kingsley Browne think that, if and when the
Supreme Court considers bans against the display of "pornographic"
materials in the workplace in order to avoid sexual harassment, the
Court will support the existing thrust of First Amendment law as it
was articulated by the Seventh Circuit in this case. Our courts have in
the past, for instance, struck down a student hate-speech code on the
campus of a state-supported school,[3] which had a similar "protection
from harm" rationale for its existence. The Supreme Court itself gave
a ringing endorsement to freedom of speech on the Internet,[4] despite
the argument that the rationale for the law prompting its decision was
to protect children from accessing inappropriate sites.

So the informed supposition is that the government cannot and
should not require that businesses forbid the display of sexually explicit visual materials by their employees. The First Amendment restrains the government from taking that kind of position, despite some

questionable lower-court decisions such as *Jacksonville Shipyards*.[5] (A court required the shipyard to forbid its employees to bring any sexually explicit material to work or to display any photographs of people in clothing not appropriate for work in the shipyard.)

Businesses, however, have a wide latitude as to what behavior they can require from their employees. The question then becomes: What should businesses do about this issue? Is there any reason businesses should take it on themselves to ban explicit pornography at work?

Maybe. Even though no conclusive evidence supports the idea that sexually explicit material "causes" violence,[6] we certainly know that seeing it disturbs many women. This is so much the case that a 1994 book by two women journalists who supported Anita Hill found corroboration of her story in an interview with a woman who could attest to the mere presence of copies of *Playboy* in Clarence Thomas's apartment.[7] And Deborah Tannen discusses the fact that "simply leaving pornographic materials in sight can be disturbing—and yes, intimidating—to women" and offers two anecdotes: one of a doctoral candidate in linguistics, who dropped off a textbook to a fellow student at his apartment and found herself surrounded by magazines left open to show pornographic pictures; the other of the only woman manager of a department store, whose colleagues left similar pictures where she was bound to find them. But what makes such pictures particularly upsetting to women? Tannen asks:

> [H]ow is it different from any other form of hazing that men in subordinate positions might use to test a new boss or "give him a hard time"? It is that pornography, or any reference to sex, reminds the new manager that she is a woman, that they are thinking of her as the object of sexual desire, and, most intimidating, that sex can be used as a format for physical attack. The graduate student who found herself surrounded by pornography in a fellow student's apartment reported that, besides humiliation, what she felt was fear.[8]

However, what we know and don't know about the effects of sexually explicit material on men and women can rightly lead us to mistrust overgeneralizations about both male brutality and female fear as a result of exposure. A *New York Post* feature in the summer of 1998 on the controversy surrounding Mayor Rudolph Giuliani's campaign to move "adult" businesses out of Manhattan's business and residential areas declared that although "one of the many issues that shaped feminism in the '70s was the fight against porn. . . . Now, the cause is almost passe." The story interviewed and photographed, apparently at random on the street, six Manhattan women (a lawyer, an auditor, a marketer, a legal secretary, a nurse, and an insurance analyst) as to what they thought of the mayor's campaign. Three were against it ("an infringement on freedom of speech"; "a really aggressive attempt to decree that New York City will be like Iowa"; "[i]t wouldn't be New York without them"). Two supported the strippers who would be affected but felt maybe they could get other jobs. And one strongly supported the mayor, but the reason she gave was that the adult businesses might cause harm to children—"I don't think it's a good idea for them to be near schools and residences"—not an explicit personal concern about pornography. The accompanying article interviewed three feminists who opposed the regulations (author Lisa Palac, American Civil Liberties Union president Nadine Strossen, and journalism professor Ellen Willis) and referred to three others who also opposed them (Camille Paglia, Susie Bright, and "sexual video-trix" Candida Royalle). It quoted only one, Phyllis Chesler, author of *Letters to a Young Feminist*, "who does not support the porn industry" but said instead, "Pornography is cruel and exploitive."[9]

Clearly, the article was selecting its material to support its angle. However, it cannot be discounted for that reason, as it had no difficulty in finding that support. Similarly, in interviewing workers and managers, one finds widely differing views on pornography. In the *Jacksonville Shipyards* case, even among the handful of women that were there, some said they did not feel oppressed by the calendars. And calling pornography part of male group culture doesn't mean that all men like it. In defense of Clarence Thomas at the time of his judiciary committee hearings, Camille Paglia found the feminist outcry against him both Victorian and anti-feminist: Victorian because it insisted on the protection of women, and anti-feminist because it asked for special treatment for them. "Many religious men, as well as women," she wrote, "find conversations about sex or pornography inappropriate and unacceptable. This is not a gender issue. It is our personal responsibility to define what we will and will not tolerate. . . . If Anita Hill was thrown for a loop by sexual banter, that's her problem."[10]

Two more points. First, this discussion applies to nontargeted displays of porn that would be on display even if no women were present. After Lois Robinson complained about the posting of calendars, sexually explicit material was handed to her, waved at her when she was working, posted by laughing men when she could see it, and left on her toolbox. Whatever the morale advantage in trying to change an all-male culture gradually, no management should allow a worker to be deliberately menaced by colleagues. As Kingsley Browne writes, even though

> the mere presence of sexual magazines in the workplace does not violate an objecting woman's privacy because it does not coerce intimacy. . . . [T]o repeatedly show her graphic pornographic pictures and relate the pictures to her might fairly be viewed as invading a sphere of personal privacy.[11]

Second, managers do have to protect themselves from suit. One 1990 district court case, *Tunis v. Corning Glass Works*,[12] was brought by a woman who complained of posted photographs of naked women, the use of "sex-based titles" such as "draftsman," and being subjected to whistles and catcalls when she was revealed as the one who complained. The plant manager acted on all her complaints promptly—he toured the entire plant to remove photographs, and when she complained again, he asked her to show a supervisor what offended her. It turned out to be a postcard taped inside someone's toolbox, which was then removed. The manager even sent out a memo saying that sex-based titles were no longer to be used. The manager stepped in again and unsuccessfully asked the union, the supervisors, and several workers to help stop the whistling and catcalls and announced that the behavior was wrong. The worker was finally let go for poor performance and brought a sexual harassment suit. The court found against her but unfortunately didn't address the issue of whether her claims could have justified a sexual harassment charge. It merely affirmed that the employer had acted appropriately. Browne, who discusses this case in the context of what he calls "the extraordinary chilling effect of the law,"[13] says this was "a strong message to employers."

In *Tunis*, the employer did everything right, and was commended by the court for having gone to such lengths to stifle the expression of its employees. . . . Although the court declined to decide whether the pictures and the gender-based language would have violated Title VII in the absence of an effective employer response, the message to employers is the same as if the court had found a violation: employers seeking to escape liability should restrict the expression of their employees, and if they seek to escape litigation altogether, they should be very aggressive in imposing those restrictions.[14]

The Supreme Court's 1998 rules making vigorous "anti-harassment policies" an employer defense against suits is certainly likely to reinforce this trend.

An acceptance of pornography is so much a part of male culture that it is not surprising that pornography would be available in an all-male workplace. When women enter such a workplace, they may have their first experience viewing such material and therefore may be startled and shocked. It is not necessarily the case that men should have predicted this and put the materials away spontaneously. But once women are present, it might be suggested that they put their calendars out of sight instead of leaving them on the bulletin boards.

Even if lawsuits were not a threat, both common civility and considerations of workplace morale would suggest it is a good idea not to allow employees to annoy and disturb one another with impunity in the workplace. For the women, the issue of pornographic materials on display is similar to (but much worse than) the issue of workplace compliments. As experts point out, even without sex-role spillover, it suddenly puts the spotlight on them as *women*, and their contemplating visual pornography alongside men tends to wipe away possible caretaker and daughter roles and leave them with no role except that of sex object. Some women feel this is equivalent to being naked in a roomful of strangers. This may be a very difficult position from which to object assertively, and management should give women encouragement and in some circumstances, object on their behalf.

But if pornography is displayed or readily available, women so offended that they want to do something about it still need to pick their way carefully. The NOW Legal Defense Fund manual says sexually explicit material "may" constitute sexual harassment and continues,

"Weigh factors such as how many pictures there are, how explicit the pictures are, if names are written on pictures or if they are left in a tradeswoman's workplace. Then decide how to respond. Male co-workers may support a campaign to rid the site of pornography because of religious or political beliefs."[15] Again, communication of one's own values is a crucial issue. Probably the best reaction to explicit sexual material in the workplace is to ignore it. But a woman manager, even if *she* doesn't care, should be willing to go out of her way to tell male workers that other women may be bothered.

When a woman does object for herself, this is an area where one-on-one, personal reactions are very important: "I feel," "I mind," "I dislike" not "you offend," "this degrades," "you should know"—and never a public dressing-down. The man may be as embarrassed as the woman, after all.

It's rare that pornography in the workplace becomes an object of concern in white-collar offices—this seems, to go by the legal cases at any rate, to be primarily a blue-collar issue. Not that white-collar workers never read pornography, but it would be likely to be someone's private reading matter, not posted to encroach on common territory. In heavily male (usually blue-collar) workplaces where it is so posted, it's best to remember that a newcomer, female or male, can't take over common territory. If a woman has been targeted by men brandishing porn, that's another matter. But generally objections are to the fact that it is visible in a nontargeted way. This is probably not harassment, and the person who wants to remonstrate would probably be best served, as the NOW manual suggests, by quietly finding others who object, including men if possible, with whom jointly to make it an issue of workplace standards and not a personal issue.

| CHAPTER NINE |

Competition and Hierarchy

Men are routinely competitive and are expected to be. This means that not only do they strive to win for the team or the company, to use Betty Harragan's analogy, but they expect to compete with other members of their teams—within rules, of course.

Browse through a shelf of business books and you will find a number that employ Harragan's "football" metaphor for business competition: *Winning through Intimidation* and *Secrets of the Master Business Strategists* are only two of them. Others have titles such as *The Aggressive Management Style* or *Powerbase*. Deborah Tannen's *The Argument Culture* is a book-length discussion of how war metaphors ("the war on drugs, the war on cancer, the battle of the sexes, politicians' turf battles")[1] have shaped much of our culture and how we approach almost every issue in an oppositional way. She even uses a special word for it: *agonism* (related to the more familiar adjective, *agonistic*), which she defines as "an automatic warlike stance . . . a prepatterned, unthinking use of fighting to accomplish goals that do not necessarily require it."[2] Though she seems to think of agonism as a masculine trait, it is certainly also present on the feminist side of the "battle of the sexes." Specifically in the sexual harassment arena, it appears in a feminist stress on the importance of bringing suit and winning through litigation, sometimes at the expense of mediation.

But many men do take to agonism naturally. This is because men and women generally learn to view the world differently, beginning with childhood and childhood games. Men usually learn to compete and to avoid losing even in a conversation; women learn to connect and to cooperate. In the first chapter of one of Tannen's books, she gives an example of how differently she and her husband responded to comments on the two-city marriage they then had. She tended to see commiseration from friends as sympathy and to accept and even to reinforce it, whereas he tended to minimize any inconvenience because he interpreted the same comments as patronizing. For him, conversations were necessary negotiations for position; for her, they were ways to give support and reach consensus.[3]

How does knowing about this difference in styles help a person who is having problems defending her position in a meeting, for instance? Here's an example.

I was at a committee meeting of a group dedicated to putting out a newsletter for a co-operative apartment complex. Two people were addressing the meeting with suggestions as to how this should be done. One was a professional woman whose freelance specialty was graphic design and who was volunteering to produce a newsletter through desktop publishing—without charge for her services, both because she would enjoy doing it and because she thought the newsletter's existence would be a good advertisement for her business.

The other person addressing the meeting was a male photographer who had worked with an out-of-town firm that he thought would do a thoroughly professional job on the newsletter. To persuade the rest of us, he denigrated the freelancer's credentials and constantly referred to the importance of "something that looks professional, not mimeographed." (The samples of work she had done were consummately professional, and no one mimeographs newsletters anymore.) He also zeroed in on the fact that she hadn't brought us a sample of the exact format she proposed and a list of the suppliers she intended to use, using this as reason to hold that we couldn't predict what she would do.

His language, and even more important, his intonation, communicated the assumption that this was a "little woman" who wasn't professional enough to know what she was doing and whom we couldn't trust to do the job.

The freelancer had beautiful general samples of her work and clearly did know what she was doing, but she was caught off guard by this attack and wasn't able to identify what was going on. She tried to answer each point factually, but he kept dancing ahead of her, repeating the damning term *mimeographed* and drowning her presentation out with his objections.

I saw that he was pulling out all the male-supremacy stops. He knew she was having difficulty answering him and was using it to his advantage to make her look the way he was describing her. So I weighed in, in the politest possible terms.

"We have two professionals here," I said, "one of whom is offering to do the job, and one who has stated that he is too busy to do it himself but has strong suggestions as to others who can do the job well. I think it would be too bad if the one who is too busy to do the job discourages the one offering to do it." I repeated this message in different ways at various times. In so doing, I managed to call attention to the manipulations of the man and communicated my support to the woman. At one point, I told everyone that I thought the woman was about to withdraw her offer, a perception that turned out to be accurate. The upshot was that she was offered the job.

My experiences as a feminist and my knowledge of communication differences enabled me to analyze the situation; no one else did. And I intervened without spouting slogans or even letting anyone know that I saw the situation as a power play to evoke stereotypical views of women.

An emphasis on differences between the sexes can go too far, as we see with the *cultural feminists,* a term often applied to Catharine MacKinnon and Andrea Dworkin as well as to others as diverse as Mary Daly and Adrienne Rich. Not all these women have supported anti-pornography ordinances—what they agree on is that women should counter male dominance by forming their own culture. This is because they assume that women have a kinder, gentler morality; that they are all nurturers; and in the world of work, that they would, when they become chief executive officers (CEOs) of the majority of the Fortune 500 companies, radically change the way in which all business is conducted. Rosabeth Moss Kanter has devoted a great deal of attention to combating that view, particularly as it affects judgments about the working life of women. "Task orientation . . . wiped out any sex differences that might be found in patterns of sociability alone."[4] Therefore, sex should be seen only as "one criterion for social placement, one sorting mechanism among others, that accounts for which positions and roles are considered appropriate for people."[5]

And there is always the temptation to have it both ways, as the woman suffrage movement did at the turn of the century. It argued that women should have the vote because they are, after all, human beings like men and equally deserving of political respect and a political voice and, at the same time, because their more delicate sensibilities would wipe out war and initiate an era of peace and plenty and sharing—in other words, because they're the same and because they're different.

But as the encounter over the newsletter shows, knowing something about how men may play to win in conversational gambits can be a great help to a woman encountering any offensive behavior, whether it involves sexual matters or just, as in that example, trying to deny a woman a job assignment. What are some of the observable differences in this area between men and women at work?

Men, but not women, compete even in ordinary conversation. Women employ what Tannen calls "rituals" to make others feel comfortable and are made comfortable in the same way by other women in return. If a woman apologizes for being two minutes late, the other woman responds that *she* was early. Each is assuming blame in a ritual way. If a competitive male rejoins with "You're always late; I've been meaning to speak to you about it," the woman is caught out—she can hardly say she didn't really mean it. "At the same time women who observe these rituals are not investing a lot of energy in making sure they themselves do not appear one-down, which means that's just where they may end up."[6] Since men characteristically do invest energy in not appearing to be one-down, when women and men interact using these characteristic approaches, the woman can appear uncertain, indecisive, even ignorant, when she is not.

Men will harass, tease, and verbally abuse each other, find vulnerable spots and use them to fluster each other—almost automatically. When called on it, they will say it was all in fun. Women, when faced with such behavior, tend to take the content seriously, rather than identifying the underlying game. Also, women try not to show that they are in authority even when they are—they feel more comfortable with an appearance of equality. As a result, men "may be seen as hostile when they are not," and women, in trying not to come on too strong, "may be seen as less confident and competent than they really are."[7]

The more of a threat a woman may be, the more competition she will invoke. A particularly interesting finding of the *Working Woman* 1992 survey on sexual harassment was that "the higher a woman is in the corporate hierarchy, the more likely she is to be harassed."[8] This is related to the ratio of men to women in upper management, which in turn is related to the so-called glass ceiling that makes it difficult for most career women to reach the corporate upper echelon. Therefore, "women in managerial and professional positions," as the survey classified them, are almost always in a work environment in which their colleagues are predominantly male. Sixty percent of such women said they had been harassed, as opposed to between 25 and 40 percent of women in more general surveys. One respondent to the survey, identified as an insurance-company executive, concluded, "The higher up you climb, the worse the harassment gets. . . . Men feel threatened and choose this behavior to deter our advancement."[9]

The implication of this quote is that such women are always harassed by superiors, or at least by equals in a neck-and-neck race who fear the women's competence. But that's not necessarily true. Although a great deal of emphasis is often put on the power of superior position in harassment cases—professors harassing students, executives harassing interns—some men gain a sense of power from being able to unsettle or fluster a woman who has existential power over them. The man can "take her down a peg or two." A 1989 survey of women professors at a university found that of the 208 professors who returned the questionnaire, almost half (47.6 percent) had experienced at least one harassing incident from a male student—the overall average of incidents per woman was 2.5. The behavior ranged from sexist comments to obscene phone calls (17 percent) and included one sexual assault. (Readers of this book will not be surprised to learn that the most effective strategy to deal with the harassment was found to be direct confrontation.)[10]

A woman who is not yet powerful may find that unpleasant behavior easily distracts her from analyzing fully what's going on. In an advice column she wrote, Harragan responded to a letter whose writer complained about a branch office where the new head was disrupting what had previously been a well-running unit with an excellent woman supervisor. The jerk was not only screaming at the supervisor, calling her incompetent, and having temper tantrums but also pestering the letter-writer for dates. She had just discovered he was doing the same thing to her best friend in the office. Harragan replied that if the man was harassing two women it might not stop there—the writer should tell all the women in the office, and not forget their excellent supervisor. "Has it occurred to you that she is being disparaged because she was the first to reject his overtures? . . . When a high-performance woman is suddenly degraded, it's a clue to something fishy, especially since poor performance reviews are the common lot of women who repulse sexual advances."[11]

As John Pryor's Likelihood to Sexually Harass (LSH) scale has informed social psychologists, men who abuse power in this way may have little finesse and little real interest in romantic rather than sexual encounters. Situations like this one are examples of using sex to throw women off balance.

If a woman coming into a workplace is upset at sexual talk, and if this is discovered and used to tease her, an easy assumption is that she is facing sexual harassment. But in dealing with the teasing, it is better to assume the best rather than the worst—the best being that the teasing represents a universal male competitive probing for vulnerabilities, rather than an attempt to discriminate against her specifically as a woman. A woman in such a position should make a special effort not to snap back, not to appear victimized, not to do anything that rewards the teasing. She should remind herself of the extent to which men do comparable things to each other, to throw each other off balance. They target vulnerability; if a person can be flustered by any sort of talk, they'll target that. Knowing what is going on can be a great help by actually changing emotional reactions from being flustered to being focused on observing behavior and analyzing an opponent's subtext. And if the teasing seems to cross the line into real hostility, there are ways short of invoking management disciplinary processes immediately that can get that point across. One union-run workshop tells women in a blue-collar environment to behave as if they are preparing a sexual harassment complaint by taking notes ostentatiously: "You'd like to do what? How do you spell your name? Can you tell me the exact time?"

Stylistic differences involving perceived status can also operate in subtler ways. Women often ask questions, both to gain information and to put the person with whom they are talking at ease. Men, by contrast, may assume that those who ask questions or allow themselves to be lectured to don't know much and therefore will sometimes go to great lengths to avoid asking questions, even when they don't have a crucial piece of information. One male instructor gave a low evaluation to a woman medical student who knew she was one of the best prepared in class because he thought she knew less than the others. When she confronted him, he told her it was because she asked questions.[12]

Finally, "whatever the motivation, women are less likely than men to blow their own horns—which means they may well not get credit for the work they have done."[13] And men may use their own rituals: ritual opposition as a way to discuss and explore ideas, and ritual challenging of a position in order to clarify it, both of which women often take personally.

Tannen has an intriguing theory that such a difference in styles goes far to explain the glass ceiling in corporations. Those who work directly with women may know the value of the work they do, but those who see them only at presentations and observe them from afar may think they are not managerial material because they don't fit the mold of exuding ever-present confidence and issuing take-charge orders. Stylistic differences in negotiating, the fact that women often use ritual apologies and ritual thanks (both of which are expected to trigger an in-kind response, and both of which leave the woman in a one-down position if they don't), and asking others for their opinion to get consensus, which can appear to be asking for advice, may all contribute to an unfair judgment. "It seems that women are more likely to downplay their certainty, men more likely to downplay their doubts."[14]

If women aren't attuned to the existence of stylistic differences and the importance that can be put on being one-up, they may find some exchanges in the workplace baffling and even distressing. After all, everyone assumes that what comes automatically is the natural way of doing things.

It's important for women not to forget that one of the ways in which many men keep score concerning their one-upmanship is by using women as a prize of the game and not merely an opponent in it. The "junky, misogynistic crack masquerading as humor" for which Maureen Dowd excoriated Senator McCain illustrates one such way of competing with another man—by attacking his women. Men also sometimes compete directly for women in a work situation, not just with them.

Unfortunately, a woman herself may be "a checker in a game," as Harragan writes—

> a female object to be manipulated in the interests of maintaining phallic supremacy in the pyramid. . . . In coldly realistic terms, this is a male-female genital-contact game within a localized setting and it makes no difference what the ostensible motivations, intentions, or emotional needs of the participants are. . . . The rules never envisioned women as independent, decisive movemakers, so the scoring system rewards only males. *Women can't win this game.*[15]

The name the men who use this game to compete with each other give to it, according to Harragan, is "fucking checkers." She claims that no individual man or woman can change the rules or the downgrading that the woman inevitably receives, unless the partners remove themselves from scrutiny by marrying each other.

Other management consultants echo Harragan's cautions for both men and women involved in any emotional relationships at the office, not just in games. One warns that "people persist in the belief that they can keep interested co-workers in the dark or, once discovered, keep them from turning that information into a weapon. It cannot be done. Sexual involvement undermines power and changes working relationships in many ways."[16]

If even some men feel that "[t]he conquest of a woman's anatomy, by whatever seductive or commanding means, is a jump-over which gives the male player possession of the captured playing piece,"[17] it may provide an additional explanation for the increased sexual harassment of women in authority positions that surveys report. In any case, it can only be helpful for women to know of the possibility.

To sum up: Many women don't know the extent of male competitiveness. A woman may not know when a man is competing with her, when his interest in her is sparked by competition, or when his view of a competitive world is leading him to interpret her way of doing things to her detriment. Competition, hierarchy, and wanting to advance in the hierarchy can be a large part of how the world of work is viewed, and sexual behavior can be just one of many tools for getting ahead. The woman who realizes this has hold of an important clue as to how deal with experiences that otherwise might throw her seriously off balance.

CHAPTER TEN

Indoctrination into Society

Men haze newcomers to the group, whether these newcomers are equals or superiors.

Subjecting people to hardships, accompanied by rewards for changing behavior, has long been known to be a very effective training technique; it's often known as *brainwashing*. One article describes brainwashing as including "induction of pain and fear, punishment of previous repertoire, invalidation of personal status, stripping of self-defense techniques, [and] reinforcement of a specific pattern of new behavior."[1] We call a process brainwashing, the authors point out, when we don't approve of it—"if we approve of the outcome, those procedures are more likely to be called initiation, or school, or the team, or the Marine Corps."[2] Almost all men experience similar induction into one or more groups as they grow up and learn that the techniques work.

In our society, the military has been the model for an induction that relies on such procedures—after all, men are the ones who go to war, almost all cultures agree on that. The institutionalized and ritualized hazing at military schools and colleges and at college fraternities is notorious. As we shall see, the presence of women in such places is making some changes, but women in military colleges, at least, know very well that hazing is coming their way. When the Citadel prepared for its legally mandated admission of women, its "Plan for the Assimilation of Female Cadets" announced, "Female cadets of the fourth class will receive the same adversative treatment as male fourth class cadets."[3]

Institutionalized hazing like that at military academies has as one of its purposes the bonding together of a new, entering group while its members encounter a ritual ordeal together. When a relatively few members of the entering group are "different" because of race, ethnic group, or sex, they may not be included in this bonding, and the ordeal may be made even harsher for them. The result may be hazing augmented to the point of abuse.

A public-relations scandal at the U.S. Naval Academy in 1988, when photographs of female midshipman Gwen Marie Dreyer chained to a urinal were circulated to the press, caused drastic changes in the Annapolis sexual harassment rules. Shannon Faulkner, the first woman admitted to the Citadel, quit in less than a week; two of the four women subsequently enrolled there in the fall of 1996 also quit, alleging "that they had been hazed by some male cadets in abusive ways. Their clothes had been doused with nail polish remover and set afire, they said, and cleanser was stuffed into their mouths."[4]

Partially as a result of the Citadel experience, General Josiah Bunting III, the new superintendent of the Virginia Military Institute (VMI), made ready for his court-ordered enrollment of women in the fall of 1997 by paying attention to the sex ratio and taking steps to allow for the real, unmalleable, physical gender difference of average height. He actively pursued the enrollment of a "cohort" of women (he aimed at thirty-five to forty) into the first class, hiring a full-time women's counselor and transferring several women from co-ed military academies into VMI's upper classes, where they could serve as mentors. He also, after discovering that "some women at the Citadel had suffered pelvic stress fractures that may have occurred while marching, decided to assign the new women to units of shorter men, saying, "They'll be able to take a shorter stride without stress."[5]

The class entering VMI in the fall of 1997 had 430 males and 30 females, a ratio close to General Bunting's hopes. Nineteen of these women had attended a summer program at the school. In the first week, when typically 5 percent of the new cadets drop out, only one woman (along with thirteen men) did so. The entering class in 1998 had thirty-four women.

The Citadel has been following suit on many of VMI's strategies. But both academies decided to include women in their general hazing rituals.

Freshmen, called "rats" at V.M.I. and "knobs" at the Citadel, will still have their heads shaved and will endure nearly a year-long regimen of initiation rites—everything from upper-class students yelling instructions at them to a grueling set of physical tests. The process, called the "ratline" at V.M.I., is designed to build character and bond each freshman class together.[6]

The U.S. Army (including West Point) has had different physical standards for men and women, standards that the Citadel also adopted. VMI, however, decided to require women to meet the same physical standards as men, described in a *New York Times* article as "60 sit-ups within two minutes, 5 pull-ups and a 1.5-mile run in 12 minutes or less."[7] Why the same standards? Perhaps to decrease gender hostility by lessening any feeling that the admission of women downgrades standards.

A 1997 article about West Point took pains to point out that it doesn't, even in the army:

> Brig. Gen. Robert St. Onge Jr., until recently West Point's commandant and second-ranking officer, so often heard that standards had been lowered since women were admitted in 1976 that he took to carrying a special chart when he visited West Point alumni clubs. The chart shows how much better physical shape today's cadet is in compared with the cadet of 1962 during the all-male era. In 1962 the average male cadet did 37 pushups and 60 situps in two minutes; the average female in the class of 1997 did 48 pushups and 84 situps. And the average male today smokes his 1962 counterpart—72 pushups and 83 situps.[8]

Note that the situp standard required of both sexes at VMI today is the 1962 average for West Point males. And note also that the average female West Point cadet today apparently does one more situp in two minutes than the average male cadet there. (One assumes that the average is always higher than the minimum standard.) But the criticism persists that different physical requirements for different genders lowers standards. In the movie *G.I. Jane*, Demi Moore, as the fictional first woman to join the U.S. Navy Seals, makes a point of refusing "gender norming" and insisting on being held to the same physical standards as the men she trains with, and she expresses concern that they won't think she measures up otherwise. In September 1997, Pentagon officials announced that, as part of "a series of policy changes meant to end the climate of discrimination," the army would set new formal physical standards for women that would be tougher than in the past. The announced reason for this was a new internal report that found "a widespread complaint among male soldiers that women are held to less demanding standards for physical fitness."[9]

Using hazing as a way of bonding together a group of newcomers continues to have its mystique. Military hazing is perhaps the most interesting form of hazing, both because it is the prototype from which all other hazing rituals seem to spring and because the American military is committed to becoming co-ed. As was evident in the cadence chants referred to earlier, the military has used the demeaning of women as a bonding ritual. Indeed, one anthropologist has gone so far as to hold, "Cross-cultural research demonstrates that whenever men build and give allegiance to a mystical, enduring, all-male social group, the disparagement of women is, invariably, an important ingredient of the mystical bond."[10] In military hazing and in fraternity initiations, the initiates have been routinely called "girls" to emphasize their weakness and outsider status. Will other bonding rituals be found to accomplish the same goal?

This form of bonding looks for vulnerabilities and finds them. The newcomers see each other's nervousness and, if they can stay the course, are accepted into the group anyway. Christopher Darden wrote in his memoir of his college days, "In some ways, the entire purpose of pledging a fraternity is the initiation. . . . I needed to subjugate myself, to learn discipline, and to be thrown together with other young men, to open myself up to other people."[11]

Deborah Tannen points out that it is the joint ordeal and the exposure of mutual weakness that forms the bond. "Looked at in this way," she says, "the goal of hazing is in a way not unlike the goal of troubles talk by which girls and women expose their weaknesses to each other in order to become closer."[12] She concludes, "Bonding through fighting, war, or structured opposition may be a facet of boys' and men's bonding through activity—doing things together—in contrast to girls' and women's typical bonding through talk."[13]

An important corollary of such institutional hazing is that it is open and publicized. Anyone wishing to join the institution knows that it is to be expected and that if one does not undergo it, one will not accepted as a true member of the ensuing group. So young women entering military academies, for instance, are not begging to be excused—they know there is a test that they intend to pass.

But equivalent initiations in workplaces are informal and unannounced. Groups of men tend to test the newcomer, male or female, in less ritualized or predictable ways, probing for weak spots. New prep-school instructors are heckled and teased. New women construction workers are told they have to wait in a certain line for their paycheck, while a pornographic movie is playing in full sight. A woman who got a job as a police photographer in a previously all-male group was sent out to the far reaches of the city on fictitious assignments. A sergeant in the paratroopers finally broke and turned a machine gun on thirteen hundred members of his paratrooper unit, killing one man and wounding eighteen. "The defense contends," said a newspaper report, "that the sergeant had mental problems stemming from harassment by soldiers under his command."[14] This wasn't legally actionable Title VII harassment, on grounds of race, religion, or sex; it was something similar to hazing. "Sergeant Kreutzer, who loved guns and had no social life, was called names like 'Crazy Kreutzer' and 'Silence of the Lambs,'" said the report.

The hazing of a single newcomer woman in an all-male working group that has been seemingly randomly formed may not be expected or even identified. There is no entering group for her to bond with—the goal is the amorphous one of being permitted to stay. If she were told she didn't belong because she was a "knob" or a "rat," she would know that she was in a class with all neophytes. When told she doesn't belong, period, she has no group to identify with except, perhaps, women who have been discriminated against. Because the hazing is sequential and singular, it is hard to perceive.

An article on racial harassment cites a parallel example:

Courts have had to decide if harassment was racially motivated. *Vaughn v. Pool Offshore* (1982) presented such a question. About one month after a black employee had commenced working, he was subjected to a practice known as "hazing," a ritual to determine whether new employees are able to stand up under stress and uncertainty. . . . His co-workers seized him, stripped him, and covered his genitals with grease. In other incidents, he was doused with cold water or ammonia while showering, had the lights cut off while bathing, and had hot water poured into his back pocket. He was referred to as "nigger," "Coon," and "black boy." Vaughn, however, had joined in similar behavior with his co-workers without apparent hostility or racial animus. In fact, the relations between the black employee and other employees were friendly and cordial. He eventually quit his job because of dissatisfaction arising from the assignment to a different job and claimed that his resignation was the result of racial behavior. . . . [T]he circuit court said that the environment was not polluted with discrimination.[15]

Lee Nason, who heads the maintenance department of the University of Massachusetts in Boston, is very familiar with hazing, both as a manager and as a former construction worker:

> Women are often told that sexual harassment, like rape, is not about sex; it's about power. This has elements of truth to it, but women often don't fully know the extent that men do comparable things to each other to throw each other off balance.
>
> Anyone new on the job gets a certain amount of grief initially. A new woman worker may feel it's aimed at her gender, but it's a rite of passage. On one of my first jobs, I was taken in hand by a supervisor who was a former M.P. He had me climbing steel all day; took me to very uncomfortable places. I considered never coming back after that first day. And the second day was even worse: I was told to lift pails of concrete over my head, which I was physically unable to do. By the third day, I had a stomachache. I kept coming, and several weeks later, when I was playing pinochle with the guys at lunch, I said to him, "I'm enjoying it now, but the first couple of days I was upset, because I couldn't do what you were asking me to do." And he said, "Of course not. Nobody could." Then he explained that his strategy was to throw the worst experiences at every new worker for the first few days, to see if they lasted.
>
> Within a month, he had me doing the same things to new guys. The idea was that since I was a *woman*, it would be even rougher on them not to be able to keep up with me.

The guys test you. They want to find out who you are. As a rite of
passage, the test is usually relatively short-lived. But sometimes women
react so strongly that they polarize the workforce against them.[16]

Hazing of newcomers can feel like an attempt to drive one from the
workplace, because in a way it is: it is a test to be passed. Unlike the
teasing and joking that can be involved in competition it has a time
limit, but it can be very hard to live through.

Note that the definition of this hazing is subtly different from the
hazing of a group—it is much more like the medieval trial by ordeal,
in which a person proved his innocence and worth by successfully enduring and passing a test of resolve. Although the institutionalization
of such hazing is not a result of discrimination, this is not to say that
no one in the group will be prejudiced against the initiate—perhaps
because of race or sex. But the cure for a general prejudice that
women can't do the job or don't belong in a particular occupation is
to pass the ordeal, to show that you *can* do the job and *can* make the
occupation yours.

All that the newcomer confronted with hazing can do is not let it be
a surprise and treat it as a rite of passage. All the male culture behaviors that we have been discussing may be thrown in one's face. One
union pamphlet on stopping sexual harassment says that

> many times the new woman in a previously all male environment is not
> just treated as "one of the boys." It is not business as usual, but rather
> the men escalate the foul language or sexual conduct to test her or make
> it difficult for her to succeed. While church picnic behavior is not neces-
> sary, intensified on-going, sexually directed conduct has been held to be
> sexual harassment. Being a woman in a nontraditional job is difficult.
> She needs support from her co-workers.[17]

What is not spelled out but rather implied here is that, for many
women, getting and keeping the job is worth it. Therefore, identifying
the behavior as sexual harassment is irrelevant, since their taking legal
or administrative action would be apt to poison the workplace for
them. Identifying it to oneself as hazing, and identifying the need for
support from co-workers, however, is another matter. It gives a new

definition of the task, which is to pass the test and to gain respect from colleagues.

One of the first women to join the Rotary Club of Westerly, Rhode Island, spoke of trial by joke:

> They test you out with jokes. . . . When they find you don't pale, they see they don't have to be pristine around you, that they can still be men.[18]

And if any of the joking is meant as hazing, you pass the test.

The drafter who got along well with her male colleagues who told sexual jokes (and even counseled them on how to treat other women) also was able to deal with a spot of visual pornography, which may have been planted to test her reaction to the Clarence Thomas–Anita Hill television confrontations about sexual harassment:

> I would open my drawer in the morning to get my stuff out of my desk. And one of the men in our group had put a picture of a black man whose name was Long Dong Silver there. Supposedly his penis is very long and hanging down. . . . I opened the drawer and slammed it shut. I was shocked. I opened it again. I didn't want any other strangers from other groups, male or female, to see what I was looking at. Of course, the guys in my little work area were just all rolling on the floor laughing because one of them had planted this in my drawer. I took it in good fashion. I laughed with them; I didn't make any disparaging remarks; I didn't condemn anybody.

Notice that the incident took place after she was comfortable with the group. Notice that she didn't want "strangers" to see what they had planted. A situation of intimacy and trust had already been created, so even if this was an attempt at hazing because of events in the news, she had already passed the acceptance test.

Now that we have a smaller military made up of volunteers, it is no longer the case that most men experience some sort of military service, as it was in generations past. So the role of confrontation and humiliation in such training is becoming less generally familiar, even to the male population. But women in particular do not understand how strongly positive some men feel about using various forms of brainwashing to build esprit de corps.

A securities trader, George Allen, while supporting his son's high school cross-country running coach in the face of charges of "gender inequity" towards members of the girls' team, tried to explain the coach's style to two women who were investigating for the school system. He concluded that they didn't understand that cross-country is "pretty much a Marine Corps drill kind of sport" and found the investigators "incredibly oversensitized." He went on, "I mentioned to them that Flynn expected a lot of these kids, that he would deride the boys and girls equally." Both investigators reacted. "They gasped at the notion that derision could be a motivation factor. . . . That was a very telling gasp, to my mind."[19]

Perhaps we may expect a confrontation in the near future within the military, between the ideas of General Bunting of VMI, who thinks such toughening is an important part of preparing for leadership, and West Point's General Christman, who says, "You can instill standards and discipline without humiliating a subordinate."[20] Intriguing questions arise. Does hazing fulfill a psychological need, as one of the few ways in which men in our culture can expose their vulnerabilities to each other in order to become close? Or does it teach bad leadership habits, as General Christman says? And if reintroduced at West Point, would it, as General St. Onge puts it, "reintroduce mean-spiritedness, viciousness, and dysfunctional leadership"?[21] And in either case, how will including the new cohort of women leaders modify the situation?

Meanwhile, here as elsewhere, old social habits linger. Many people want to change customs such as hazing; they may one day be able to do so. But the issue for a woman entering a nontraditional workplace and for a manager overseeing worker relations is to understand what is the case here and now—and to react to it to their advantage. Kingsley Browne summed the problem up when he wrote, "Failure to understand male psychology has led many women to assert that they just want to be treated like men, while the fact is that, for very fundamental reasons, men often do not treat each other very well."[22]

We shouldn't forget that male group culture is no longer appropriately characterized as a white Anglo-Saxon Protestant male group culture. This section began by pointing out the positive nature of emphasizing a common denominator that can include and even bond together people of various interests and backgrounds. But if that common denominator involves putting down, embarrassing, insulting, and demonizing women as a process that "everyone" can relate to, what hope does this hold out for the ultimate inclusion of women as equal colleagues in the workplace?

The change is happening already; the secret of this bonding is out. The workplace is no longer the supposedly serious place where men can go in order to get away from the distractions of women. It is being revealed to women that, on the contrary, the workplace is a place where men have fun and do things together, where a scatological vocabulary is assumed; a place full of dirty jokes, dirty pictures, insults, horseplay, and subjecting others to "rites of passage." Put that way, it sounds almost childish.

The fact that a lot of women don't think this atmosphere is much fun is irrelevant; the specific culture of many workplaces is changing and will continue to change. As members of other groups got into workplaces that were unfamiliar with them, mutual stereotypes were exploded and many of them discarded. The same thing is happening with women. Men are discovering that there are women who can do the job, and women are discovering that there are men who can be helpful and who wish them well. Workers in workplaces that are "balanced," in Rosabeth Moss Kanter's terminology, rarely if ever report sexual harassment. The real point to be made is that the impulse towards common denominators and a certain confusion about the entrance of women is understandable and not, initially at least, necessarily hostile. Rather, both sides may lack knowledge of what to expect. Women who inform themselves about male culture and are prepared to communicate their feelings without hostility when faced with things that bother or offend them will be doing their part to bring about a truly integrated workplace. Such a workplace may, in fact, be more enjoyable for everyone.

PART III

What's to Be Done

CHAPTER ELEVEN

Can Sexual Harassment
Be Forestalled?

The outpouring of media attention and the hundreds of social science studies that have made sexual harassment their focus in the twenty-odd years since it first came to general notice are almost unprecedented. Not only that, but corporations have devoted highly paid time to training programs and other ways in which to eliminate the problem. All of which raises the question: Why is sexual harassment still an object of controversy? Why hasn't it been eliminated, except as an occasional criminal matter similar in frequency to embezzlement? No one sits and debates whether the laws against embezzlement go too far.

Part of the reason sexual harassment is still with us may be that many top managements have not taken the issue as seriously as they take embezzlement. One expert, Barbara Gutek, predicted in 1985 that enough had been learned in the previous decade to make it "possible by the middle 1990s to eliminate sexual harassment, leaving a more productive and professional workplace for everyone."[1] Her action plan postulated that corporations would act on two main assumptions: that the support of management was crucial to success in this endeavor, and that the workers would believe in this support only if an anti-harassment stance was incorporated into the reward structure. In other words, people who assist in eliminating sexual harassment would be rewarded, and those who practice it would be punished, with the issue included in some way in all performance appraisals.

By the end of the 1990s, however, sexual harassment had not been eliminated by most managements. It is also the case that Gutek's two suggestions have not been universally applied. Instead of being rewarded for assisting in eliminating sexual harassment by reporting it, many women still say they are punished for complaints and face reprisals.

One of the early surveys—this one of over twenty-three thousand civilian employees of the federal government, conducted by the U.S. Merit Protection Board and reported in 1981—found that not only did few employees who said they were harassed make either formal or informal complaints (2.5 percent and 11 percent, respectively) but that, while about half the people who made formal complaints felt the report made the situation "better," 33 percent reported that the situation became "worse."[2]

A decade later, there were enough reported reprisals against women complaining of sexual harassment within the federal Department of Veterans Affairs (VA) offices that Joseph Kennedy of Massachusetts called for "congressional hearings into sexual harassment within the VA" in 1992. On top of complaints of serious harassment—a woman being thrown to the ground by a supervisor, who lunged on top of her; a woman whose supervisor pulled a car in which they were riding off the highway and forced her face into his groin—there were indications that the complaint-reporting system was backfiring.

One woman said that the day after she filed a complaint, "her alleged harasser stormed into her office, shouting at her and pointing his finger in her face." Another said, "Everywhere I turned, the door slammed in my face. . . . It was reprisal after reprisal." A registered pharmacist was reduced to reviewing charts in the medical records office. Another woman was moved to a small isolated room and given no work to do for six weeks. A woman who had been in charge of quality assurance and risk management for an entire medical center was moved to an office in a basement, and her title was changed.[3]

The online newsletter *DataLine* has posted some "real-life examples of sexual harassment," reported soon after the Anita Hill–Clarence Thomas confrontation, which include the following:

A veteran civil servant with an impeccable performance record was promoted to work for a man who made advances and tried to touch her. When she refused him, he began a campaign that included leaving "sex toys" in her locker. When she filed a complaint, the campaign escalated to include vandalism of her personal property and physical abuse (hitting and shoving). When her boss's friends threatened her, she backed down.[4]

Cronyism in the chain of command that can override formal procedures intended to protect the complaint process exists in private industry as well as in the government examples cited here. Top management has not been uniformly known to take harassing behavior seriously, no matter what procedures are put in place.

What have companies done to forestall sexual harassment, and how effective has their action been? Some have felt that there is nothing they need to do: a fair atmosphere is all that is necessary. I met an old friend recently, who is now the vice president of a computer software company. On hearing that I was writing this book, he told me that he has a well-run company, so they had never had an experience with sexual harassment. He looked rather taken aback when I mentioned that nevertheless his company might do well to institute a grievance procedure, because of the 1998 Supreme Court decisions naming that as a necessary defense to a sexual harassment suit. However, he immediately saw the point, nodded, and said, "You mean, to protect ourselves." Even though I suggested it, I'm not really sure, however, whether modeling company policy on the law is always productive.

As we have seen throughout this book, what companies take very seriously is the possibility of lawsuits. But a lot of steps taken to guard against this possibility have proved counterproductive. To protect themselves, the securities industry has included binding arbitration clauses in employment contracts, to preclude suits. But several legal decisions and a 1998 Senate Banking Committee hearing put the status of such clauses in doubt, at least for Wall Street firms. At issue has been the composition of the arbitration panels run by organizations such as the New York Stock Exchange and their competence to judge fairly. The panels have been criticized by both employee groups and women's organizations, especially with regard to their handling of civil rights claims. Merrill Lynch abolished its compulsory arbitration procedure; Smith Barney changed the composition of its arbitration panels; and when Tonyja Duffield sued Robertson Stephens and Co.

for prohibiting her through such an agreement from bringing her sexual harassment claims to court, the Ninth Circuit ruled in her favor in the summer of 1998. It said that such agreements force "American workers to choose between their jobs and their civil rights."[5]

Some companies are asking employees to sign "consensual relationship agreements," stating that the relationship is welcome and promising that they will not bring a sexual harassment suit should it end unhappily. Other companies, as I mentioned earlier, are initiating a ban even on dating between employees. These attempts to eliminate sex from the workplace have been especially criticized. In March 1998, Judith Vladeck, the New York employment lawyer who brought one of the first harassment suits in the early 1970s, deplored this development to a writer for the *New York Times*:

> There are real concerns about so sanitizing the workplace that you're removing any pleasure in the relationships among people who work together. . . . That's not what the law requires, and I don't think women want a sanitized workplace. I think what the law says is that if you hit on me, and I say, "No way, Buster," I'm entitled to have you accept my rejection of you, and it shouldn't interfere with my work.[6]

Something is missing from such management attempts to control the situation: a positive goal, rather than the negative one of minimizing legal damage by demanding that employees promise in some way never to sue. A better approach, as discussed somewhat in chapter 5, is trying to go beyond the law to make the workplace a better place. If, as the courts and the court of public opinion seemed to be saying to President Clinton in 1998, when his behavior with Kathleen Willey and Paula Jones was called into question, a single grope or a single demand for oral sex is not legally actionable sexual harassment, then companies have to make clear that this is still behavior that will not be considered acceptable—there is no "free grope." Ways to do this include signals such as an explicit "no reprisals" policy and perhaps steps to expedite complaints. Some companies are beefing up their reporting procedures by hiring an ombudsman to deal with people outside the chain of command. Others have initiated an "open-door" policy that will allow complaints to be made to any manager, not just to someone in the complaining employee's particular hierarchy.

These are good correctives for a policy that has been too narrowly tailored to the law. But the new policy needs to be explicit and to be put in the context of general harassment, which can become a problem whenever the diversity of workplaces changes dramatically. Managements that are serious about communicating to their employees that they disapprove of harassment might well start to promulgate more exact policies that draw distinctions, somewhat along these lines:

Every workplace may find that it includes people who enjoy tormenting others. Some of this behavior, when it is intended to create (or does create, when observed by a reasonable person) a hostile atmosphere, has been ruled by the courts to be illegal workplace discrimination when directed at a member of a "protected category." Federally protected categories include race, color, religion, national origin, citizenship, gender, age over forty, and disability. New York State protected categories also include sexual preference and marital status.

The most talked-about offense in this area is sexual harassment. We will not tolerate instances of sexual harassment, by which we mean targeted and repeated abusive or offensive actions and/or talk to do with sex that interferes with the work of another. (We have posted current EEOC guidelines as examples.) Single instances of unwanted sexual touching or unwelcome demands for sexual acts will also not be tolerated and will be subjected to disciplinary action. We also will not tolerate harassment in general. If any employee is the subject of harassment of any sort (e.g., racial, religious, national), management will intervene and investigate, and the incident will at a minimum go in the record of the offending employees.

The private lives of employees are their own concern, and any arrangements for socializing or dating that are mutually acceptable will not be scrutinized by the company. However, if an employee feels herself or himself the object of a one-sided pursuit that is distracting from work and bothersome, management will intervene if requested and take action, including the possible transfer of one or both parties.

We also will not tolerate cruelty or disrespect for the values of others just because those others do not happen to fall within a protected class and therefore such behavior does not expose us to lawsuit. We expect our employees to treat each other with civility and mutual respect; not to use

derogatory epithets in referring to one another; to recognize that in get-
ting to know one another they may have to accommodate different ways
of talking and may unintentionally give offense; and to pay attention to
requests for moderating behavior or language that offends others. Boor-
ishness and cruelty are not what we expect from our employees. We will
investigate promptly any violations of these principles and will subject of-
fending employees to disciplinary action, up to and including dismissal.

As this suggested policy statement indicates, it's important today to
pay attention to harassment that is not targeted at women. Corporate
diversity has become a hot issue, and Rosabeth Moss Kanter's work on
tokenism and population ratios can be applied to the dynamics of
groups that differ in ways other than gender. It's not as easy as it
might seem to run a diversified workplace. Goodwill is not enough,
and beginning a program of diversification can create all the new
problems that tokenism and skewed populations bring. When dealing
with the presence of groups other than women (whose numbers in the
general population are relatively equal to those of men), it is important for managers to note that the point at which workplace populations become balanced is not directly related to their representation in
the general population, which is the figure government agencies
sometimes use when inquiring into illegal discrimination. You can
have the proper nondiscriminatory percentages in your population
and still not have the right population mix for balance. The percentage
of black noncommissioned officers in the military, for instance,
reached 31 percent (30 percent is often considered the point at which
a skewed population is tilted and approaches balance) in 1990, when
the percentage of blacks in the population as a whole was somewhat
less than 12.5 percent.

Perhaps it is salutary to notice that when Texaco, Inc., was successfully sued in the mid-1990s for racial discrimination (after a board
member made public the language directors had used to refer to black
employees during a board meeting that the member had secretly
taped), the company had been mounting an effort to diversify its
workforce. According to an article in *Investor's Business Daily*, an expert stated that some of the supposedly racist comments for which
Texaco was sued and agreed to settle were not actually racist—the ref-

erence to "black jelly-beans" that was widely quoted in the media at the time of the suit, for example, is apparently "a well-known metaphor common to diversity consultants." Texaco was considered at the time to be a leader in diversity efforts, had been running a diversity program for three years, and had hired the highly respected president of the American Institute for Managing Diversity as a consultant. The article came to a surprising conclusion:

> Texaco's fate was actually an outgrowth of its diversity efforts. Some executives were concerned that the company's diversity programs were spurring racial separation. Some blacks at Texaco were demanding a different national anthem, for instance, according to executives' words transcribed on the tape.[7]

Going back to Kanter, we see how this could have happened. Since taking diversity past the token stage can engender hostility towards those who have now become a threat to the dominants, a successful attempt to diversify means a newly unsettled workplace that can be calmed only by increasing the minority population in the direction of balance (or by returning the population to uniformity, but in today's business world that is not a viable option). If the diversification extends to management, its dominant members will also feel some hostility—which can exist as an emotion side by side with a knowledge of the excellent business reasons why the workforce population should be newly diverse. In other words, the objectionable language might not have been used at all if the effort to diversify had never been made. And on the other side, as the number of tokens increases towards minority status, they may make demands that call attention to differences.

This means a newly diversified workplace may have just begun its task of integration. Since in some respect such a workplace will be population skewed, this may be precisely the time when knowledge of what ratios do to groups and some directed information sharing of values between members of different populations is most particularly needed. The solution may have to include not only information but altering the population ratios so that changes are made by adding sizable groups all at once, as General Bunting insisted on doing with women at VMI.

To install a working anti-harassment procedure, management needs also to pay attention to just and proportional punishment. In many companies, initially the problem was that offenders received only a slap on the wrist. More recently, the concern has been that those accused are dismissed too quickly, without proper attention to a fair and objective investigation process. Because courts disagree on what adequate remedial action on the part of an employer is, firms may err in the direction of unnecessarily severe punishment. Non-union companies would do well to adopt the union requirements that, in the interests of fairness, they must inform the accused, investigate the truth of the charge promptly, interview others who might be witnesses or know something about either side's credibility, and take prompt action when the investigation has been completed.

The standard of evidence may vary. An examination of labor arbitration decisions to judge the fairness of penalties for sexual harassment found that, of the eleven decisions examined, two arbitrators used as a standard the preponderance of the evidence, seven required clear and convincing evidence for termination, and two required that the case be proved beyond a reasonable doubt. (The last two cases involved accusations of moral turpitude.) All the decisions applied the seven tests for a just-cause firing that arbitrator Carroll R. Daugherty first made public in a 1966 case.[8] Since they concern fairness in any workplace, not just one with a labor agreement, they are worth reprinting here:

1. Did the company give the employee forewarning or foreknowledge of the possible or probable disciplinary consequences of the employee's conduct?
2. Was the company's rule or managerial order reasonably related to (a) the orderly, efficient, and safe operation of the company's business and (b) the performance that the company might properly expect of the employee?
3. Did the company, before administering discipline to an employee, make an effort to discover whether the employee did in fact violate or disobey a rule or order of management?
4. Was the company's investigation conducted fairly and objectively?
5. At the investigation did the "judge" obtain substantial evidence or proof that the employee was guilty as charged?

6. Has the company applied its rules, orders, and penalties evenhand-edly and without discrimination to all employees?
7. Was the degree of discipline administered by the company in a par-ticular case reasonably related to (a) the seriousness of the em-ployee's proven offense and (b) the record of the employee in his service with the company?[9]

If management does install an explicit policy of mutual respect, re-ward the reporting of violations, and punish offenders fairly, will this eradicate sexual harassment? My contention is that, to reach that goal, it will also need to inform itself about the social-studies findings re-ferred to in this book. One branch of government seems to be manag-ing to forestall problems by doing things right in many of these re-spects. The way in which the U.S. Army has dealt with racism provides very hopeful news for those people and organizations that would like to do better in eliminating group hostility, including sexual harass-ment. World War II, "the war to save democracy," was fought with segregated American troops. After that war, President Harry S. Tru-man integrated the armed forces in 1948. But it was more than twenty years later, during the Vietnam War, that the armed forces finally began systematically attacking the issue of racism. The Pentagon opened the Defense Race Relations Institute at Patrick Air Force Base in the 1970s; the army began "sensitivity training" at about the same time; and the navy created stiff new rules against racial bias, and senior officers who didn't uphold them were threatened with dismissal.[10] And the population ratios began to approach balance. Military leader-ship was becoming integrated—the number of senior black noncom-missioned officers grew from 14 percent of all noncoms in 1970 to 31 percent by 1990, while the percentage of black commissioned officers tripled during the same period.[11]

Here again, we see that the percentage of senior black noncoms reached the point of moving from being tilted to being balanced (gen-erally placed at 30 percent), so that, according to Rosabeth Moss Kan-ter's thesis, by the late 1990s they were in a position to be considered primarily as individuals; whereas women, who were limited by law to 2 percent of the armed forces before the draft ended in 1973, by 1998 made up only 14 percent of the army, 17 percent of the air force, 5 percent of the Marine Corps, and 13 percent of the navy.[12] These figures have reached the point at which a new population is no longer token but still represents an external threat to the dominant group, and therefore, one may expect more stereotyping and more hostility on the part of the dominant group.

Race, in the military at least, is no longer a similar threat. In the late 1990s, according to Thomas E. Ricks, "[t]he Army . . . enjoys far better race relations than any other major social institution in the country." In an article published in *The Atlantic* at the end of 1996, he quoted both white and black soldiers as to how "the Army has built equal opportunity (EO) into its way of life." This comment came from a white Texan sergeant major: "There's black, white, Hispanic—and military. That's a new ethnic group." A black sergeant told Ricks that "the last time he encountered racism in the Army was 'way back in 1980.' He said he sees it all the time in the civilian world." A white infantry commander recounted the only racial incident he could recall in a recent year, when a white sergeant yelled a racial epithet at a recruit: "The sergeant is out of the army now. . . . He was unfit to be a NCO."[13]

Many authorities believe the military is only now facing up to the issue of sexual harassment as discrimination, and that once it puts its mind to it, the armed forces may surprise us all with how well they can do as an institution in eliminating behavior they *want* to eliminate. By the mid-1990s, every branch of the military had an anti-harassment policy, and hot lines to report harassment and receive advice were set up by the navy in 1992, by the air force in 1994, and by the army in 1996 and 1997.[14] The navy also instituted a Standing Committee on Military and Civilian Women in the Department of the Navy and starting training courses in sexual harassment for all recruits.[15]

Still, partly because of the exclusion of women from combat and therefore from access to promotion, there are relatively few high-ranking female officers in the armed forces. When the Secretary of the Army appointed a special panel of five men and four women from the officer and civilian ranks of the military to review policies on sexual harassment in late 1996, many panel members were strong advocates of further gender integration and felt that sexual harassment incidents are reinforced by the existence of what one female retired officer called "all-male macho units." In this view, growing reports of harassment show the need to open to women the thousands of combat positions still closed to them. The *New York Times* reported, "Until women are treated as equals, these advocates say, men will continue to mistreat women, and the exclusions block women from advancing along the three main routes to senior leadership: armor, infantry and field artillery."[16]

One of the reasons for an optimistic prediction that the military will move to make successful changes is that, although it no longer has the power to draft civilians, it is still an all-encompassing, twenty-four-hour-a-day environment. What can ordinary business managements do to similarly influence social behavior? To put the question another way: How can they make the transition of workplaces to a more balanced population of women with a minimum of disruption?

Management consultant Peter Drucker predicts that demographics will be the main business concern for at least the next two decades. At the same time that "knowledge work" is becoming crucial in business, the people of the developed world are not reproducing themselves, so a shortage of knowledge workers, as opposed to manual workers, is already with us.[17] These underpopulation demographics mean that not only the armed forces (which could not continue on a volunteer basis without the contributions of women) but most civilian businesses are going to have to recruit more and more women. There is no choice but to diversify many jobs that have traditionally been all male.

To recruit capable women, these workplaces will need to become more woman-friendly. Changing sex ratios will inexorably bring positive changes, but businesses can also take two interim approaches: (1) Help women to become more assertive and to speak out without hostility when they feel offended, and alert them to the fact that most of the hostility they may encounter is encouraged by skewed or tilted ratios and will change when these ratios become more balanced. (2) Take strong steps to control situations in which predators feel free to disguise their motives, and alert them to the fact that they can't get away with being predators. This would definitely include a climate of opinion emanating from top management that differences are to be respected.

Some companies are moving aggressively in this direction. But at the same time, regulations and legal penalties have been increased, which has only increased hostility between male and female workers. And many managements are patting themselves on the back for doing all they must by informing employees of legal penalties and the ways to complain and bring suit. As we will see, most training programs are focused on what the law requires, how to spot examples of illegal behavior, and what must be done to comply with the law. Even some of the research as to which training programs are effective is focused on these objectives.

Managements may take employee relations seriously and try to forestall sexual harassment, or they may not. Fortunately, employees don't have to wait for the ideal management to install the ideal program. What can they themselves do to forestall being sexually harassed? As examples show us, some women have been able to protect themselves even in very sexually charged and potentially hostile workplaces. The rest of us can profit from articulating what they have done and can help other women to do likewise.

If one is trying to instruct oneself, the first step is to understand different styles and be willing to concede that difference is not necessarily wrong. Try to learn to read metamessages. Categories are not rigid— all men (or all Greeks or all Italians) are not necessarily alike—but identifying a pattern of behavior, even if you are not sure how it is caused, enables you to have a perspective in dealing with it. A man from a southern European family background, for instance, may be exuberant and touchy-feely towards *everyone*, and when he puts his arm around a female worker, he may mean nothing sexual at all. The worker is certainly entitled to respond by explaining (in private) that this is a transgression on *her* space that makes her uncomfortable, but it is not necessarily the subject for a lecture on Respect for Women.

The next step is to look at the sex ratio in your workplace and estimate its effects. After you have evaluated your workplace dynamics, as well as the styles of those you will be dealing with, you can begin to take action to establish yourself. Experienced workers in nontraditional jobs suggest that a woman coming into an all-male workforce should do two things immediately.

First, establish your competence. Make it clear that you deserve your job. The men you work with may push you very hard to find out what you know; do not take it personally, and do not assume it is a sign of discrimination.

Second, it is crucial that you make a real effort to get a network of friends. If other women are in your workplace, seek them out and try to find out what their take is on the advantages and pitfalls there. Also, break up the existing male solidarity by actively cultivating sympathetic men who want to see women treated fairly. Your strongest allies may be family men with working daughters, who are also supportive of their wives (not all men with working wives are supportive of them). As one architect told me, "You have to have places you can go that are safe for you."

Dottie Jones of the United Automobile Workers (UAW) women's department, who conducted training sessions for union men on sexual harassment for some years, suggests that men with sisters are also concerned with fairness towards women. The UAW produced a training video in 1992 called *Would You Let Someone Do This to Your Sister?*[18]

Don't forget that it's not necessary to confide your dreams and fears to a man for him to consider himself your friend; doing things together (telling jokes, playing cards) and bantering in a friendly fashion will do it, since most men bond through activities (and joking and horsing around are activities) rather than through talk and shared intimacies, which are more important to women. (One manual for blue-collar women refers indirectly to this when it advises, "Evaluate for yourself how familiar you will get with your co-workers. Sometimes when you make your personal life an open book you may regret it later.")[19]

A member of management can solicit support from those whom she supervises as well as from peers but should be cautious about soliciting support from her bosses. That could invoke one of the main things a woman in a nontraditional job should avoid: the perception that she has a special in. You should also, as previously mentioned, never communicate that you expect to be treated like a lady; that is an extremely counterproductive statement, because it can be taken to imply that you want it both ways—to be one of the boys in getting the job but also to be treated better than they are.

The *New York Times* published a roundup of sexual harassment case histories after the 1998 Supreme Court decisions, in order to interpret what the new rulings might mean. One example is of a female supervisor at a construction company who "prides herself on being able to deflect the sexual bantering common on the job." When a new district manager brought in to solve a problem starts calling her at home and then makes a verbal pass, takes her to lunch and touches her hand, arrives when she is working late to insist she go out with him, and later kisses her, she panics. Instead of saying anything to him, she develops health problems, misses work, and finally leaves her job and sues. She didn't use the company's sexual harassment process, apparently because of her previous tolerance of sexual bantering and her reputation for being unflappable, which she doesn't want to lose.

The *Times* asked an expert if the supervisor would win her case, and he said probably not, since she knew the complaint procedures and didn't use them.[20]

This case shows the importance of allies. If the supervisor had realistically looked at her position as one of the few female supervisors in construction, she should have started earlier to build a circle of friends at work to whom she could communicate her values. Her seeming unflappability over sexual topics would be a good asset for her to offer to such a circle. That wouldn't have guaranteed she would have someone to whom she could completely open up when the district manager first made his move, but at least she wouldn't have felt so isolated. It seems possible that she felt more at risk because she had allowed the sexual banter to continue, as if now she had no right to complain about anything.

Although she could deal with sexual talk from her subordinates, apparently the arrival of a star manager superior to her left this woman feeling so isolated that she could neither reply to him in an assertive way nor speak to anyone else. Her only recourse seemed to be to flee, and to seek help only from legal personnel who had not known her before.

What happened may not even have been true sexual harassment: the story seems to indicate that the man genuinely developed interest in her over a period of time that he showed in mildly increasing ways, which she tried to ignore instead of deflect. This behavior only encouraged him, on the principle that the absence of a "no" means "keep going." It's a very sad story, one that illustrates the importance of finding ways to be assertive that are not insulting to the other person but still make your point clear. If she had known how to do that, she might still have her job—and even her reputation for being "unflappable."

However, predators do exist, and at times the firm hand of authority is required. Legal experts suggest a series of steps in that case. A wrap-up article in the *New York Times* lists the following:

Read your company's policy.
Speak directly to the harasser.
Document all actions and comments.
Speak up to company management (in person and in writing).
Get support, from friends and perhaps from a lawyer.
Refrain from the urge to sue.
Move on.
Don't bank on a big monetary award.[21]

A word more about documentation, which I haven't discussed before this. The obvious immediate reason to document is that which started all the concern with sexual harassment: unemployment insurance. Documentation can prove "constructive firing." Should a woman find someone's behavior so obnoxious that she decides to quit her job, advises Doris Ng of Equal Rights Advocates, a San Francisco organization, "she would have a viable argument that she didn't quit per se, but was really forced to quit in terms of how he treated her."[22]

For a person who has difficulty confronting a harasser, it is often suggested that you write a letter to him instead, saying exactly what behavior bothered you and that you want it to stop, with dates on which the behavior occurred and accounts of any requests to stop that you have made. Some advisers to employees even suggest that you write the letter, take it by hand to the offending person, and watch him while he reads it. Others suggest the letter be sent by certified mail. It is important to keep a copy of the letter, and perhaps to send a copy to higher management. If you are making any sort of complaint to management, any corroboration of what the behavior that you object to was can be important. This will prove what you thought he did and that you objected to it on a certain date.

Union pamphlets and manuals in particular stress the importance of establishing a paper trail. Examples would be dated notes describing what was said or done to you, and what you replied, that also list the names of any witnesses; a diary; and copies of any letters about such incidents that you sent to the offending party. If you file a complaint through the union, all this will help inform the union shop representative who will be representing you to management. The NOW Legal Defense and Education Fund even suggests, for your own protection, that if your company gives written performance evaluations, you should mail a copy of your good evaluation to yourself and *don't open the envelope*, keeping it as proof of your good record on a certain date in case the evaluation changes after you make a sexual harassment complaint.

Documentation makes a lot of sense, but the support of others in the workplace is even more crucial. If you ever come to the point of making a serious complaint, the work you have done in establishing a network of allies and a sense of your competence will be essential to help you carry on from day to day.

As I indicated in chapter 1, those close to the issue seem to agree with one of the *New York Times*'s points: "Refrain from the urge to sue." Suits tend to drag on for years; they're expensive (even if you get a lawyer to take a case on a contingency basis, you will have to pay "costs"); and few people find the outcome at all satisfactory. Aleeza Strubel of the NOW Legal Defense and Education Fund also says many people get bogged down on the EEOC level; they don't know that when you've filed a complaint with the EEOC, after 180 days you are entitled to a right-to-sue letter saying you may sue on your own, whether they've reviewed your case or not. When I spoke to Strubel, I asked her if she knew of better solutions, since bringing suit has so many problems, but she didn't go outside legal parameters. Mediation is an option, she said, but for that you also really need an attorney. Administrative agencies (not just the EEOC but state and city commissions) are not brokering settlements because they have such a backlog.[23]

In the case of lesser but still rankling incidents about which you may not want to complain formally, throughout this book I have suggested possible responses to offensive and distressing encounters. These range from Ken Palmer's eight strategies for deflecting sexist talk to Shereen Bingham and Lisa Scherer's suggestion of a clear, detailed, but non-aggressive objection that includes facework. There's a cornucopia of possible responses out there for those who are looking for them. One Radcliffe student, in response to a professor who, infuriated by her knitting through his lecture, informed her in class that "Sigmund Freud has discovered that knitting is simply a sublimated form of masturbation," told him, "Professor, when I knit, I knit, and when I masturbate, I masturbate."[24] A marine sergeant finally stopped her commanding officer from pressuring her to sleep with him by going with him to a hotel and, after he undressed and went into the bathroom, leaving with his clothes, which she gave to the military police when she returned to base.[25] The possibilities for creative personal responses are endless.

One common denominator among those who feel they have responded successfully seems to be attitude: an attitude that clearly recognizes negative values such as sexism or predation in the person one is dealing with and protects oneself from them without extending their aura to color the entire world—or workplace. The protagonists in the *Robinson* and *Tunis* cases seemed consumed by a contrasting vision that men *should not* have a culture that is different from women's and therefore must be stopped by a rule or a law. Both women were vilified by their colleagues for their crusades and ultimately left their jobs, so the result was not satisfactory to them personally; and even though Robinson (unlike Tunis) won her decision, it is unlikely that the Jacksonville Shipyards became friendlier to women as a result of the encounter.

People who embark on such crusades become the instruments of vengeance and punishment, with the perhaps unstated desire to make the world a better place. Vengeance and punishment may seem satisfactory and may sometimes be justified, but they don't change the world. If the idea is to lessen hostility in the workplace, an incremental approach in which women go into new fields, show that they are talented and competent, gain respect for their values and their differences by an assertive but friendly drawing of the line, and set the stage for the employment of many more women is what will bring lasting change.

CHAPTER TWELVE

What's Wrong with Sexual Harassment Law?

Workplace harassment, including sexual harassment, is a relatively young area of concern. But what should be done about it? At what point of intensity does it become clear that there should be legal recourse against such behavior? It is certainly not acceptable for one person to extort sexual services from another through threats of economic reprisal. That doesn't mean, however, that the "casting couch" model of employment policy, in which special privileges are offered to employees willing to add such extracurricular activities to their job description, has necessarily been made liable to civil suit: favoritism is not against the law. Many feminists today agree that prostitution should be decriminalized—so if one should be able to exchange sex for economic benefit on the street, why make it illegal to do the same thing in the workplace? Present sexual harassment law tries to avoid this particular dilemma with the concept of "welcomeness." It seems paradoxical that a sex-for-job-benefit solicitation in the workplace may be legally free and clear if accepted, but the same overture when the offerer has read the signals wrong can be grounds for a lawsuit. So a man can't really know if he is putting his company in jeopardy until the woman reacts.

These and other dilemmas raise the question: What *is* the place of the sexual harassment law? A mounting tide of criticism from a legal perspective is now becoming apparent to the general public. One area of controversy is the identification of sexual harassment as discrimination. Court watchers, for instance, do not consider that the opinion in the Supreme Court same-sex harassment case *Oncale v. Sundowner Oil* necessarily means Oncale will win his suit when he brings it. From the very beginning, the fact that sexual harassment is part of discrimination law has meant that the accused harasser must be shown to be discriminating on the basis of sex. An equal opportunity harasser is not liable, case after case has decided. A supervisor who swears at men and women alike, who demeans both men and women in public, and who inflicts his vile temper on both genders won't be found guilty of sexual harassment. Courts have explicitly said that if there was ever a bisexual quid pro quo harasser who required both men and women to accede to his sexual demands, he could not be convicted under Title VII. *Oncale v. Sundowner* finally exposed this Procrustean bed of discrimination law to serious question. Even the *Washington Post* "urged Congress to uncouple sexual harassment from sex discrimination" after the *Oncale* case came down.[1]

This was not the first time that the coupling of sexual harassment and discrimination law had been questioned. As early as 1990, the *Yale Law and Policy Review* published an article by Ellen Frankel Paul, a professor of political science and the deputy director of the Social Philosophy and Policy Center at Bowling Green State University. Paul held that the strange case of the bisexual harasser was only one of several reasons that sex discrimination is a "defective paradigm" for sexual harassment.[2] It is also not consonant with the motivation of Congress in passing the anti-discrimination law: "They were fashioning a *civil rights* law . . . not a law proscribing just any kind of oppressive act that one person might commit against another."[3] Sexual harassment was not an injury that occurred simply because an individual was a member of a group and therefore lacked "an essential attribute of discrimination: that is that *any* member of the scorned group will trigger the response of the person who practices discrimination."[4]

Discrimination also means treating members of a despised group worse than others. But in homosexual harassment, the perpetrator picks a member of his own group; that is clearly a "preference phenomenon." But isn't "the archetypical case of male to female harassment" also a matter of preference?[5] Further, according to Paul, making the employer liable, as discrimination law does, flies in the face of common-law rules that hold employers liable for an employee's acts only if they are directly authorized or in some way further the employer's business. But the employer in the sexual harassment case is also a victim of the harasser's act: in quid pro quo, "the manager . . . attempts to bribe the woman with the employer's assets."[6] Finally, Paul points to the difficulty of line drawing between welcome and unwelcome acts, and in crude workplaces, between harassment and behavior that is acceptable to men but not to women, even when not targeted at them.

For all these reasons, she suggests that federal law be replaced by a state tort of sexual harassment, created by either the courts or the legislature. Such a remedy, she holds, would replace the problems of the present discrimination approach with "an individualist approach that stresses the victim's right to privacy, to freedom from physical assault or the threat of it, and to freedom from the infliction of severe emotional distress."[7] It would also be more just in that it would punish the actual perpetrator, rather than the company for which he worked.

More recently, in a long article in the *New Yorker* deploring the trend towards applying sexual harassment legal concepts to consensual relationships, Jeffrey Toobin hailed law professor Vicki Schultz for doing what he called "some of the most thoughtful and original work in the field of sexual harassment."[8] Schultz's take is in some ways the polar opposite of Ellen Paul's—she wants a legal approach to sexual harassment that is *more* strictly based on discrimination. We should be banning not sex but sexism in the workplace.[9] "[T]he popular view of harassment is both too narrow and too broad," writes Schultz. "Too narrow, because the focus on rooting out unwanted sexual activity has allowed us to feel good about protecting women from sexual abuse while leading us to overlook equally pernicious forms of gender-based mistreatment. Too broad, because the emphasis on sexual conduct has encouraged some companies to ban all forms of sexual interaction, even when these do not threaten women's equality on the job."[10]

Both Paul and Schultz are trying to deal with the seeming contradiction between the first quid pro quo cases, with their emphasis on job selection according to the applicant's or employee's sexual willingness, and many of the hostile environment cases that have an almost Luddite flavor of wanting to destroy a perceived threat to existing workplace conditions (in this case, the introduction of women) by any means possible. Paul thinks the problem is that judges saw that quid pro quo was reprehensible behavior that should be against the law and were willing to seize the opportunity to outlaw it as discrimination when presented with such an argument—even though it didn't fit. Schultz thinks the application of discrimination fits better than Paul sees it as doing but that the courts erred "by locating the problem in the sexual character of the advances rather than in the workplace dynamics of which they were a part,"[11] and that this has led them to discount sexist treatment that is not overtly sexual. Whatever their reason, the courts chased off after sexual behavior as the evil from which women need protection, and companies are following suit.

It is not only the identification with discrimination law that troubles some legal experts. Two Supreme Court justices became concerned that a separate standard was evolving, treating sexual harassment differently from other forms of harassment within discrimination law. The *Burlington* and *Boca Raton* Supreme Court sexual harassment decisions were not unanimous; both decisions were seven to two, with Justices Thomas and Scalia dissenting. The dissents objected that the Court had created a standard of liability for hostile environment sexual harassment that was different from the standard for racial harassment, and claimed that both forms of harassment should be dealt with identically. They advocated, in the words of an article in *The Economist*, a "negligence standard" for liability, by which "the burden of proof should lie with the plaintiff, who should be required to show that the employer acted unreasonably in not trying to stamp out or remedy harassment."[12] Instead, as discussed in chapter 2, the Court for the first time held companies vicariously liable for the hostile environment created by a supervisor, unless they could meet the burden of raising an affirmative defense.

Some observers also cite differences in opinions between one jurisdiction and another as warning signs of a coming showdown between sexual harassment and the freedom of speech guaranteed by the First Amendment. Harassment law seems to say that certain words and images in a workplace can create a hostile environment for which the courts can punish an employer. The First Amendment says that "Congress shall make no law" abridging freedom of speech, and a long line of legal decisions holds that this means in particular that rules dealing with speech must be "viewpoint neutral." According to established First Amendment law, as was discussed in chapter 8, government may not prefer one viewpoint (for example, that women belong in fire fighting) to its opposite. But that is what all harassment law does. The courts have rarely addressed this contradiction in harassment cases, perhaps because it is not the government that says what may not be said or shown in the workplace; rather, it is the employer who is seeking to limit liability. As Eugene Volokh puts it:

> Harassment law suppresses speech not by directly penalizing employees who say offensive things, but by threatening employers with liability if they do not punish such employees themselves. This indirect speech restriction is every bit as potent as a direct one. Companies, fearing liability, implement policies prohibiting a particular kind of speech and providing for disciplinary measures. Employees, fearing discipline, avoid expressing the proscribed speech. The employees are as deterred by this as they would be by the threat of a lawsuit aimed directly at them. And this suppression of harassing speech by employers was precisely the aim of the EEOC and of many of the courts that developed harassment law.[13]

Law professor Kingsley Browne goes further in his monumental article "Title VII as Censorship: Hostile-Environment Harassment and the First Amendment," where he states:

> Had courts squarely faced the first amendment issue in hostile-environment cases, they could not have employed the EEOC guidelines as they did without creating a new exception to the first amendment. The standard for hostile-environment harassment cases is strongly viewpoint-based and can be upheld only by a showing of government interest of the highest order. No currently recognized first amendment doctrine can explain the analysis in these cases.[14]

It is extremely possible that the Supreme Court sometime in the future will apply an explicitly free-speech analysis to lower-court decisions, or even to the EEOC guidelines. Can the law as we know it withstand such an analysis? Some observers hold that what will then be needed is a more rigorous definition of harassment, which will leave much of the existing law in place. Eugene Volokh, for instance, points out that First Amendment precedents do not forbid use of the law against physical conduct, discrimination in job assignments, quid pro quo harassment, and unprotected speech such as slander and threats. In a web site devoted to free speech and harassment, he has posted a discussion of what he considers "Permissible Harassment Restrictions," in which he suggests that unwelcome "one-to-one" speech will continue to be permissibly restricted: he likens it to unwanted mail and phone calls, both of which may be blocked by legal authorities. However, "one-to-many" speech (posters, public conversations with willing listeners) should be protected, in his view.[15]

Volokh makes clear that, in his opinion, hostile environment one-to-one speech must meet three criteria to be held constitutionally punishable: the speaker must know the speech is unwanted; it must be said to a particular employee who is in a protected category, and because of that category (he lists "race, sex, religion, or national origin"); and it must create "a hostile work environment."

Another proposal has been made by Feminists for Free Expression (FFE), a free-speech organization that has filed several amicus (friend-of-the-court) briefs in this area. FFE submitted the following definition to the Supreme Court in its amicus in the *Harris* case:

> Title VII liability should be imposed only for a pattern or practice of speech or conduct targeting a specific employee or employees, which a reasonable person would experience as harassment, and which has demonstrably hindered the employee in his or her job performance.[16]

This definition would not collide with Volokh's one-to-one proviso, but it also attempts to make it clear that simple offensiveness doesn't create a hostile work environment—an issue that Volokh seemingly leaves up to more subjective perception. According to FFE, the speech or conduct must be targeted and repeated (a pattern or practice), must meet a reasonable-person test, and must have had an effect on job performance.

Other free-speech advocates go even further. Kingsley Browne summarizes his disagreement with Volokh as follows: "My position is that even censoring one-to-one speech cannot be justified under the First Amendment, at least not under the vague harassment standard that currently exists. . . . [A] one-on-one rule would not substantially improve the situation, because the fundamental problem with harassment regulation is not that employers sometimes lose lawsuits but rather that employers are under strong incentives to censor their employees, and this would be only slightly reduced by a limitation to one-on-one speech."[17]

One employment lawyer, Richard Dooling, suggests that there are grave questions to be raised about Title VII itself. But he concludes, "If it is too early in the season of public opinion to call for a repeal of Title VII, the time is ripe at least for pruning its most unworkable and unenforceable sections." Where Volokh says that protecting one-to-many speech and still banning one-to-one speech in the workplace would leave workers with protection against a number of harassing behaviors, Dooling goes further and points out that such behaviors are forbidden by other civil and criminal laws, and workers would be protected "if Congress passed an amendment to Title VII which simply confined its interpretation to its original plain language, namely, prohibiting discrimination in the terms and conditions of employment." Tort law would still be available to bring the individual harasser to justice.[18]

Even a woman who identifies herself as a "liberal feminist" wrote at the end of 1998 that she now regrets she ever joined with those "so eager to 'educate the public' about sexual harassment . . . that they were willing to overlook the frightening precedent being set" by the Clarence Thomas hearings, in which "a man's political career was nearly ended and his private life pawed through while an entire nation watched." Judith Shulevitz concluded an article comparing contemporary sexual harassment law to another feminist mistake, the turn-of-the-century social purity movement, with the following question:

> So should we do away with all forms of sexual harassment law? Or just parts of it—the hostile work environment clause, say, or the gender-biased evidentiary rules? It will take years to find the best place to draw the line, and we'll never get it perfectly right. The important thing is to realize that it's way past time to move it.[19]

Even stranger than the seeming conflict between speech and protecting workplace equality is the real conflict between two areas of law that govern workplace relations, employment law and labor law. When a woman named Barbara Lawler had to walk past a line of jeering men who shouted lewd language at her on her way to work at the Georgia Kraft company, the courts told the company it was forbidden to discipline the men. Why? Because she was an executive, and the men were on strike.[20] Walter Olson has called attention to this little-known section of the National Labor Relations Act:

> The expressing of any view, argument, or opinion, or the dissemination thereof, whether in written, printed, graphic or visual form, shall not constitute or be evidence of an unfair labor practice under any of the provisions of this subchapter, if such expression contains no threat of reprisal or force or promise of benefit.

"Note its careful language," writes Olson in his discussion of sexual harassment: "protected speech not only will not constitute an unfair labor practice in itself, but cannot be introduced as evidence of such. Perhaps it's time to introduce a similar principle into harassment and discrimination law."[21]

Is it conceivable that the law might actually be amended in one of these suggested ways? It would take a mounting tide of public outrage, one would think, to get Congress to act in such a fashion, especially when the beneficial intent of the law is so widely assumed. Since widely quoted polls show that a majority of voters indicate they wouldn't vote to ratify the text of the Bill of Rights today, it seems like a long shot. In such a case, private policy and private action would take a form very different from their present, almost slavish reliance on the law as it now exists.

CHAPTER THIRTEEN

The Larger Picture

When I started to write this book, I saw the issue of sexual harassment in the workplace as just another area, like protective labor legislation, where legal measures had been instituted without a full understanding of their consequences, and where not enough feminist attention was being paid to the nonlegal alternative of what women could do to help themselves and each other. I assumed that the negative impact of the law on freedom of speech was essentially a bad mistake but the accidental creation of well-meaning people that would be corrected when enough scholarly analysis had accumulated to prod the Supreme Court to pay attention. But the impact of another speech controversy challenges that assumption. This controversy is over a deliberate attempt to eradicate certain kinds of speech, and it raises a question of intent about sexual harassment law as well. Also, this other speech controversy is gaining visibility that may very well lead to public outrage over all attempts to regulate speech.

Hundreds of our colleges and universities have adopted speech codes that, in the name of protecting the weak, forbid offending members of certain protected classes—mainly women, blacks, and gays, although Native Americans, Hispanics, Asians, and Jews are often added to the list. Conspicuously not forbidden is the "harassment" of white males, heterosexuals, and members of Christian religious groups, including Catholics, all of whom are taken to need no protection because they represent the dominant culture. These codes, which some free-speech feminists had thought were fading away after at least one well-publicized court case,[1] are still being adopted by prestigious institutions, even with growing enthusiasm. Harvard Law School, for instance, adopted "Sexual Harassment Guidelines" in

October 1995 that ban speech "creating an intimidating, demeaning, degrading, hostile, or otherwise seriously offensive . . . educational environment."[2]

This phenomenon is generally known as "political correctness on campus"—speech rules that teachers and students are expected to follow. What is not so generally known is that these rules have teeth. A majority of the thirty-six hundred colleges and universities in the United States punish students and teachers alike for speech offenses through secret disciplinary hearings, which do not grant the due process for the accused that is required in legal proceedings.[3] The results can end careers and change futures.

A book published in the fall of 1998 called *The Shadow University* examines in exhaustive detail the implementation and the implications of these codes, as well as the strong support (at least, lip-service support) they have received from both professors and administrators. Written by history professor Alan Charles Kors and criminal defense attorney Harvey A. Silverglate, the book is unequivocally critical of what the authors label "current thought reform." The authors identify four core beliefs of those bent on reform: (1) An individual's moral status is determined not by behavior or character but by the group into which he or she has been born. ("An individual is not an autonomous moral being, but a member of a racial and historical group that possesses moral debt or credit.") (2) "There is only one appropriate set of views about race, gender, sexual preference, and culture," and disagreement with the official set of views is "not an intellectual disagreement, but an act of oppression or denial" that deserves punishment. (3) "All behavior and thought are 'political,' including opposition to politicized 'awareness' workshops." (4) The only possible reason that faculty or students would object to being required to attend such workshops is that they desire "the continued oppression of women and of racial or sexual minorities."[4]

These beliefs, in practice, have led to separation of groups on campus. There are separate cultural centers for various minorities; there is censorship through speech codes and indoctrination through required workshops, as well as in the classroom. And administrations have enforced the rulings of secret hearings by denying tenure, revoking tenure, suspending teachers without pay and students from classes necessary for graduation, stripping suspects of their housing and campus jobs, and expulsion.

Increasingly, people are being viewed primarily in terms of their group membership. Such a view has an unsavory history in the twentieth century. Paul Johnson, who before he wrote *Modern Times* was a prominent British socialist and editor of the *New Statesman* (1965–1970), wrote an eloquent "Farewell to the Labour Party" that the *New Statesman* published in 1977. In it, he deplored what he saw as the growing "left-wing fascism" in the party he had once loved because he had seen it as championing the individual. Now, he claimed, the party wanted to deal with individuals only through the groups to which they belonged—their unions. At the time he was writing, the Labour Party was claiming that there was no room in society for the self-employed who worked without trade-union membership—membership in the approved group—and one of its leaders even said in public that "it must be made impossible for self-employment to exist." This meant, Johnson pointed out, that creativity would be destroyed: "[T]he self-employed include scientists and inventors, writers and musicians, painters and sculptors, men and women who make films and TV programmes, design ballets and write songs—the essential creators who keep civilization going." Turning its back on all these people, the Labour Party, wrote Johnson, "has taken over the collectivist philosophy of the union bosses. . . . Those who do not fit in, who, for one reason or another, do not have a union card, or the right union card, become non-persons and, if awkward, enemies of the state." He went on to say that as the Labour Party "drifted into collectivism, I have come to appreciate, perhaps for the first time in my life, the overwhelming strength of my own attachment to the individual spirit."[5]

Something like the atmosphere that Johnson deplored in the Great Britain of the late 1970s seems now to be permeating many U.S. campuses. Policies to ensure "equality" are applied and enforced unequally, depending on the group membership of the individuals involved. The rallying cry for these policies seems unexceptional—it is to eradicate sexism, racism, and homophobia. Who could be *for* such things? But to accomplish the goal, words that hurt must be punished, derogatory speech against the purportedly powerful must be encouraged, and the person caught in the middle, who doesn't quite fit into any group category, must be crammed into the most likely pigeon-hole. Thus, a student resident adviser (RA) who thinks his religion keeps him from wearing a pink triangle to show solidarity with homosexuals during orientation week loses his RA job. Roman Catholic Hispanics who object to anti-Catholic signs ("Keep Your Rosaries Off Our Ovaries") at the women's center are considered traitors to their group. Students who are the products of mixed marriages and therefore won't identify with anti-white slogans have no recourse.

In a chapter called "Marcuse's Revenge," Kors and Silverglate trace the genesis of such phenomena to Herbert Marcuse's essay on "Repressive Tolerance,"[6] which they characterize as stressing the importance of "intolerance against movements from the Right and toleration of movements from the Left."[7] They summarize his view as holding that "freedom is a zero-sum game,"[8] in which liberty for one side can be gained only by taking liberty away from the other. Freedom of speech does not, therefore, benefit the powerless. Those in power (defined as the Right—white male Christian heterosexuals) have silenced those out of power. To transform society in a "progressive" direction, the balance must be shifted; the powerful must now be silenced to allow dissenting voices to be heard. These ideas since have become commonplace on literally hundreds of campuses and are implemented in the speech codes and in "separatist racial residences and support programs."[9] (They also informed the Critical Race Theory movement that began at Harvard in 1981, and they have been echoed in the work of Catharine MacKinnon.) Administrators pay lip service to all this because the so-called powerless are the very students apt to cause trouble if crossed, because they are organized into militant groups. Administrators see no comparable danger of an uprising in favor of individualism.

Furthermore, "[c]ampus life begins with the sorting out of students into oppressors and victims." Those who have supposedly been brainwashed by the culture are to be re-brainwashed. *The Shadow University* claims that "[m]ost colleges and universities with significant populations of racial minorities hold separate orientations for them, introducing them, before they have even begun their academic lives, to their official identity, their official advocates, and their official spokesmen and spokeswomen."[10]

Marcuse has triumphed on campus, according to Kors and Silverglate, but these ideas "have not noticeably taken root in the 'real
world' outside the academy,"[11] where they see the opposing idea that
everyone's speech should be protected as gaining more and more acceptance.

Are Kors and Silverglate right about this acceptance? The picture is
a little more complicated. Yes, it is generally accepted that most speech
should be protected, but it is also generally accepted that "equality,"
as in the Fourteenth Amendment phrase "equal protection of the
laws," means that people should be protected from discrimination.
These two principles sometimes seem to be in conflict.

Legal scholars have considered First Amendment rights to be
among those that are in a "preferred position" in contemporary times,
compared to the rights of property and freedom of contract so
strongly defended by late nineteenth- and early twentieth-century
courts. When Franklin Delano Roosevelt's threat to pack the Court
with New Deal supporters led to "the switch in time that saved nine"
and a strong New Deal supporter, Hugo Black, was appointed to the
Court in 1937, an era ended.

Professor Henry Abraham of the University of Virginia described
the ensuing change in a 1982 book: "What the post-1937 judiciary
did was to *assume* as constitutional all legislation in the proprietarian
sector *unless* proved to the contrary by a complainant, but to view
with a suspicious eye legislative and executive experimentation with
other basic human freedoms generally regarded as the 'cultural freedoms' guaranteed by the Bill of Rights—among them speech, press,
worship, assembly, petition, due process of law in criminal justice, a
fair trial."[12] Elsewhere, he calls this "a double standard of judicial attitude, whereby governmental economic experimentation is accorded
all but *carte blanche* by the courts, but alleged violations of individual
civil rights are given meticulous judicial attention."[13]

Notice the term *civil rights*. Abraham uses the terms *civil rights* and
civil liberties in his book but doesn't clearly distinguish between them.
One distinction I would make is that *civil liberties* refers to those areas
of individual "cultural freedoms" that have nothing to do with the existence of the state, liberties that are to be preserved by insulating
them as much as possible from legal interference and regulation.

These today certainly include speech, press, religion, and assembly. The term *civil rights*, in contrast, traditionally has referred to state-created rights that limit the state's power in order to ensure that it treats all its inhabitants fairly in their access to the legal and political machinery. The right to vote, for instance, requires the existence of a state, as do certain guarantees in the Bill of Rights, such as the right to a fair trial or a grand jury indictment for a capital crime. The original Civil Rights Act in 1866 gave this sort of civil rights (including the right to own title to property, make a will, testify in court, and bring legal suit) to freed slaves because they had been denied those rights in slavery. States could no longer discriminate against such persons in certain enumerated ways. (This act did not deal with voting.)

By the time of the Civil Rights Act of 1964, a change in definition had occurred. It was no longer only the state that was required to treat its inhabitants fairly; for the first time, the actions of private institutions and companies were also required to be fair. The two most controversial sections of the act dealt with forbidding employers and labor unions in companies that employed more than a certain number of people (originally one hundred; today, fifteen) to discriminate against workers on certain grounds (race, color, religion, sex, or national origin) and with forbidding privately owned businesses—"public accommodations" such as restaurants, hotels, stores, and theaters that offered their services to the general public—to discriminate among potential customers.

The public accommodations section of the act did not spark lasting controversy. But discrimination in employment proved harder to measure and define. What was originally intended in the Civil Rights Act of 1964 to be a mandate for fairness towards the individual has become, through a succession of Supreme Court decisions, a way of dealing with people according to group identity. Those in some groups are "protected" by the law; those in others are not.

With the change in the concept of civil rights to focus on abridging the permissible actions of the employer rather than the actions of the state, "freedom from discrimination" indeed became a zero-sum game. The freedom of action that some workers gain in this way must of necessity remove some freedom of action from the employer. When we called earlier workplace laws "economic regulation," we knew very well that we were restricting the possible actions of the employer, and we said that economic rights were not absolute. However, freedom from discrimination is no longer looked at as an issue of economic regulation. It is now considered a "cultural freedom," like freedom of the press or freedom of religion. But civil liberties such as freedom of the press or of religion are not, in their essence, zero-sum games: for me to speak, no one is required by law to keep silent or even to listen. Civil liberties are not creatures of the law, as "freedom from discrimination" is.

In the process of shifting part of the meaning of civil rights, we avoid admitting the existence of this zero-sum game. We want to forget that the law limits the employer's economic choices to the extent that it expands those of the protected employee. This forgetfulness is facilitated by the fact that today's culture generally accepts the regulation of property as at worst an unimportant inconvenience but looks much more severely on the regulation of cultural freedoms. So we think of freedom from discrimination as a cultural freedom that benefits everyone, because we accept the regulation of the workplace on which it depends as only an inconvenience to the employer—the curtailing of a secondary right.

We should question holding that this right is secondary. John Locke, the seventeenth-century philosopher whose *Two Treatises of Government* so strongly influenced the thinking of the authors of the Declaration of Independence and the U.S. Constitution, held that our basic rights were "life, liberty, and property," in the phrase later used in both the Fifth and the Fourteenth Amendments. As Henry Abraham put it in his discussion of preferred freedoms, "Any quest for an obvious, clear line between 'property rights' and 'basic human rights' is, of course, doomed to fail, because by definition and implication *both are guaranteed freedoms* under our national and state constitutions."[14] In fact, property rights and what we today call cultural freedoms are inextricably intertwined. We are physical beings, and no freedom can exist without physical components—that is, the freedom to own and control property. Newspapers and religious institutions must have property rights in order to exercise their First Amendment rights—they need presses and ink and buildings and vestments and money for salaries. The First Amendment may in fact *be* the most important element of the Bill of Rights, because it can be looked at as the amendment that crosses over from protecting ideas to protecting property, showing the necessity of both protections: freedom of speech is the right to think and express yourself, but freedom of the press is the right to try to *merchandise* that thinking, and liberty is lost to the extent that either area is subject to abridging laws.

However, this is not today's thinking. Activists and politicians alike express equivalent admiration for free speech (which Marcuse wrongly considers to be a zero-sum game) and for fairness (which, as currently defined, *is* a zero-sum game). Since "fairness" depends on economic regulation to enforce it, free speech loses in this equation. If one were, like Marcuse, convinced that representatives of the dominant culture must be censored in order to transform society to benefit the oppressed, a good way to jump-start this idea out of academia and into what Kors and Silverglate call the "real world" would be to connect it in some way with existing workplace regulation, perhaps by making it part of that regulation itself.

Of course, there has not been a conspiracy to destroy free speech; nothing so simple. But when we accept the end-state of fair behavior, which has to be achieved by passing laws to make us be fair to one another, as the equivalent of free speech, which the Constitution says Congress "shall make no law" to abridge, we have set the stage for mandating away some of our freedom. A kind of Gresham's law of political principle is involved here: If it somehow enhances freedom to use the law to obtain fairness in employment, why not find a way to use it to ensure "fair speech"? And that is what Catharine MacKinnon did in the mid-1970s. In fact, the idea of regulating speech that targeted protected classes found its first acceptance in employment law.

So if one had thought in 1975 (to pick an example) that the speech of members of the general culture must be censored in order to better the lot of women by destroying male dominance, one could not improve on what Catharine MacKinnon has done with her work on sexual harassment law. The times were ripe. The hostile environment concept has now redefined much of men's speech towards women that has to do with sex or gender as discrimination when it takes place in the workplace, so that businesses can be punished for allowing it to exist. The importance of "protecting the weak" from discrimination has taken us from the marketplace to the marketplace of ideas in one easy, almost unnoticed jump. And, voilà! Title VII is used by the courts as a largely unrecognized federal censorship law—and the employers themselves have been recruited as the censors.

While this was happening in the "real world," it was easy to take the concept back to the campus. The employment law that has sprung up to enforce fairness already had the requisite approach, which now works so well on campus, of dividing people into groups. The Supreme Court has decided, even though the language and legislative history of Title VII explicitly ban preferences and quotas, that anti-discrimination laws intended to protect certain classes of people more than others. This view has been extended to other laws, such as the 1990 Americans with Disabilities Act (ADA). It was applied to campuses by invoking another part of the 1964 Civil Rights Act, the 1972 Education Amendments to Title IX—which some have also used to explain the need for campus speech codes.

Protected classes on campus include, not coincidentally, most of the same classes that employment law protects: racial and ethnic minorities, those with disabilities, and, of course, women. (There are some differences. Victims of homophobia are not yet protected in federal law but are under campus speech codes. One group that is conspicuously unprotected on campus is members of Christian denominations, even though Title VII forbids religious discrimination.) In general, when campus codes began in the 1980s, we already accepted that the courts had defined some classes of people as too vulnerable to protect themselves and therefore needing legal (or on campus, official) protection.

The Shadow University does not make such a connection, I hasten to add; it is my own. Kors and Silverglate seem more concerned with the idea that workplace concepts shouldn't be legally applied to interfere with academic freedom than with seeing much continuity between the two venues. In fact, they say that "[o]ther than this blurring of speech and conduct, however, the EEOC guidelines on sexual harassment represented a fairly routine exercise of long-standing employer/employee legal concepts."[15] This, of course, bears out my point that the "long-standing legal concepts" have already blurred distinctions necessary to freedom (between state action and private action, for instance) that once were clear. Civil liberties are not rightly understood as grants from government. They are legal principles that have been withdrawn from "political controversy, to place then beyond the reach of majorities and officials," as Justice Robert Jackson once said;[16] areas of activity in which the government acknowledges our rights and promises to leave us alone.

How can we save ourselves from the implications of this situation and of this law? Kingsley Browne, in an article written for a forthcoming book, thinks that those who hold that the impact of hostile environment law on speech is "routine" make the mistake of watching only the outcomes of litigated cases. But these "are merely the tip of the iceberg," he cautions. The real action is occurring on the shop floor and in the office suites, in what employers are doing to avoid the impact of the law. These avoidance techniques raise grave First Amendment concerns of viewpoint discrimination as well as vagueness. Employers now have to curtail people's speech about race, religion, gender, and ethnicity, because if they don't, they are vulnerable on two counts: "employer liability and the totality-of-the-circumstances standard," by which a number of remarks from different people can add up to liability. Incremental changes in the law won't do, cautions Browne, nor will simply adding individual actor liability to the existing law. Requiring that speech be targeted at a specific person or group of persons to be actionable would do something, but not enough.

The only hope he seems to see is something very close to the tort solution recommended by Ellen Frankel Paul. Browne puts it this way: "Remaining First Amendment difficulties notwithstanding, an individual-liability system would eliminate some of the chief evils of the current regime. It would reduce the pressure on employers to impose draconian speech codes." It is time to recognize, he concludes, that our present law has installed "a regime that cannot be countenanced under the First Amendment."[17]

If we decide that this existing regime must be scrapped, what of the criticism that sexual harassment law, imperfect as it may be, has helped women and at least called attention to problems that used to be swept under the rug? This is in part true; but it doesn't follow that any such benefits will be lost if we replace federal law with state torts. Egregious behavior will still be liable to egregious damages—even, when the behavior has been employer sanctioned, from employers.

Popular culture indicates that along with any beneficial attention it may have brought to real problems, the whole concept of hostile environment decisions has polarized and damaged male–female relations. Very real and open hostility between men and women is expressed in current books and magazines, to say nothing of movies and plays. One filmmaker, Neil La Bute, whose movies *In the Company of Men* and *Your Friends and Neighbors* explore casual cruelty towards women by middle-class men, has explicitly admitted that focus on harassment has exacerbated this hostility. In an interview, he posited that growing insecurity and "a shift in romantic expectations" away from permanent marriage in the direction (as he put it) of expressing contempt "has been brought to the fore in recent years by debates about politically correct language and sexual harassment."[18] So even the way in which the law has called attention to these problems may have turned out to be counterproductive.

It's too early to tell if current revelations about campus speech codes will reinforce the criticisms being made about sexual harassment law and make legislative or judicial change possible. What is becoming clear is that the very mechanisms that have been instituted, both in academia and in our courts of law, with such high hopes to revolutionize society and create better relationships, are instead sowing anger and mistrust. Isn't it time for a change?

CHAPTER FOURTEEN

Training for Success

The mechanism that businesses have installed to create better relationships is the company training program. But most of these, having been instituted to comply with the law, focus on the law. Some programs are called "diversity training," some are called "sensitivity training"; one I went to was called a "Harassment and Abuse Seminar." One executive who has not installed such a program had this reaction: "Everything I have heard and read about various kinds of diversity training makes them sound like a Reign of Terror imposed upon us by wrong-headed laws. Do we really have to subject employees to video tapes and role playing when they ought to be producing something useful?" Management training courses, however, are part of the spirit of the age. Four thousand people showed up at a Training '99 conference in Chicago, where they heard, among other treats, a speech by British comic actor John Cleese, who is a founder of a London-based maker of training materials that have been used by more than "27,000 organizations, including I.B.M., AT&T, and General Electric."[1] Cleese's best-selling videos include such topics as sales techniques, the dynamics of meetings, conducting job interviews, and bad service. The American Management Association also offers courses on a number of business techniques, including assertiveness training for leaders. Companies such as U.S. Steel expose workers to courses such as "values training."

So sexual harassment training didn't appear in a vacuum. With such a penchant for courses and presentations, it is small wonder that when American business was faced with a requirement that office behavior should change, it believed a course would fit the bill. However, diversity or sensitivity courses are certainly different from other management courses. For one thing, they are often obligatory for everyone, unlike courses for managers who are interested in a particular area of business. For another, they can emphasize the negative. "Trainers," said one woman trainer to me, "often blast males."

Certainly, I have found no evidence that the term *diversity* in such courses is defined as it has been on campus—as an official disavowal of racism with respect to protected groups that has little regard for diversity of thought or for people who don't fit easily into the protected categories. One trainer told me that diversity training began as an effort to explain to employees who might be going overseas how different cultures operate; then it was expanded to deal with gender. However, now, she explained, "diversity is about discrimination. The emphasis is not on 'How do we work together?' The issue is usually couched as 'Something wrong is going on and we have to fix it.' I teach gender communication," she continued. "I do believe it has to be neutral. But most people who train in this area have an agenda." What sort of agenda? "The mind-set is: 'We are not prejudiced. If we are, it's bad.' Whereas, you have to start with the assumption that we are all prejudiced. When a client says to me that he's concerned about male bashing, I say, 'I am a woman, and that's a possibility. So if I step over the line, you let me know.'"[2]

This trainer is not a lawyer, but most trainers are, because what most companies want is legal training. One member of a New York law firm that has run training programs in hundreds of companies for about a decade told me that the difference between his course and sensitivity training is that his course is informative; it doesn't try to change people's basic attitudes and behavior. It tells them what is against the law, and therefore what they shouldn't do in the office. He doesn't say to a client, "You need to question your assumption that women are objects."

The new director of diversity for a large national company told me that for about seven or eight years, the company had included sexual harassment in a two-day course on principles of respecting others; but as of early 1999, it had decided to give managers a separate two-hour "Leadership and Sexual Harassment Prevention" course, in order to implement a new zero-tolerance policy. This policy meant that nowhere in the offices should "*Playboy* or *Hustler*" be found, that there should be no sex-based jokes, and that managers were warned about "verbal abuse, sarcastic over-the-edge remarks, and to be careful about kidding." To implement this policy, the trainers use case studies to help people understand the responses of others.

Sometimes companies provide their employees with nonlegal programs on related subjects, such as an offering from the Minneapolis-based Theatre at Work that reportedly "dissects anger-provoking issues like sexual harassment and racism through short plays performed through groups of employees. A facilitator then leads a discussion of the play's relevance to the workplace."[3]

There is no consensus on what sort of training is effective. One 1997 journal article examined results of multiple training methods—in this case, a combination of case analyses, commercial videotape episodes, and a questionnaire—and concluded: "Subjects were found to be more sensitive to incidents of possible sexual harassment when videotape episodes were combined with case analysis." However, the authors also found that "trainees may misidentify who is the potential victim in a particular case . . . or may not attend to all the facts," and somewhat to the dismay of the authors, some subjects recommended that both parties in the episode (target as well as harasser) be fired.[4] Clearly, this was not a formula for a dynamite new training program!

And of course, some of the material that the more interactive training programs may dig out of employees could ultimately be used against the company. In one 1992 case, a company-run program to educate managers against the use of stereotypes asked managers to volunteer stereotypes they had heard. But when a sexual harassment suit was later brought against the company, the plaintiff was able to quote several of the stereotypes of women that managers came up with for the course as evidence that helped prove her case of intentional discrimination.[5]

Sensitivity training is intended to "sensitize" people about language and even looks that are perceived as harassing and often may use exercises to make its points. These have sometimes come in for criticism. One woman professor complained, in a *Wall Street Journal* op-ed piece after the June 1998 Supreme Court decisions on sexual harassment liability, about the increased training sessions the decisions would spawn:

But who's harassing whom when I'm forced to attend "sensitivity training" seminars and reveal my personal feeling to co-workers with whom
I don't even exchange recipes? At one Fortune 500 company, a sensitivity consultant instructed employees to conduct the following "group
exercise." "I want all of the men to sit down on the floor in the center
of the room. You are not allowed to speak while sitting down. The
women are to stand around the men in a circle and begin to whistle and
make sexist comments about the appearance and anatomy of the men."
What if I don't *want* to talk about my colleagues' anatomy?[6]

What also if the men don't react as the consultant obviously expected,
with embarrassment and distress, but rather think this is cute and
funny?

Some such sensitivity sessions involve dredging up and expressing
negative feelings, a technique complained about to a *Los Angeles Times*
writer by a white senior at Temple University "who chose Temple because of its diversity":

> He and other students think the school needs to do a better job helping
> diverse students come together. Temple's required classes on racism, he
> says, often boil down to arguments between blacks and whites. . . .
> "They bring out hate inside you that you don't want to feel."[7]

A 1993 journal article complained about "the lack of any attention
to the evaluation of intervention—in particular, the training programs
that have recently become ubiquitous" and said there were three possible aims for such programs. The unanswered question is, "Should
training programs attempt to increase knowledge, change attitudes,
modify behavior, or some combination of the three?"[8] The lack of
outcome evaluation, the authors suggest, is because the very existence
of the programs, no matter how effective or ineffective, is a defense in
a lawsuit.

Some feminists have become concerned that the extent to which
women have sought new protections may be regulating us out of the
marketplace. Robyn Blumner devoted a column to provisions in recent legislation, as well as "the expansive reading of sexual harassment
by both the courts and the EEOC," that are making it more and more
expensive for companies to hire women. She suggests that "there will
come a point when employers decide women employees are just not

worth the potential liability. . . . And we women will have done it to ourselves."[9]

Supporting such a view is the reaction of one web site to the Court's 1998 "expansive" decisions on sexual harassment liability. After the rulings made the issue of having procedures in place key to a defense, the site posted suggestions for companies that included taking "extreme care in both the *selection* and training of the people it employs" (emphasis added)—which could be taken to mean not only that companies would do well to try to screen out men who score high on John Pryor's Likelihood of Sexual Harassment (LSH) scale but also that they might avoid hiring vulnerable women as well. It further recommended, "Require every employee, CEO included, to attend training to both identify and fairly investigate harassment. Refresh that training at appropriate intervals."[10]

Some programs aggressively attempt to modify male behavior. Professor Vicki Schultz of Yale has remarked on a training program for masons near the university "where they are teaching the men what they call the 'five-second rule.'. . . That means that men are not allowed to look at a fellow worker who is a woman for more than five seconds because to do so might be sexual harassment."[11]

But the most usual kind of training focuses on increasing the knowledge that workers have of sexual harassment, which often, but not always, includes providing information for targets on what to do when harassed. The information is available in various forms. Some companies use commercial videotape presentations that may follow shots of a person giving information with scenes dramatizing various encounters that may or may not be harassment. For instance, *Sexual Harassment in Healthcare: Relearning the Rules*[12] has people identified as various health care workers (nurses, orderlies, social workers, doctors) speaking about their personal life, their reactions to language, and propositions in the workplace. This is followed by an authority telling the audience about the two types of sexual harassment that the law "clearly defines," and telling targets in particular to take four steps: Confront, Report, Document, and Seek Support. Scenes include a male orderly getting low ratings from his female nurse supervisor because they used to date but he broke it off and a guy who makes out the work assignments because he is senior on the shift trying to make time with one of the other nurses, both designed to emphasize that any worker in a position of power can make a quid pro quo demand. The authority gives a long list of what may create a hostile environment: words, gestures, jokes, "unwelcome flirting," even job favoritism. The scenes go into more ambiguous areas to indicate the possible offensiveness of neck massage, and one shows two women being whistled at—one likes it; one doesn't. A man who asks another for details about his love life is told these questions are "probably illegal." Harassment, he is told, "doesn't necessarily have to involve homosexuality; it just has to make you uncomfortable."

The video goes over the four steps again, in more detail. Confront, don't gloss over. "Explain how you feel; explain that the behavior is illegal." Report to management. Document while it's fresh in your mind what happened, where, and your response; send a dated return-receipt letter to the harasser. And finally, get support from a relative or friend, because talking helps. The conclusion of the presentation is that "the rules of appropriate conduct have to be relearned."

The tape captures the attention more than a lecture could do and has the virtue of giving some specific advice to targets, but it focuses on illegality while creating a not universally accepted impression of what is and is not illegal. Some of this information doesn't reflect the consensus of the legal community and overexpands the area of actionable behavior. "Favoritism," meaning that a supervisor is romantically involved with a worker and seems to favor her, is not illegal, for instance—it is only when favoritism based on sexual favors is widespread in a company that it has sometimes been construed as implying a hostile environment issue for those left out. And the law about same-sex harassment is by no means as clear as the tape implies.

This tape and others aimed at a more general audience are meant to be shown to all workers in a company. Some on the market are intended for supervisors and focus specifically on how to conduct an interview with a complaining target and the subsequent investigation. These, too, generally combine short dramatized examples with an authority explaining a short list of action points: Take the complaint. Inform and interview the accused. Conduct an investigation. Recommend and carry out a disciplinary action.[13] Often these points are printed out on the screen while the authority elaborates on them.

Another kind of video is exemplified by a tape produced by the Bureau of National Affairs (BNA), called *A Costly Proposition*. This one has no authority figure lecturing; it is all dramatized vignettes occurring in widely differing employment areas—a documentary film crew, a music promotion business, and three office situations in nonspecific areas of business that feature, in turn, a clerical worker, a woman boss who wants to promote a man she used to be involved with, and an incident between two colleagues at a convention.[14] All these scenes are purposely ambiguous and clearly meant to inspire audience discussion in the context of a lecture presentation on behavior, law, and company policy. It is also well produced and well acted. (A young Wesley Snipes plays a part in one of the episodes.)

Printed materials are also available for workplaces that want to do training in house. Educational institutions can subscribe to an *Educator's Guide to Controlling Sexual Harassment*[15] on a continuing basis and keep updated monthly supplements in a loose-leaf notebook. The section in the guide on "Training" provides two module courses into which the institution is told to insert its own sexual harassment policy. One course is designed for workers and the other for managers and supervisors. Each is meant to last about two hours and provides lesson plans, outlines, handouts to be reproduced, materials for projection, and evaluation forms.

The worker course includes a Personal Behavior Checklist (for potential offenders) and a list of Informal Methods to Stop Misconduct (for potential targets) The latter list suggests five methods:

1. Tell the offender his behavior is unwelcome and tell him to stop.
2. Adopt an icy "Miss Manners" approach.
3. Refuse to answer personal questions.
4. Put a copy of your company's sexual harassment policy on his desk.
5. Write him a letter giving a factual account of his behavior, saying how it made you feel; say what you want to happen next, and either deliver it in person or mail it. Keep a copy.

The manager course includes material on liability issues and a List of Dangerous Words—not, as you might think, swear words and endearments but phrases managers should not use to complainants. Examples are "Boys will be boys" and "No big deal."

As presented, the suggested target behavior mixes responses that have not been shown to be effective (avoidance and indirection) with two effective and clear strategies (nonhostile confrontation and a carefully detailed letter). It seems confusing to suggest that noncommunication and clear communication might be equally effective, or equally satisfying.

An example of a training workbook is available from the Labor Institute in New York, called *Sexual Harassment at Work*.[16] Although stating that it is for "working people," it was really developed for women workers, intended as the basis for a course for them that a facilitator at a union or workplace could run. It can be used, however, by mixed groups or even, says a note, "with a little bit of creativity,"[17] by men alone.

The curriculum is divided into twelve activities, each containing a task or set of tasks to be undertaken by small groups of participants. Each group then reports back to the group as a whole, and the facilitator summarizes what is to be learned or explored. Informational fact sheets to be copied and handed out are also included, as well as a summary the facilitator may use to sum up at the end of the session. The tasks include questions for discussion, and each small group elects a reporter to take notes on the discussion and report to the facilitator, who then uses the notes as a basis for general discussion. The activities include two topics not included in many training courses—Racism and Sexual Harassment and Sexual Orientation and Sexual Harassment— as well as three activities dealing with what workers can do to combat sexual harassment. Finally, additional resource material is provided in several appendixes.

The Labor Institute works largely with unions, and a number of union women are credited in the acknowledgments. The fact sheets include a lot of material on unions, and the tasks often involve union situations ("[R]oleplay that you are a shop steward hearing a complaint").[18] Unions are often in the somewhat strange position of having to defend both workers involved in a formal sexual harassment dispute; a union representative presents the complaint to the company for the complaining member, and then, if action is taken against the accused, the union also makes sure the procedure has been fair to him and has followed the requirements of the union contract. To avoid being in this conflicted position, unions want to do everything they can to discourage complaints against co-workers, and the material in *Sexual Harassment at Work* emphasizes informal procedures and even includes a fact sheet on the alternative dispute resolution (ADR) mediation developed by the Teamster's Union, whereby member-to-member disputes can be discussed in a neutral setting. At one time the Labor Institute trained shop stewards and union representatives in how to deal with sexual harassment. But when I visited the office in the fall of 1998, I was told that although the National Council for Research on Women still lists them as giving such courses, they no longer offer training.

This course contains a lot of good material, although necessarily, some information in the fact sheets of all such published courses may be slightly out of date and, without the presence of an informed trainer, won't be corrected. I particularly like the fact that the course provides for both a legal definition of sexual harassment and a "working" definition of harassment that is not legally actionable but may require response.

But in many executive's minds, there's no substitute for the presence of a live authority who can answer questions on the spot. Probably the majority of training courses are formally given by lawyers whom the companies have hired for this purpose, and are performed on company time. Often the company requires everyone to take such training and provides for periodic refresher courses. Two that I attended were designed by a large New York City law firm for a company's managers and workers, respectively.

The company in question was small, with only thirteen managers, of whom two were missing from the session. Three young lawyers made the presentation, which began by pulling information (a definition of sexual harassment) out of the participants rather than by lecturing. The focus was on what a complaint procedure should be, and here very specific information and direction was given: In receiving a complaint, take it seriously; listen carefully and take notes; ask who, what, when, where, how, also how often and even why. (Why do you think this occurred?) Ask the person, What do you want done about your complaint? Also ask if the complainant has talked to anyone, and tell her not to talk to anyone from now on. Remember that you have a "legal duty" to investigate, even if asked not to, and that you can't guarantee confidentiality or any specific action except investigation. But you can and should guarantee that there will be no retaliation for the complaint, either from management or from the accused. If the accused tries to retaliate, he should be fired.

These trainers also insisted that the person taking the complaint get the complainer to sign a written statement verifying the complaint. If she won't, they advised, work on changing the wording of your notes until she signs. If she wants to take it home, fine. If she wants to show it to a lawyer, fine. But make it clear that you can't in good faith take action to remedy the situation if she won't sign.

The most attention in this session was paid to taking the complaint, with a volunteer then role-playing doing so and one of the lawyers acting as the complainer. But specific points were also made about the ensuing investigation: Determine the best person to make the investigation. Always have two people present in interviewing the accused and any witnesses. Find out if there have been any similar incidents or complaints; and talk to everyone who knows about the incident "and then put a lid on it," because stories have a tendency to grow. Finally, do not approach the accused by saying there has been an accusation; ask if he knows the complainant and ask him to tell about his relationship with her. Eventually, you will say, "There are allegations."

The group was small and there was a great deal of discussion and questions. Ninety percent of the time you won't have to fire anybody, the managers were told. If you find yourself in a "he said, she said" situation and can't prove that anything untoward occurred, you warn and watch. The remedy for a proven incident might be as simple as telling the person to stop it. The trainers were asked what to do if men say a woman is "harassing" them by wearing revealing clothes; they responded, "It is perfectly appropriate to ask both men and women to wear appropriate dress." One thing that startled me was that the lawyer playing the target in the role-playing said that she had said *nothing* to respond to the man she was complaining about; she "just looked at him." The trainers said managers can't expect people to tell someone to stop: "Some people just can't do it." The manager who was role-playing protested but was told that the offender might be expected to know he had crossed the line "from her body language."

The next course was given to twenty-one employees, and again it began by getting the attendees to express opinions about sexual harassment. The trainers opened with the idea of the illegality of general abuse of members of protected categories, of which sexual harassment in just one form. They pointed out that there are differences between federal and state law, in categories covered and in definitions. "Employment at will" means that a person can be fired for anything *but* being in a protected category—your boss can fire you because he doesn't like your red hair but not because he doesn't like your race or gender.

One question that came from the floor regarded what to do about a photographer the company had used who had "touchy-feely" Tourette's syndrome—he poked and patted people he was photographing. The trainer led the ensuing discussion towards the recognition that the situation indicated a possible conflict—with no resolution—between the Americans with Disabilities Act, which forbids firing because of a disability, and the sexual harassment guidelines that require employers to take action to end sexual harassment. Then stress was laid on the fact that your computer and your E-mail at work are not yours. The trainer told a cautionary tale of two Smith Barney executives who were fired for sexual harassment because they were E-mailing sexual jokes to each other that both enjoyed, using their office computers.

The elements of a legal definition for sexual harassment were introduced with a statement that there is a difference between what is sexual harassment and what makes you uncomfortable. The elements of a "hostile work environment" listed were that behavior had to be severe, pervasive, unwelcome, and appear so "to a reasonable person." Although the one who behaves has to know behavior is unwelcome in order for the behavior to be labeled harassment, the target still doesn't have to say "stop," the audience was told. The company policy was reviewed, and examples were given of the importance of using the complaint procedure by discussing people who hadn't used theirs or had used it too late. Particular questions were asked about this company's specific issues and problems, and there was a stress on the fact that "welcome behavior is always welcome." The final advice of the trainers before they showed three episodes from the BNA film for discussion was to "listen to the inside voice that says, 'Maybe I shouldn't.' Harassment occurs when you hear it and you do it anyway. And you do it again and again."[19]

These particular courses were sensible, clear, and obviously enjoyed by those who attended, who seemed glad of the opportunity to ask questions and air some of these issues. The advantages of such a course over the less-expensive tapes and printed materials and handouts are obvious. Some of the tapes implied or even stated, for instance, that confidentiality should be promised, when clearly all that is possible in an investigation is discretion. Updates in the law and current events were discussed at the beginning of the live presentation, and any misunderstandings on the part of the participants could be swiftly corrected and explained through the expertise of the team.

My reservation about the courses involved the descriptions of passivity and avoidance in women as something that must be accepted, a point to which I return in the next chapter. I later privately asked the trainer why he had done this, and he replied, "That was a conscious decision. We decided that it would cut against the company's interest to ask for any sort of assertive response, because there is a slim chance that a woman could say in a suit, "[I]n the company's training I was told that I had to say no, and I couldn't, so I didn't feel I could report the incident.'"

Not all such programs are well received. Reports I have heard from other businesspeople have expressed resentment and annoyance at being required to discuss such issues in a session and even to go back for "refresher" training. There are instances of people who have made a point of refusing to attend, including one Pentecostal Christian, Enrique Oppenheimer, who was the subject of a Nat Hentoff column in 1994. Oppenheimer had worked for eighteen years in New York City's Department of Housing Preservation and Development and refused to attend the mandated "sexual harassment prevention training course" because he felt that the government was interfering with his free exercise of religion by compelling him to participate in a competing code of behavior. "As a practicing Christian," he explained to Hentoff, "I take from the Bible the mandate from God as to how to behave with my fellow humans." This constitutional challenge to the course distressed his superiors, who held hearings on his refusal and offered various compromises that Oppenheimer turned down. When it came to light that several other employees, including the judge at one of his hearings, had somehow quietly avoided the course, he was not prosecuted but was asked to stipulate that he had "received" some written materials on harassment from the course; he didn't have to be tested on them or even read them, so he agreed to that. As Hentoff put it, "Oppenheimer accepted the department's surrender."[20]

The purpose of all this training seems to be to get people—usually men—who have found certain behaviors rewarding to give them up, and to get other people to think they should complain about or report the first group. But something is indeed missing in this approach. Suppose we applied these current sexual harassment training principles to heavy drinkers. We would teach everyone that the word *drunk* was primarily a legal term, and that legal guidelines define it as unwelcome drinking of alcoholic beverages to excess, excessive invitations to drink alcoholic beverages, repeated requests for alcoholic drinks, or creating an "uncertain environment" associated with drinking that interferes with co-workers or makes it hard for them to do their jobs. We would read scenarios or show films of people taking drinks in different circumstances and of how they then behaved, and we would then discuss which of these people were drunk. Did this particular scenario show drinking "to excess"? Did the description of last night's bender in another scenario create an "uncertain environment" for the listener? Could we infer from the fact that the protagonist staggered and fell down that he was truly drunk? We would "sensitize" people to drinking and encourage them to smell each other's breath and to keep logs of how many drinks their colleagues took. Finally, we would inform everyone of the procedures for complaining about drunkenness and how to sue the company.

Certainly, seeing depictions of unpleasant drunken behavior might deter many borderline drinkers from overindulging. But would it be surprising if, instead of giving up drinking, some people who might be considered hard-core drinkers felt their right to a private life was being interfered with and defiantly drank more? Would it be surprising if people for whom drinking was a problem found the program of no help? And finally, would it be surprising if the net result of the training was to make employees suspicious of each other and to polarize them into one group that righteously reported others and another whose members were mutually overprotective about their drunkenness? Would you expect that such a program would wipe out the possibility of lawsuits against the company under the law against drunkenness?

We have been doing the equivalent of this for too long. We seem to have reached a plateau, stuck in a regime that isn't achieving the objectives either of feminism (to make working conditions beneficial for women) or of management (to guard against lawsuits). And the experts know it. I was told separately by both the librarian of a large educational library that specializes in labor relations and the co-author of a sexual harassment training workbook that they no longer read the new books that are published on sexual harassment, because "they are all the same." In what way? I asked. They define sexual harassment, discuss sexual harassment law, and say what to do if you're sexually harassed, both authorities responded.

It is time for a rethinking of what we are doing about human relations, starting with a revamping of the law. And yes, there is a place for training—but a different kind of training. It should not be compulsory, for starters. What seems to be missing is any discussion of the motivation of behavior, of the interactive nature of behavior, and, perhaps most of all, of how people can deal with offensive and distressing behavior in others.

CHAPTER FIFTEEN

Towards a Feminist Theory
of Training

Obviously, in an era in which legal liability is tied to the establishment of training programs and complaint procedures, managements will ignore the law at their peril. For the foreseeable future, training programs are with us. It is possible to improve many training materials and courses, but it would probably be foolhardy for a company of any size to decide to eliminate them completely.

But we can stop insisting that, in this area alone, working people are supposed to be legal experts. The law is and should be an engine of last resort, not a guide to everyday life. Actually, if a company really wants to eliminate sexual harassment, an emphasis on the law is self-defeating. That's because federal sexual harassment law is no direct threat to offenders, is overbroad and vague, and is resented as intrusive into private behavior.

Federal sexual harassment law exempts the actual actors from suit. Some states and localities make harassing supervisors liable, implicitly or explicitly, but those allowed to be sued under Title VII are only employers and companies. Since the people whose behavior will invoke the punishment are the employees who work for the companies, one would think it behooves companies to find other ways to motivate them in training than exhorting them to comply with the law. Yet sexual harassment training is often called "compliance training." Compliance just says, "Don't get *us* in trouble." Reliance on it as a motivator can even be seen by employees as punitive, self-serving, and counterproductive.

The law is overbroad and vague. The purpose of law is to define forbidden behavior and promulgate guidelines for its punishment. But as was discussed in chapter 2, sexual harassment law isn't statutory law. We're talking civil suit here, and only when a person crosses the borderline of outrageousness does it become at all clear that the behavior is forbidden. Statutory law is almost always self-evident: there is no workplace uproar over what embezzlement is, or physical assault or forgery. Even most of the rules that a company itself may institute—dress codes and no-smoking rules, for instance—while not necessarily self-evident, are clear once they are instituted. The rules say, we have too many mechanics (or nurses or managers) to recognize individually, so we want you to dress a certain way so that we or the public can recognize you on sight; or, some people have problems when other people smoke, and certain areas pose fire hazards, so you can smoke in this specified place but nowhere else. Such rules of conduct, like the law of theft or fraud or assault, are easy to define and easy to follow, and employees know they will be disciplined if they don't do this or they do that.

But sexual harassment? As we have seen, current training programs spend a lot of time agonizing over what the definitions of the offense might be and show employees and managers scenarios of events, which they then discuss and disagree about. (Some research projects have done the same thing and recorded the different reactions of men and women or of people who have been targets of reported harassment and those who have not.) The programs also familiarize everyone with the EEOC guidelines and tell them how to bring suit; but of course, all companies want employees not to bring suit but rather to resolve sexual harassment problems out of court. Targets would benefit by such resolution, too. According to those who deal with women who do bring suit, it is a little like spending your life trying to win the lottery—your chances of making it big are minuscule, and you can end up losing most of your friends should you win.

Another difficulty in dealing with sexual harassment as a legal problem is that almost all people accused of harassment, from the one whose joke is misunderstood to the hard-core opportunistic harasser on John Pryor's Likelihood of Sexual Harassment (LSH) scale who believes in rape myths, *don't believe they are hurting anyone.* And we know from our experiences with alcohol and drug prohibition that people whose behavior is regulated and who don't believe they are hurting anyone else overwhelmingly evade and resent the regulations. Company rules such as bans on smoking or requirements to wear uniforms are different, partly because they are time-and-place specific— they are not attempts to reach into and change an employee's lifestyle and govern the way in which co-workers deal with each other, on and off the job. Therefore, I submit, we can expect that attempts to change sexually offensive behavior towards co-workers by invoking the law will always contain a large counterproductive element.

We can see a feeling that personal lives are being intruded upon in some of the reactions to training programs. Some of the training programs I examined include room for discussion of such issues as "Have feminists gone too far?" and "Do these regulations violate free speech?" The programs say no, but a lot of people in the media (and in some workplaces) say yes. The reasons are not difficult to understand. If you tell people that the way in which they relate to each other naturally is against the law, their immediate reaction is to think the law intrusive. If, by contrast, you tell people that they may have misunderstood each other but that they can learn to communicate more clearly, you are offering them a new skill without blaming half of them in advance.

The subject is workplace relationships; an emphasis on compliance plucks the issue of sexual harassment out of the general context of employee relations and focuses on it in a quasi-legal and ultimately confusing way. This is not to say we can do nothing to help those who feel themselves to be targets. But perhaps we should pay more attention to what we actually have learned about human sexual relations at work and how research in communications, group composition, and gender studies might inform us further.

Rita Risser opens her research report on the *New Law of Sexual Harassment* by quoting a manager who attended a mandatory sexual harassment seminar that Risser was running, who reminded her that in the 1970s, people were told in similar seminars that they must hug their employees—now they are being told they must not.[1] If you are running a company, do you focus on warmth and openness or on bad behavior and avoiding offense? Fashions change.

Risser has seen it happen; she gave her first seminar on the subject in 1982, long before most people had come to the conclusion that it might be a good idea to *prevent* sexual harassment. Relatively recently, she changed the title of the seminars she has been giving to managers and employees since the early 1980s from "Understanding Harassment" to "Respectful Workplace" and "Values to Work By." This reflects a change in content, from an emphasis on complying with the law to what she now sees as more fundamental: an emphasis on being aware of the values of other people and communicating your own. "We are really doing more communication styles," she says today.[2] She does it in an interesting and valuable way.

One exercise she uses involves a small group, usually a mixed group of men and women, minorities and whites, and people of different ages. These people are asked how they feel about a number of issues: for example, "swearing, being touched, having your space invaded, hearing your colleagues speaking a language other than English, having people talking about religion in the workplace." She says that inevitably there are differences, "even if I've got twenty white men in a room"; and inevitably, everyone has a point of real sensitivity. Once this is discovered, the discussion turns to what to do about that.

At one seminar, a woman said that she likes dirty jokes and ethnic jokes, she swears, and she doesn't mind being touched—"but she was adamant that people should not speak any language other than English." Someone else in her group had no problem with people speaking other languages, but he was adamant that "ethnic jokes are completely inappropriate." When this sort of difference emerges in a seminar—and it always does—people realize that the issue is: How do we explain to each other what our sensitivities are and perhaps negotiate so that we all feel we are respected?

If our experience tells us that workplace relations are generally not completely happy, then some sort of training program could be a good thing. First of all, the company should follow Rita Risser's example and not call it compliance. Call it something like "Getting Along in the Modern Workplace."

Second, if attendance is mandatory (and it seems to be received wisdom that it should be), make sure that it takes place on company time, not on workers' time off. One legal expert discovered to her dismay that a man in a plant in which she was running a training program had been told that, after working six days in a row, he had to come in for the training on his day off or be fired.

Third, work out what you want the program to accomplish. Like an alcoholic intervention, one goal is to prove to the person exhibiting the behavior that the behavior is in fact hurting someone, the target. You want to highlight certain workplace behaviors that men assume are positive but women report as negative and get men to realize that the very people they are trying to interact with want them to stop doing these things. You also want to get women to respond in ways that encourage the men to stop. You could borrow the idea from "Respectful Workplace" of a sample list of behaviors (swearing, telling dirty jokes and talking about sex, telling religious jokes, making cracks about members of other groups [ethnic, gender, sexual orientation, etc.], hugging or patting, asking for a date, paying compliments, "stealing a kiss," and so on) and discuss *them*, not fictitious scenarios. Go around the circle and have participants (both men and women) say which behaviors they find acceptable and which they really feel bad about. You may want to do exercises in which people role-play how they might respond to such behaviors and what they think the outcome would be. Encourage feedback from everyone. You certainly want to give the men in the group an opportunity to explain their assumptions and their view of all this.

When you have dealt with a number of such issues, then you have to explain the company's policy and the company's decision to require mutual courtesy and respect—and finally, the company's complaint procedures and how all of this fits into existing sexual harassment law, including the EEOC Definitions and Guidelines. But the law can be put in the wider context of communication, as that which protects you when communication gets out of hand, rather than as the sole reason one should examine and discard certain ways of relating to people.

The most helpful kind of training course would be based on such ideals of communication and self-help, rather than focused on either legal information or "sensitivity." Many companies now have ethics officers, and some include issues of sexual harassment in a larger context of ethics. The Boeing aerospace company, for instance, has installed a training program called "Questions of Integrity: The Boeing

Ethics Challenge," in which supervisors present to employees a list of
fifty-four ethical problems that have multiple-choice answers. The
program sets problems of harassment in a wider context that includes
such issues as dealing with customers and suppliers, observing that a
product may have been damaged by someone else, and being insensi-
tive to the values of co-workers, for instance, by wearing a pro-choice
T-shirt.[3]

Some of the examples that have surfaced in this book point to another function that a training course in job relationships could have
for some companies in today's society: to explain and practice exercises in what might be considered the ordinary rules of civility. As a
1996 column by Todd Seavey complained, "Traditional notions of civility, such as the near-dead ideal of the gentleman, rule out most of
the behavior against which the average woman now sees feminism as
the only shield."[4] I am suggesting courses not in etiquette but in very
basic interpersonal skills, which some people may never have been
taught.

We know that in today's society there is widespread dissatisfaction
with public schools, and some educators in the inner cities are trying
not only to teach content to students but to reach out to their unpre-
pared parents in the community, to help them with life tasks as rudi-
mentary as cleaning a room and keeping track of money. Companies,
too, are finding that they can help make up for inadequate-content education with courses for employees. Could there be a need to make up
for inadequate life-skills education in a similar fashion? One blue-collar manager in a company that hires a lot of ex-felons told me her
problems included men who seldom shaved and came to work in torn
and dirty clothes ("looking like someone you would not want to meet
in a dark alley," she said), and some who seemingly never bathed. "I
had to tell one of the drivers once that it was inappropriate for him to
pee in the garage in public in front of women. He was real shocked by
this, because this was new!"

Some of the behavior that is distressing to women in the workplace
may be due to a similar lack of knowledge—not knowing what other
people, especially women, have a right to expect, not because it's required by law but because it's civil. There is also, of course, a cohort
of young employees who come out of a public-school culture (middle-

class as well as inner-city) that considers it cool for boys in high school and junior high not to care what girls expect—even to show each other that they disrespect girls, by attacking them verbally and sometimes even groping them.

Backgrounds vary in every conceivable way—by class, religion, education, culture, and ethnicity—and today we are all mixed together in the workplace and have to get along somehow, despite the fact that we all have different standards of how to behave. In this sort of workplace, dealing with harassment primarily in terms of complying with the law is, at the very least, superficial.

But the most telling argument against a legal focus in training is that the view of woman that is created thereby is, inevitably, of woman as passive. The rationale is that the law must *do something* for woman. Environments that may seem acceptable to men will be unpleasant for a woman to encounter, and the law must protect her. For advocates of protective labor legislation, from the turn of the century until the ERA ratification fights, it was unacceptable that a woman might be asked to perform difficult and dirty work; the law should forbid her to comply, even if she wanted to. Today, as a woman leaves the home and goes out into the workplace, the law must be at her side, or force management through the possibility of penalties to be at her side, in a way men have not required in order to shield her from the hurtful behavior of those whom she may encounter, even if she says she can cope. And suppose she can't? Why decide that the law must be the one to confront the offender? Why not, instead, help her to do something for herself? One unfortunate reason that companies don't do more to help in this way is, as we saw in the previous chapter, the possibility that encouraging women employees to be assertive on their own behalf might jeopardize the employer in a lawsuit.

As far back as the U.S. Merit Systems Protection Board survey in 1981, "there were substantial and strong correlations between measures of the strength of the most assertive response and the severity of the harassment and between strength of response and the victim's psychological welfare as a result of the harassment."[5] But we still seem to have difficulty in getting from *a* to *b*, from abstract knowledge of what to do to actually doing it. Women are prone, says one writer, to "learned helplessness."[6] This certainly would suggest that a focus on modifying behavior might be a worthy goal for training programs—on modifying the behavior of targets, not, as the present focus has it, of potential harassers. Some researchers have even suggested assertiveness training.[7]

Once more, it *should* be the woman, and not the man, whose behavior is modified. Because we are talking about women wanting to enter male workplaces that are permeated by male culture. When you want to do something new, it makes sense to learn about it: it's stupid to go into unknown territory without a map and proper equipment. We are also talking about women who want men to change and not to behave in harassing ways, and there are only two ways to effect such a change: either tell them what you want or get someone else to force them into acceptable behavior. If you find it difficult to tell them— again, why not learn how? In fact, the idea is for both men and women to learn something by establishing clear communication.

Perhaps the training many women need, which is essentially feminist training, shouldn't be done by management—at least, not while existing law is in place. One organization that has the motivation to help female employees get access to such training, at least in some workplaces, is the union. When it comes to sexual harassment, unions want resolution rather than confrontation, because in the event of a formal complaint they may have to defend both parties. A study of union defenses of sexual harassers in a union work environment found that the typical defense *raised by the union* to an incident was either denial of the event or blaming the victim. A comment on this study suggested that unions could help targets defend themselves instead: "Rather than utilizing denial or blame, there are in fact, a spectrum of positive responses that can be called upon in cases of sexual harassment. . . . [I]n laying out this repertoire of options, I attempt to help the complainant understand that she/he is *empowered* to become an agent of action and to respond effectively to sexual harassment in the workplace." The first option suggested is: "Develop the capability, in the harassee, to effectively deal with the problem on her/his own,"[8] either by personal confrontation or in writing. The author then goes on to stress the elements that should be learned: confront, speak your feelings about what happened, say "stop."

Everyone knows it would be ideal if all targets knew how to do that. But assertive behavior, like manners, is a skill to be learned; it is not innate. So the question remains: Who's going to teach it? If the company is non-union, and if it's problematic for such programs to be initiated by management, what about women's organizations? One of the values that the resurgence of feminism brought to discussions of social change in the 1960s and 1970s is a focus on the possibility that women can wield social power without waiting for legal power. One of the early achievements of NOW was to bring together more than one hundred thousand women into consciousness-raising groups all over the country. Feminism in the 1970s didn't look on situations that negatively impact on women as management problems or as requiring women to bring individual lawsuits; rather, it organized ways in which women could help women. If it is true, as the evidence brought together in this book seems to bear out, that perhaps hundreds of thousands of women are made miserable by offensive workplace experiences that they don't know how to deal with—then feminists should be helping them to deal. Like the original NOW, we should be organizing the equivalent of consciousness-raising groups; like the early women executives in the 1960s and 1970s, we should be organizing women's clubs and networks where we can trade strategies and put each other in touch with possible mentors; we should suggest to women in nontraditional workplaces that they ask offices and shops to give them time and space to meet and discuss these challenges. And there should be feminist training courses available, on a self-help basis or perhaps through such organizations as the YWCA.

As I read the guidelines and workbook materials for sexual harassment training, I come across gleaming nuggets of common sense that could be incorporated into such courses:

Role-Playing. Set up a situation in which people can role-play what their reactions might be and get feedback from a working group: reactions to a friend's distress; reactions to another employee's language; reactions to an accusation of offensive behavior.

Checklists. Make a checklist of what you think your own behavior towards others should be.

Free Speech. Discuss what free speech is and should be. When is a right to say something more important than the negative impact on others of what you say? What about politeness and consideration? Is there a difference between a political forum and an organization like a company? If so, what is it?

Support Groups. For women who feel at a disadvantage when they are outnumbered in the workplace: start your own support group. Tell the members of your group if you are having unusual difficulty with a co-worker who keeps making remarks you dislike, and invite them to come around *en masse* and take notes. If you have such a group, seek out new women coming into the workforce and show them the ropes.

Feminists could offer a great service if they helped working women to network with each other, to share concerns about unpleasant communication, and to role-play and brainstorm about how to respond to such communications in ways that could satisfy them and not escalate any unpleasantness. You might want to research feminist consciousness-raising groups and what they have done in the past to help women in the workplace: this is a technique that women found of inestimable help to them in breaking into new jobs in the 1970s.

But a truly feminist training program needs to go even further if it is to support women. You want to give workers a new kind of information—information on how the workplace is changing, on population ratios, on the advantages and seeming disadvantages of having to interact with people who are very different.

The single hardest thing to do seems to be to confront offensive behavior and tell the offender clearly that you would like him to stop. Too few attempts have been made to give people practice in what may be needed most: assertive, nonhostile communication techniques. You might want to give people information about communication differences—between ethnic groups as well as between genders. You might not only have a general discussion of free speech and its importance in American life but also explore the use of counterspeech to answer speech that is offensive. You might want to emphasize different techniques of assertive communication and practice them.

A truly innovative training program based on such ideas could reverse the depressing trend towards rule-ridden behavior in the workplace and replace it with an emphasis on people-knowledge, communication, conflict resolution, community, and, above all, individual responsibility.

Implied in this discussion is a breaking down and subdividing of the concept of *sexual harassment*. Originally, this was a useful term that distinguished really unwelcome behavior at work from welcome courting behavior. Now, it has been hijacked by lawyers. When a man's act of exposing himself to a woman he doesn't know while making a request for oral sex can rightly be called "not sexual harassment" by a judge, we need to reexamine our vocabulary.

We probably have to let the term stand for the legal concept that is continually being refined and evolved by the Supreme Court, and that soon may be the province of a state tort rather than of federal discrimination law. But I suggest that researchers and management trainers refuse to let this term be so broad that it includes rape and sexual assault, both of which are already actionable by law. (Lawyers may not want to adopt this suggestion, since the 1991 Civil Rights Act allows legal fees for the winners of a "sexual harassment" case, which rape and assault civil suits generally do not.)[9] Then we need another concept for behaviors at work that are not necessarily illegal but that some people find offensive and wish would stop. It would include material that is undoubtedly protected by the First Amendment, from pornography to swear words to endearments, as well as hugs and pats from people whose culture encourages such behavior as ordinary courtesy. "Sexually offensive behavior" has been suggested for this area by at least one training workbook.[10]

Sexual harassment is a subject about which the Left told us for years that we should have a society that requires men to be more caring towards women, while the Right told us that too much regulation would hamper the goal of a freer society. In the aftermath of President Clinton's travails, the Left seemed to be more concerned with freedom and the Right with caring. In fact, what all the debates about laws and regulations and speech codes are showing is a passionate desire in a majority of us to bring about a society that can be at once both caring and free. If we hold to that vision, perhaps we can put the law on the back burner, which is its rightful place.

NOTES

Notes to Introduction

1. *Robinson v. Jacksonville Shipyards, Inc.*, 760 F. Supp. 1486 (M.D. Fla. 1991).

Notes to Chapter 1

A large part of this chapter is based on an article of mine published in the newsletter of the Association of Libertarian Feminists: Joan Kennedy Taylor, "A Challenge to Feminism—Sexual Harassment," *ALF News*, no. 59 (Summer 1996): 1.

1. Philip Weiss, "Don't Even Think about It. (The Cupid Cops Are Watching.)," *New York Times Magazine*, 3 May 1998, 44.

2. Alex Kuczynski, "In Offices, an Excuse to Mention S*x," *New York Times*, 1 February 1998, sec. 3, 1, 5.

3. Ronni Sandroff, "Sexual Harassment in the Fortune 500," *Working Woman*, December 1988, 69ff.

4. Ronni Sandroff, "Sexual Harassment: The Inside Story," *Working Woman*, June 1992, 47ff.

5. Ibid., 51.

6. Ibid., 48.

7. Ibid., 49.

8. Ibid., 50.

9. Ibid., 51.

10. Linda Greenhouse, "Court to Examine Sex Harassment," *New York Times*, 8 March 1998, 22.

11. John Cloud, "Sex and the Law," *Time*, 23 March 1998, 49.

12. Ibid., 52.

13. Susan Estrich, "Sex at Work," *Stanford Law Review*, 813 (1991), reprinted in Kelly Weisberg, ed., *Applications of Feminist Legal Theories to Women's Lives: Sex, Violence, Work and Reproduction* (Philadelphia: Temple University Press, 1996), 725–732.

14. Catharine MacKinnon, "Harassment Law under Siege," *New York Times*, 5 March 1998, A29.

15. Gloria Steinem, "Feminists and the Clinton Question," *New York Times*, 22 March 1998, sec. 4, 15.

16. Cloud, "Sex and the Law," 52.

17. Deborah Tannen, *Talking from Nine to Five: Women and Men in the Workplace: Language, Sex and Power* (New York: Avon Books, 1995), 250–251.

18. Peter Elstrom, with Edith Hill Updike, "Fear and Loathing at Mitsubishi," *Business Week*, 6 May 1996, 35.

19. Rita J. Simon, Jennifer Scherer, and William Rau, "Sexual Harassment in the Heartland? Community Opinion on the EEOC Suit against Mitsubishi Motor Manufacturing of America," in Cathy Young, ed., *Rethinking Sexual Harassment: A Women's Freedom Network Special Report*, Women's Freedom Network Working Paper 3 (Washington, D.C.: Women's Freedom Network, 1998).

20. *Lynch v. Des Moines*, 454 N.W. 2d 827, 834 (Iowa 1990).

21. *Loftin-Boggs v. Meridian*, 633 F. Supp. 1323 (S.D. Miss. 1986).

22. *Swentek v. USAir, Inc.*, 830 F. 2d 552, 557 (4th Cir. 1987) All three cases referred to in notes 20, 21, and 22 are cited by Kingsley R. Browne in "Title VII as Censorship: Hostile-Environment Harassment and the First Amendment," *Ohio State Law Journal* 52 (1991): 542–543. He writes: "The courts in *Lynch, Loftin-Boggs,* and *Swentek* seem to permit employees in a protected class to engage in the same conduct that they later complain of and then to 'touch base' and declare that they prefer to participate no longer. That seems less an antidiscrimination principle than a principle of special treatment, which is more likely to lead to resentment than acceptance of women and minorities in the workplace" (543).

Notes to Chapter 2

1. 42 U.S.C. section 2000c.

2. Walter Olson, *The Excuse Factory: How Employment Law Is Paralyzing the American Workplace* (New York: Free Press, 1997), 50–51.

3. Ibid., 61.

4. *Rogers v. EEOC*, 454 F. 2d 234 (1971) at 238. See Ellen Frankel Paul, "Sexual Harassment," *Encyclopedia of Applied Ethics*, vol. 4 (New York: Academic Press, 1998), 90; and Kingsley R. Browne, "Title VII as Censorship: Hostile-Environment Harassment and the First Amendment," *Ohio State Law Journal* 52 (1991): 485.

5. Elvia R. Arriola, "'What's the Big Deal?' Women in the New York City Construction Industry and Sexual Harassment Law, 1970–1985," *Columbia Human Rights Law Review* 21 (1990), reprinted in Kelly Weisberg, ed., *Applications of Feminist Legal Theories to Women's Lives: Sex, Violence, Work and Reproduction* (Philadelphia: Temple University Press, 1996), 780–781.

6. Ibid., 781.

7. Bonnie Bullough and Vern L. Bullough, "Sexual Harassment," *Free Inquiry*, Winter 1991/92, 5.

8. Kelly Weisberg, "Introduction," "Sexual Harassment" section in Weisberg, ed., *Applications of Feminist Legal Theories to Women's Lives*, 729.

9. Catharine A. MacKinnon, *Sexual Harassment of Working Women* (New Haven: Yale University Press, 1979), 1.

10. *Corne v. Bausch and Lomb, Inc.* 390 F. Supp. 161 (D. Ariz. 1975) at 163.

11. Ibid.

12. *Williams v. Saxbe*, 413 F. Supp. 654 (D. D.C. 1976).

13. *Alexander v. Yale University*, 459 F. Supp. 1 (D. Conn 1977). The case was brought under Title IX of the Education Amendments of 1972 to the Civil Rights Act, which prohibits sexual harassment in schools that receive federal money. Almost all colleges and universities, as well as public schools, receive such funds.

14. 477 U.S. 57 (1986).

15. Ibid. at 69.

16. The EEOC and court cases before *Meritor* had imposed liability on employers for quid pro quo harassment by supervisory personnel, holding that decisions about the victim's employment status were decisions that the supervisor made as an agent of the employer. See *Katz v. Dole*, 709 F. 2d. 251 (1983).

17. 510 U.S. 17 (1993) at 22.

18. 201 *Daily Labor Report* E-1 (October 18, 1988).

19. Eugene Volokh, "Was Wright Wrong? Who Knows?" *Wall Street Journal*, 3 April 1998, A18.

20. Linda Greenhouse, "High Court Widens Workplace Claims in Sex Harassment," *New York Times*, 5 March 1998, 1.

21. *Oncale v. Sundowner Offshore Services, Inc.*, 118 S. Ct. 998 (1998) at 1002.

22. Greenhouse, "High Court Widens Workplace Claims in Sex Harassment," 1.

23. Rita Risser, "The New Law of Sexual Harassment: Everything You Know Is Wrong," in Cathy Young, ed., *Rethinking Sexual Harassment: A*

Women's Freedom Network Special Report, Women's Freedom Network Working Paper 3 (Washington, D.C.: Women's Freedom Network, 1998), 27.

25. Rita Risser, *Sexual Harassment Law—It's Not What You Think* (Santa Cruz, Calif.: Fair Measures, 1999), 6.

25. *Smith v. St. Louis Hospital,* 109 F. 3d 1261 (8th Cir. 1997), described in Risser, *Sexual Harassment Law,* 14.

26. *Burlington Industries, Inc. v. Ellerth,* 118 S. Ct. 2257 (1998) at 2270; identical wording in *Faragher v. City of Boca Raton,* 118 S. Ct. 2275 (1998) at 2292.

27. One textbook says the following about vicarious liability: "In one sense this is strict liability, since the new person who is held liable is without any fault of his own, and becomes liable only by reason of his relationship to the actual wrongdoer. In another, it is not. The foundation of vicarious liability is still, as the law stands, negligence or other fault on the part of someone; and what the law does is to broaden the liability for that fault by imposing it upon an actual defendant who is himself without fault. Whether it is to be called strict liability or not is perhaps a pointless quibble over the meaning of the term" (William L. Prosser and John W. Wade, *Cases and Materials on Torts,* 5th ed. [Mineola, NY: Foundation Press, 1971], 553–554).

28. Linda Greenhouse, "Court Spells Out Rules for Finding Sex Harassment," *New York Times,* 27 June 1998, 1.

29. Anita K. Blair, "Harassment Law: More Confused than Ever," *Wall Street Journal,* 8 July 1998, A14.

30. "United States: Men, Women, Work and Law," *The Economist,* 4 July 1998, 21.

31. Rita Risser, in a private conversation with the author, 18 May 1998.

32. Robyn E. Blumner, "Sexual Harassment and the First Amendment: A Feminist Perspective," in Young, ed., *Rethinking Sexual Harassment,* 25.

33. Risser, "New Law of Sexual Harassment," n. 4–5.

34. Kate O'Beirne, "Bread and Circuses: Paula Jones, for the Defense," *National Review,* 20 April 1998, 28.

35. John Koch, "The Interview: Wendy Kaminer," *Boston Globe Magazine,* 31 August 1997, 10.

36. Catharine A. MacKinnon, "Harassment Law under Siege," *New York Times,* 5 March 1998, A29.

37. Quoted in Henry Louis Gates, "The Naked Republic," *New Yorker,* 25 August and 1 September 1997, 117.

38. Gloria Steinem, "Feminists and the Clinton Question," *New York Times,* 22 March 1998, sec. 4, 15.

Notes to Chapter 3

1. Rita Risser, "The New Law of Sexual Harassment: Everything You Know Is Wrong," in Cathy Young, ed., *Rethinking Sexual Harassment: A Women's Freedom Network Special Report*, Women's Freedom Network Working Paper 3 (Washington, D.C.: Women's Freedom Network, 1998), 27.

2. I am dealing in this book with the model of sexual harassment as a male-on-female issue, because 90 to 95 percent of the reported incidents are male on female. This choice leads, in turn, to what could be taken as overgeneralization about not just men's role in harassing situations but the behavior in general of "men" and "women," as well as to an examination of what is known about how their behavior patterns differ. This is not to be interpreted as indicating advocacy on my part for a position on sociobiology or gender psychology or the proper roles of men and women in society. It certainly should not be interpreted as male-bashing. Individuals differ, and within each gender pattern of behavior are individuals who behave like the opposite gender, as well as every possible variation in between. Often the patterns that scholars have observed and identified are used in argument as if they are straitjackets with which triumphantly to dispose of individual differences. Such is not my intention. When I make generalizations about "male culture" or "girls trained from childhood to react in a certain manner," I do not intend to imply that all males or all girls participate in the observed pattern. But there are observed and observable patterns that significantly divide by gender, and they can be useful and even comforting to recognize.

3. Rosabeth Moss Kanter, *Men and Women of the Corporation* (New York: Basic Books, 1993), 6.

4. Ibid., 248–249.

5. Ibid., 315–316.

6. Barbara A. Gutek and Bruce Morasch, "Sex-Ratios, Sex-Role Spillover, and Sexual Harassment of Women at Work," *Journal of Social Issues* 38, 4 (1982): 55.

7. Ibid., 58.

8. Ibid., 63.

9. Irene Padavic and Barbara F. Reskin, "Men's Behavior and Women's Interest in Blue-Collar Jobs," *Social Problems* 37, 4 (1990): 613–628.

10. Ibid., 624–625.

11. Ibid., 625.

12. Ibid., 617.

13. Helen T. Palmer and Jo Ann Lee, "Female Workers' Acceptance in

Traditionally Male-Dominated Blue-Collar Jobs, *Sex Roles* 22, 9/10 (1990): 607–626.

14. Jane Gross, "Now Look Who's Taunting. Now Look Who's Suing," *New York Times*, 26 February 1995, sec. 4, 1.

15. This is not hyperbole; the "goals and timetables" that all government contractors must meet for the hiring of women and minorities are government quotas that are enforced by the Office of Federal Contract Compliance Programs of the U.S. Department of Labor.

16. From an E-mail message received by freedom@well.com, 28 February 1998, 23:17:24.

17. Risser, "New Law of Sexual Harassment," 27.

18. Wendy Shalit, "Feminism Lives! In Sexual Harassment Law There Is a Nugget of Truth That Keeps Feminism Vital," *National Review*, 6 April 1998, 37.

19. See Deborah Tannen, *You Just Don't Understand: Women and Men in Conversation* (New York: Ballantine Books, 1991), 182–183, 185, 259–260.

20. Edward Lafontaine and Leslie Tredeau, "The Frequency, Sources, and Correlates of Sexual Harassment among Women in Traditional Male Occupations," *Sex Roles* 15, 7/8 (1986): 433–442.

21. Kanter, *Men and Women of the Corporation*, 317.

22. Shereen G. Bingham and Lisa L. Scherer, "Factors Associated with Responses to Sexual Harassment and Satisfaction with Outcome," *Sex Roles* 29, 3/4 (1993): 263.

23. Ibid., 248.

24. Marilyn Moats Kennedy, *Powerbase: How to Build It/How to Keep It* (New York: Macmillan, 1984), xii.

25. Wendy Grossman, *Net.wars* (New York: New York University Press, 1997), 108.

26. James E. Gruber, "How Women Handle Sexual Harassment: A Literature Review, *Sociology and Social Research* 74, 1 (1989): 6.

Notes to Chapter 4

1. Deborah Tannen, *That's Not What I Meant! How Conversational Style Makes or Breaks Relationships* (New York: Ballantine Books, 1992), 29–30.

2. Ibid., 40.

3. Susan Estrich, "Rape," *Yale Law Journal* 95 (1991): 1087–1184, reprinted in Kelly Weisberg, ed., *Applications of Feminist Legal Theories to Women's Lives: Sex, Violence, Work and Reproduction* (Philadelphia: Temple University Press, 1996), 434.

4. Ibid., 436.

5. Ibid. 441.

6. *Goldberg v. Maryland,* 41 Md. App. 58, 395 A. 2d 1213 (1979) at 1219.

7. *Commonwealth of Pennsylvania v. Berkowitz* 537 Pa. 143, 641 A. 2d 1161 (1994) at 1164.

8. Mary Becker, Cynthia Grant Bowman, and Morrison Torrey, eds., *Feminist Jurisprudence: Taking Women Seriously* (St. Paul: West Publishing Co., 1994), "Text Note: Repeal of Marital Rape Exemptions," 241.

9. Ibid., 241–242 and n. 18.

10. Lois Pineau, "Date Rape: A Feminist Analysis," in Weisberg, ed. *Applications of Feminist Legal Theories to Women's Lives,* 484–494.

11. Nancy Friday, *My Secret Garden: Women's Sexual Fantasies* (New York: Pocket Books, 1998), 8–9.

12. Ibid., 11.

13. Shere Hite, *The Hite Report* (New York: Dell, 1976), 301. References to this report in the following paragraphs are cited in the text.

14. Gina Kolata, "Women and Sex: On This Topic, Science Blushes," *New York Times,* 21 June 1998, sec. 15, 3.

15. The staff of the Institute for Sex Research, Indiana University: Alfred C. Kinsey [and others], *Sexual Behavior in the Human Female* (Philadelphia: W. B. Saunders, 1953); see also Alfred C. Kinsey, Wardell B. Pomeroy, and Clyde E. Martin, *Sexual Behavior in the Human Male* (Philadelphia: W. B. Saunders, 1948).

16. William H. Masters and Virginia Johnson, *Human Sexual Inadequacy* (Boston: Little, Brown, 1970) and *Human Sexual Response* (Boston: Little, Brown, 1966).

17. Pineau, "Date Rape," 489.

18. Ibid., 493–494.

19. See Peggy Reeves Sanday, *Fraternity Gang Rape: Sex, Brotherhood, and Privilege on Campus* (New York and London: New York University Press, 1990).

20. See Neil Malamuth, M. Heim, and S. Feshbach, "Sexual Responsiveness of College Students to Rape Depictions: Inhibitory and Disinhibitory Affects," *Journal of Personality and Social Psychology* 38 (1980): 399–408; Neil Malamuth, "Rape Proclivity among Males," *Journal of Social Issues* 37, 4 (1981): 138–157; Neil Malamuth, "Factors Associated with Rape as Predictors of Laboratory Aggression against Women," *Journal of Personality and Social Psychology* 45 (1983): 432–442; Neil Malamuth, "Aggression against Women: Cultural and Individual Causes," in N. Malamuth and E. Donnerstein, eds., *Pornography and Sexual Aggression* (New York: Academic Press, 1984).

21. John B. Pryor, "Sexual Harassment Proclivities in Men," *Sex Roles* 17, 5/6 (1987): 269–290.

22. John B. Pryor, Christine M. La Vite, and Lynette M. Stoller, "A Social Psychological Analysis of Sexual Harassment: The Person/Situation Interaction," *Journal of Vocational Behavior* 42, 1 (February 1993): 75.

23. Elaine Sciolino, "The Nation's Problems with Sex and Power," *New York Times*, 4 May 1997, sec. 4, 4.

24. Ibid.

Notes to Chapter 5

1. Deborah Tannen, *Talking from Nine to Five: Women and Men in the Workplace: Language, Sex and Power* (New York: Avon Books, 1995), 243.

2. Betty Lehan Harragan, *Games Mother Never Taught You: Corporate Gamesmanship for Women* (New York: Rawson Associates Publishers, 1977; reprint, New York: Warner Books, 1978).

3. Ibid., 23.

4. Ibid., 78.

5. Mary Coeli Meyer, Jeanenne Oestrich, Frederick J. Collins, and Inge Berentold, *Sexual Harassment* (New York, Petrocelli Books, 1981), 138–139.

6. Barbara A. Gutek, *Sex and the Workplace* (San Francisco and London: Jossey-Bass Publishers, 1985).

7. Ibid., 99.

8. Ibid., 100–101.

9. Karen B. Williams and Ramona R. Cyr, "Escalating Commitment to a Relationship: The Sexual Harassment Trap," *Sex Roles* 27, 1/2 (1992): 47–72.

10. Michelle Cottle, "When a Boss Turns Abusive," *New York Times*, 29 November 1998, sec. 3, 11.

11. Rita Risser, in a private conversation with the author, 18 May 1998.

12. Nancy Lloyd, "Helen Gurley Brown: Still the Same Ol' Tease," *Modern Maturity*, May/June 1997, 56.

13. Harragan, *Games Mother Never Taught You*, 374–379.

14. Celia Farber, "The Trial," *Salon*, June 1997. Archived at http://www.salonmagazine.com/june97/spin490609.html; accessed 19 November 1998.

15. Barbara A. Gutek and Bruce Morasch, "Sex Ratios, Sex-Role Spillover, and Sexual Harassment of Women at Work," *Journal of Social Issues* 38, 4 (1982): 70.

16. Ibid., 73.

17. Meyer et al., *Sexual Harassment*, 134.

18. Rita Risser, "The New Law of Sexual Harassment," in Cathy Young, ed., *Rethinking Sexual Harassment: A Women's Freedom Network Special Report*, Women's Freedom Network Working Paper 3 (Washington, D.C.: Women's Freedom Network, 1998), 28.

Notes to Chapter 6

1. R. W. Apple Jr., "Introduction," in Gerald Gold, ed., *The White House Transcripts: Submission of Recorded Presidential Conversations to the Committee on the Judiciary of the House of Representatives by President Richard Nixon* (Toronto, New York, and London: Bantam Books, 1974), 2–3.

2. Betty Lehan Harragan, *Games Mother Never Taught You: Corporate Gamesmanship for Women* (New York: Warner Books, 1978), 110.

3. From Freedom Forum online, at http://www.freedomforum.org/speech/1998/4/24manson.asp/.

4. E.g., *In re Joseph T.*, 430 S.E. 2d 523 (S.C. 1993).

5. Daniel Seligman, "PC Comes to the Newsroom," *National Review*, 21 June 1993, 30.

6. Alyssa Katz, "It's a Man's Word," *Village Voice*, 6 July 1993, 16.

7. Eric Schmitt, "War Is Hell. So Is Regulating Sex," *New York Times*, 17 November 1996, sec. 4, 5.

8. Carol Burke, "Dames at Sea," *New Republic*, 17 and 24 August 1992, 16.

9. Ibid., 18

10. Edward Lafontaine and Leslie Tredeau, "The Frequency, Sources, and Correlates of Sexual Harassment among Women in Traditional Male Occupations," *Sex Roles* 15, 7/8 (1986): 433–442.

11. Rita Risser, *Research Report: The New Law of Sexual Harassment, December 1996* (Santa Cruz, Calif.: Fair Measures, 1996), 3–4.

12. Rita Risser, in a private conversation with the author.

13. Barbara A. Gutek, *Sex and the Workplace* (San Francisco and London: Jossey-Bass Publishers, 1985), 178.

14. Michael Winerip, "The Beauty of Beast Barracks," *New York Times Magazine*, 12 October 1997, 48.

15. Ibid.

16. Mitchell Zuckoff, "A New Word on Speech Codes," *Boston Globe*, 21 October 1998, 1 and A12. On Monday, 1 March 1999, the faculty senate of the University of Wisconsin at Madison rescinded its classroom speech code. See Lester H. Hunt, "Repealing the Codes of Silence," *Liberty* 13, 5 (May 1999): 35–38.

17. Michael Janofsky, "Race and the American Workplace," *New York Times*, 20 June 1993, sec. 3, 1.

18. Harragan, *Games Mother Never Taught You*, 110ff.

19. Deborah Tannen, *Talking from Nine to Five: Women and Men in the Workplace: Language, Sex and Power* (New York: Avon Books, 1995), 273.

20. Betsy Freeman, "Breaking the Code," *Savvy*, June 1988, 94.

21. Quoted in a review of Frances K. Conley's *Walking Out on the Boys* by Susan Jacoby, "Hospital Harassment," *New York Times Book Review*, April 1998, 38.

22. Ibid.

Notes to Chapter 7

1. Maureen Dowd, "The Joke's on Him," *New York Times*, 21 June 1998, sec. 4, 15.

2. Dr. Adele Scheele, "Subtle Sexism," *Working Woman*, July 1992, 17.

3. *Fair v. Guiding Eyes for the Blind*, referred to in Vicki Schultz, "Sex Is the Least of It: Let's Focus Harassment Law on Work, not Sex," *The Nation*, 25 May 1998, 13.

4. NOW Legal Defense and Education Fund and Association for Union Democracy, Women's Project, *Manual for Survival: For Women in Nontraditional Employment* (New York: Association for Union Democracy and NOW Legal Defense and Education Fund, 1993), 11.

5. Kenneth Cooper, *Stop It Now! How Targets and Managers Can Fight Sexual Harassment* (Ballwin, MO: Total Communications Press, 1985), 113–127.

6. Edward J. Harrick and George M. Sullivan, "Racial Harassment: Case Characteristics and Employer Responsibilities, *Employee Responsibilities and Rights Journal* 8, 2 (1995): 82.

7. Deborah Tannen, *The Argument Culture: Moving from Debate to Dialogue* (New York: Random House, 1998), 184–186.

Notes to Chapter 8

1. *Robinson v. Jacksonville Shipyards, Inc.*, 760 F. Supp. 1486 (M.D. Fla. 1991).

2. Kingsley R. Browne, "Title VII as Censorship: Hostile-Environment Harassment and the First Amendment," *Ohio State Law Journal* 52 (1991): 524n. 254. The case referred to is *American Booksellers Assn., Inc. v. Hudnut*, 771 F. 2d 323 (7th Cir. 1985).

3. *Doe v. University of Michigan*, 721 F. Supp. 852 (E.D. Mich. 1989).

4. *Reno v. ACLU*, 117 S. Ct. 2329 (1997).

5. *Robinson v. Jacksonville Shipyards, Inc.*, 760 F. Supp. 1486 (M.D. Fl. 1991).

6. The Meese Commission's investigation of the social science research failed to confirm either that pornography had become more violent and widespread than it had been in 1970 or that it can be shown to be the cause of anti-social behavior, even though the commission report came to both conclusions. A detailed examination of the evidence is provided in chapter 3, "Standard Deviation: Research Literature on Sexually Explicit Material and Social Harms," of a book by Marcia Pally, *Sex and Sensibility: Reflections on Forbidden Mirrors and the Will to Censor* (Hopewell, NJ: Ecco Press, 1994).

7. Jane Mayer and Jill Abramson, *Strange Justice: The Selling of Clarence Thomas* (Boston: Houghton Mifflin, 1994).

8. Deborah Tannen, *Talking from Nine to Five: Women and Men in the Workplace: Language, Sex and Power* (New York: Avon Books, 1995), 259.

9. Elizabeth Cohen and Samme Chittum, "XXX-treme New Feminists," *New York Post*, 21 July 1998, 23.

10. Camille Paglia, *Sex, Art, and American Culture* (New York: Vintage Books, 1992), 47–48.

11. Browne, "Title VII as Censorship," 530.

12. *Tunis v. Corning Glass Works*, 698 F. Supp. 452 (S.D. N.Y. 1988).

13. Browne, "Title VII as Censorship," 508.

14. Ibid., 509.

15. NOW Legal Defense and Education Fund and Association for Union Democracy, Women's Project, *Manual for Survival: For Women in Nontraditional Employment* (New York: Association for Union Democracy and NOW Legal Defense and Education Fund, 1993), 25.

Notes to Chapter 9

1. Deborah Tannen, *The Argument Culture: Moving from Debate to Dialogue* (New York: Random House, 1998), jacket copy.

2. Ibid., 8.

3. Deborah Tannen, *You Just Don't Understand: Women and Men in Conversation* (New York: Ballantine Books, 1991), 24–25.

4. Rosabeth Moss Kanter, *Men and Women of the Corporation* (New York: Basic Books, 1993), 340.

5. Rosabeth Moss Kanter, "The Impact of Hierarchical Structures on the Work Behavior of Men and Women," in Rachel Kahn-Hut, Arlene Kaplan

Daniels, and Richard Colvard, eds., *Women and Work: Problems and Perspectives* (New York: Oxford University Press, 1982), 235.

6. Deborah Tannen, *Talking from Nine to Five: Women and Men in the Workplace: Language, Sex and Power* (New York: Avon Books, 1995), 146.

7. Ibid., 23.

8. Ronni Sandroff, "Sexual Harassment: The Inside Story," *Working Woman*, June 1992, 48.

9. Ibid.

10. Elizabeth Grauerholz, "Sexual Harassment of Women Professors by Students: Exploring the Dynamics of Power, Authority, and Gender in a University Setting," *Sex Roles* 21, 11/12 (1989): 789–802.

11. Betty Lehan Harragan, "Sexual Harassment in the Office: Telling All Is the Best Defense," *Savvy*, September 1980, 22.

12. Tannen. *Talking from Nine to Five*, 26.

13. Ibid., 155.

14. Ibid., 36.

15. Betty Lehan Harragan, *Games Mother Never Taught You: Corporate Gamesmanship for Women* (New York: Warner Books, 1978), 351.

16. Marilyn Moats Kennedy, *Powerbase* (New York: Macmillan, 1984), 173.

17. Harragan, *Games Mother Never Taught You*, 350.

Notes to Chapter 10

1. Donald M. Baer and Stephanie B. Stolz, "A Description of the Erhard Seminars Training (*est*) in the Terms of Behavior Analysis," *Behaviorism* 6, 1 (Spring 1978): 59.

2. Ibid., 60.

3. "Citadel Etiquette," *New York Times*, 11 August 1996, sec. 4, 7.

4. Eric Schmitt, "A Mean Season at Military Colleges: Beleaguered, Embarrassed, Marching On," *New York Times*, 6 April 1997, sec. 4A ("Education Life"), 30.

5. William H. Honan, "The Man with the Plan: 'You Learn What to Avoid,'" *New York Times*, 6 April 1997, sec. 4A ("Education Life"), 33.

6. Schmitt, "Mean Season at Military Colleges," 30.

7. Ibid.

8. Michael Winerip, "The Beauty of Beast Barracks," *New York Times Magazine*, 12 October 1997, 49.

9. Philip Shenon, "Army Plans to Require Women to Meet Higher Fitness Goals," *New York Times*, 14 September 1997, 30.

10. Peggy Reeves Sanday, *Fraternity Gang Rape: Sex, Brotherhood, and Privilege on Campus* (New York: New York University Press, 1990), 19–20.

11. Christopher A. Darden, with Jess Walter, *In Contempt* (New York: ReganBooks, 1996), 72–75, quoted in Deborah Tannen, *The Argument Culture: Moving from Debate to Dialogue* (New York: Random House, 1998), 189.

12. Tannen, *Argument Culture*, 189–190.

13. Ibid., 193.

14. "Witness Says Sergeant Vowed to 'Mow Everyone Down,'" *New York Times*, 11 June 1996, A18.

15. Edward J. Harrick and George M. Sullivan, "Racial Harassment: Case Characteristics and Employer Responsibilities," *Employee Responsibilities and Rights Journal* 8, 2 (1995): 88–89.

16. Lee Nason, in a private interview with the author, April 1996.

17. *Stopping Sexual Harassment: An AFSCME Guide* (Washington, D.C.: n.d.), 10.

18. Quoted in J. Peder Zane, "In Some Cities, Women Still Battle Barriers to Membership in All-Male Clubs," *New York Times*, 8 December 1991, 38.

19. Frank Ahrens, "Coach Flynn's Toughest Race: He Was Used to Winning. Then Came the Charge of 'Gender Inequity,'" *Washington Post*, 8 September 1998, B1.

20. Winerip, "Beauty of Beast Barracks," 48.

21. Ibid., 49.

22. Kingsley R. Browne, "An Evolutionary Perspective on Sexual Harassment: Seeking Roots in Biology rather than Ideology," *Journal of Contemporary Legal Issues* 8 (Spring 1997): 75.

Notes to Chapter 11

1. Barbara A. Gutek, *Sex and the Workplace* (San Francisco and London: Jossey-Bass Publishers, 1985), 178.

2. Shereen G. Bingham and Lisa L. Scherer, "Factors Associated with Responses to Sexual Harassment and Satisfaction with Outcome," *Sex Roles* 29, 3/4 (1993): 247–248.

3. Susannah Pugh and Pat Cahill, "Sexual Harassment on the Job," Springfield *Union-News Extra*, 18–19 September 1992, 1E–2E.

4. "After Hill v. Thomas," *DataLine* 1, 4, October 1991, at http://cyberworks.com:70/Oh/dataline/editorials/pstanita.html; accessed 13 October 1997.

5. Jeffrey Keegan, "Appeal in Sex Discrimination Suit May Land Arbitra-

tion Issue in Supreme Court: Critics, Congress Turn up the Heat on an Important Street Policy," *Investment Dealers' Digest,* 3 August 1998, 3–4.

6. Tamar Lewin, "Debate Centers on Definition of Harassment," *New York Times,* 22 March 1998, 28.

7. Matthew Robinson, "Diversity's Double-Edged Sword: It Can Expand Markets, but also Split Work Forces," *Investor's Business Daily,* 20 February 1997, 1.

8. David S. Hames, "Disciplining Sexual Harassers: What's Fair?" *Employee Responsibilities and Rights Journal* 7, 3 (1994): 207–215.

9. David A. Dilts and Clarence R. Deitsch, "The Tests of Just Cause: What Price Predictability in Arbitral Decision Making?" *Employee Responsibilities and Rights Journal* 5, 1 (1992): 15.

10. Eric Schmitt, "The Military Has a Lot to Learn about Women," *New York Times,* 2 August 1992, sec. 4, 3.

11. Richard Rayner, "The Warrior Besieged," *New York Times Magazine,* 22 June 1997, 29.

12. Ibid., 27.

13. Thomas E. Ricks, "The Great Society in Camouflage," *The Atlantic,* December 1996, 24, 28–30.

14. Eric Schmitt, "Army Shuts Off Phone Line for Sex-Harassment Reports," *New York Times,* 14 June 1997, 6.

15. Constance Jones, *Sexual Harassment* (New York: Facts on File, 1996), 32.

16. Eric Schmitt, "Role of Women in the Military Is Again Bringing Debate," *New York Times,* 29 December 1996, 14.

17. Peter Drucker, "The Future That Has Already Happened," *The Futurist,* November 1998, 16ff.

18. This video was recommended when Dottie Jones spoke on "A Trade Union Response to Sexual Harassment in the Workplace" at a policy breakfast seminar in New York City for Cornell University's New York State School of Industrial and Labor Relations, 31 January 1992.

19. NOW Legal Defense and Education Fund and Association for Union Democracy, Women's Project, *Manual for Survival: For Women in Nontraditional Employment* (New York: Association for Union Democracy and NOW Legal Defense and Education Fund, 1993), chap. 1.

20. Margot Slade, "Tales from the Front Line of Sexual Harassment," *New York Times,* 19 July 1998, sec. 4, 3.

21. Barbara B. Buchholz, "After the Talk or the Touching Gets Too Personal, Where to Turn?" *New York Times,* 2 March 1997, 11.

22. Quoted in Michelle Cottle, "How to Break the Chains," *New York Times,* 7 February 1999, sec. 3, 11.

23. Aleeza Strubel, in a telephone interview with the author, 29 September 1998.

24. Edward L. Pattullo, "Sex and Secrecy at Harvard College," *Harvard Magazine,* January–February 1992, 70.

25. Eric Schmitt, "War Is Hell. So Is Regulating Sex," *New York Times,* 17 November 1996, sec. 4, 5.

Notes to Chapter 12

1. Cathy Young, "Groping toward Sanity," *Reason,* August–September 1998, 24–31.

2. Ellen Frankel Paul, "Sexual Harassment as Sex Discrimination: A Defective Paradigm," *Yale Law and Policy Review* 8, 2 (1990): 333–365.

3. Ibid., 346.

4. Ibid., 350.

5. Ibid., 352.

6. Ibid., 356.

7. Ibid., 360.

8. Jeffrey Toobin, "The Trouble with Sex: Why the Law of Sexual Harassment Has Never Worked," *New Yorker,* 9 February 1998, 55.

9. She was not the first to take this position. See the prescient Nadine Strossen in chapter 6 of *Defending Pornography* (New York: Scribner, 1995), 119–140.

10. Vicki Schultz, "Sex Is the Least of It: Let's Focus Harassment Law on Work, Not Sex," *The Nation,* 25 May 1998, 12.

11. Ibid.

12. "Men, Women, Work and Law," *The Economist,* 4 July 1998, 22.

13. Eugene Volokh, "Freedom of Speech and Workplace Harassment," *UCLA Law Review* 39 (1992), reprinted in Mary Jo Frug, ed., *Supplement to Women and the Law* (New York: Foundation Press, 1997), 34.

14. Kingsley R. Browne, "Title VII as Censorship: Hostile-Environment Harassment and the First Amendment," *Ohio State Law Journal* 52 (1991), 512–513.

15. Eugene Volokh, "Freedom of Speech and Workplace Harassment," *UCLA Law Review* 39 (1992): 1791ff. Excerpted on http://147.142.26.is/faculty/volokh/harass/PERMISSI.HTM; accessed on November 17, 1998.

16. Brief of Amicus Curiae, Feminists for Free Expression in support of

Petitioner, at 31n. 50, *Harris v. Forklift Systems, Inc.*, 114 S. Ct. 367 (1993) (no. 92-1168).

17. Kingsley Browne, E-mail message to the author, 18 November 1998.

18. Richard Dooling, "The End of Harassment?" *National Review*, 4 May 1998, 26–27.

19. Judith Shulevitz, "Don't Take It So Personally: Feminism's Boundary Problem," *Slate*, posted 2 October 1998; see http://www.slate.com/Features/Feminism/Feminism.asp; accessed 5 October 1998.

20. Walter K. Olson, *The Excuse Factory* (New York: Free Press, 1997), 249.

21. Ibid., 263.

Notes to Chapter 13

1. *Doe v. University of Michigan*, 721 F. Supp. 852 (E.D. Mich. 1989).

2. Alan Charles Kors and Harvey A. Silverglate, *The Shadow University: The Betrayal of Liberty on America's Campuses* (New York, London, Toronto, and Singapore: Free Press, 1998), 151.

3. Ibid., 309.

4. Ibid., 215.

5. Paul Johnson, "Farewell to the Labour Party," *New Statesman*, 9 September 1977, 329–332.

6. Herbert Marcuse, "Repressive Tolerance," in Robert Paul Wolff, Barrington Moore, Jr., and Herbert Marcuse, *A Critique of Pure Tolerance* (Boston: Beacon Press, 1969, c. 1965), 81–123.

7. Kors and Silverglate, *Shadow University*, 76.

8. Ibid., 84.

9. Ibid., 198.

10. Ibid., 194.

11. Ibid., 71.

12. Henry J. Abraham, *Freedom and the Court: Civil Rights and Liberties in the United States* (New York and Oxford: Oxford University Press, 1982), 13.

13. Ibid., 10.

14. Ibid., 13.

15. Kors and Silverglate, *Shadow University*, 88.

16. *West Virginia State Board of Education v. Barnette*, 319 U.S. 624 (1943).

17. Kingsley R. Browne, "The Silenced Workplace: Employer Censorship under Title VII" (article presented at a Yale Symposium on Sexual Harassment in February 1998; unpublished manuscript copy in the possession of the author).

18. Alex Kuczynski, "Between the Sexes, It's World War III," *New York Times*, 19 July 1998, sec. 9, 1, 8.

Notes to Chapter 14

1. Adam Bryant, "A Rebuff to the Ministry of Silly Bosses," *New York Times*, 7 February 1999, sec. 3, 1.

2. Elizabeth Rodenz, owner of the San Francisco firm Executive Round Table, interview with the author, December 1998.

3. Bruce Felton, "When Rage Is All the Rage: The Art of Anger Management," *New York Times*, 15 March 1998, sec. 3, 15.

4. Kenneth M. York, Lizabeth A. Barclay, and Amy B. Zajack, "Preventing Sexual Harassment: The Effect of Multiple Training Methods," *Employee Responsibilities and Rights Journal* 10, 4 (1997): 277–289.

5. *Stender v. Lucky Stores, Inc.*, 803 F. Supp. 259 (N.D. Cal. 1992).

6. Marianne M. Jennings, "Who's Harassing Whom?" *Wall Street Journal*, 6 July 1998, A14.

7. Richard T. Cooper, "College Rethinks Commitment to Serving Poor," *Los Angeles Times*, 13 April 1998, A13.

8. Louise F. Fitzgerald and Sandra L. Shullman, "Sexual Harassment: A Research Analysis and Agenda for the 1990s," *Journal of Vocational Behavior* 42, 1 (February 1993): 17–18.

9. Robyn E. Blumner, "Women's Worst Enemies," *St. Petersburg Times*, 4 October 1998, sec. D, 1.

10. Thea Joselow, "Workshop: New Workplace Liability: How Does It Shake Down for Business Owners?" at http://women.connect.com/info/business/workshop/jul09; accessed 12 July 1998.

11. Quoted in Jeffrey Toobin, "The Trouble with Sex," *New Yorker*, 9 February 1998, 55.

12. *Sexual Harassment in Healthcare: Relearning the Rules*, videotape produced by Envision, Inc., 1201 16th Avenue S., Nashville, TN 37212; 35 minutes; copyright 1993.

13. *Handling the Sexual Harassment Complaint: For Managers and Supervisors*, videotape produced by AMI, American Media Incorporated, 4900 University Avenue, West Des Moines, IA 50701; copyright 1990.

14. *A Costly Proposition*, VAMC/UD BNA Communications, 9439 Key West Ave., Rockville, MD 20850; 32 minutes, copyright 1993.

15. Bernice R. Sandler, *Educator's Guide to Controlling Sexual Harassment* (Washington, D.C.: Thompson Publishing Group, 1993–1996).

16. Sharon Szymanski and Cydney Pullman, *Sexual Harassment at Work: A Training Workbook for Working People* (New York: The Labor Institute, 1994).

17. Ibid., 4.

18. Ibid., 116–119.

19. Courses given by David R. Lagasse, Esq., Meredith Steigman, Esq., and Denise Campbell, Esq., for Winthrop, Stimson, Putnam & Roberts, to the managers and workers of a small nonprofit company in New York City on October 16, 1998.

20. Nat Hentoff, "'He Would Prefer Not To': The Man Who Refused to Go to Sexual Harassment Prevention Class," *Washington Post*, 24 September 1994, sec. 1, 16.

Notes to Chapter 15

1. Rita Risser, *Research Report: The New Law of Sexual Harassment* (Santa Cruz, Calif.: Fair Measures, 1996), 1.

2. Rita Risser, in a private conversation with the author, 18 May 1998.

3. "Corporate Profits, Charting a Course to Ethical Profits," *New York Times*, 8 February 1998, sec. 3, 1 and 9.

4. Todd Seavey, "Ladies and Gentlemen: Feminism," *New York Press* 9, 18 (April 1996): 17–23.

5. Jay A. Livingston, "Responses to Sexual Harassment on the Job: Legal, Organizational and Individual Actions, *Journal of Social Issues* 38, 4 (Winter 1992): 13.

6. Rebecca A. Thacker, "A Descriptive Study of Behavioral Responses of Sexual Harassment Targets: Implications for Control Theory," *Employee Responsibilities and Rights Journal* 5, 2 (1992): 155.

7. E.g., Karen B. Williams and Ramona R. Cyr, "Escalating Commitment to a Relationship: The Sexual Harassment Trap," *Sex Roles* 27, 1/2 (1992): 47–72—"literature on date rape has suggested that assertiveness training can be an effective intervention . . . because women are uncomfortable with saying 'no,' assertiveness training also may be effective for curbing some forms of sexual harassment."

8. Merle Waxman, "Constructive Responses to Sexual Harassment in the Workplace," *Employee Responsibilities and Rights Journal* 7, 3 (1994): 244.

9. Michael D. Weiss, "Rethinking Sexual Harassment: A Lawyer's View," in Cathy Young, ed., *Rethinking Sexual Harassment: A Women's Freedom Network Special Report*, Women's Freedom Network Working Paper 3 (Washington, D.C.: Women's Freedom Network, 1998), 30.

10. Sharon Szymanski and Cydney Pullman, *Sexual Harassment at Work: A Training Workbook for Working People* (New York: The Labor Institute, 1994), 22.

INDEX

ABOUT THE AUTHOR

Joan Kennedy Taylor is the National Coordinator of the Association of Libertarian Feminists, a founding member of Feminists for Free Expression, and author of *Reclaiming the Mainstream: Individualist Feminism Rediscovered*. She lives in New York City and Stockbridge, Mass.